CANOEING AND CAMPING

DATE DUE

Beyond the Basics

Second Edition

Cliff Jacobson

Illustrations by Cliff Moen

The Globe Pequot Press

Guilford, Connecticut

Cover design by Saralyn D'Amato
Page design by Lisa Reneson
Front cover photographs: *upper left:* Stuart Osthoff, *Boundary Waters Journal*; *lower right:* © Bob Firth

Library of Congress Cataloging-in-Publication Data
Jacobson, Cliff.
    Canoeing and camping: beyond the basics / Cliff Jacobson; illustrations by Cliff Moen. — 2nd ed.
        p.   cm.
    Includes index.
    ISBN 0-7627-0668-6
    1. Canoe camping.   I. Title.

GV790.J33 2000
797.1'22—dc21   99-087384

Manufactured in Korea
Second Edition/Second Printing

Dedication

To my Aunt Ruth, who always believed I would succeed.
You will always have a special place in my heart.

Acknowledgments

A special thanks to Cliff Moen, Dr. Bill Forgey, Charlie Wilson, and all my canoeing friends. Thanks also to *Canoe & Kayak* magazine, and *Pennsylvania Angler & Boater* magazine for permission to use portions of my articles that have appeared in these publications.

Contents

WHAT'S NEW IN THIS EDITION?

When the first version of this book (*Wilderness Canoeing & Camping*) appeared in 1977, Kevlar canoes, bent-shaft paddles, and dome tents were hot new items. Paddlers had just begun to discover the joy of lean quick canoes, lightweight gear, and the "Minnesota switch" style of paddling. The late Harry Roberts, who edited the highly revered *Canoesport Journal* in the late 1980s, polarized the canoeing industry by bad-mouthing the slow, doggy canoes that were popular at the time. Harry lovingly referred to these canoes as "pushers," "boring dishpans," "tin cans," and "barking dogs." His classic line was: "You can learn to turn a fast canoe, but no amount of learning will make a slow canoe fast." Some big-bucks canoe companies took insult and canceled their advertising in *Canoesport Journal*. The magazine couldn't withstand the income loss and it soon went out of business.

Well, Harry, it's the year 2000 and canoe companies have listened up. Now quick canoes that turn are available from scores of companies. Yesteryear's whitewater racing hulls have evolved into hot wilderness touring canoes. Personal-sized solo canoes, which were an odd sight in the 1980s, are the sports cars of today. Carefully alloyed composites and the use of design innovations such as "shouldered tumblehome" have resulted in canoes that are lighter, livelier, stiffer, stronger, and more beautiful than those you wrote about in *Canoesport Journal*.

Polyethylene and Royalex canoes have consumed the paddling world, and good folding canoes are here at last. Bent-shaft paddles are commonplace; they're even used in rental fleets. And Global Positioning Systems, satellite photos, and computers have changed the way we travel. The most complex waterway is an easy challenge if you understand today's technology.

The sad note is that most outdoorspeople continue to believe that things are more important than skills. Well-heeled campers have plenty of toys but few know how to use them. Witness the recent story of a couple who became lost in a large national park. They had a cell phone, map and compass, and GPS. Their trail map did not have coordinate reference lines so they couldn't plot a GPS fix. The couple phoned authorities for help and read off the latitude and longitude numbers to them. The authorities gave the couple a compass heading to follow home.

In this new Y2K revision, you'll find two new chapters, plus slick tricks for rigging canoes and tarps and stormproofing your camp; new recipes and cooking tips; a bold, well-researched new plan for addressing aggressive bear behavior; plus updates on all the basic skills you need to comfortably canoe the backcountry.

Sad to say, some of the new equipment is not up to snuff. I mourn the passing of the wonderful

Bendonn oven, Gerber Shorty knife, Shoe-Bug repellent jacket, tank-tough Optimus 111B stove, and Silva compasses with aluminum dials. Today's moderately priced dome tents leak in rain and blow down in wind (high-priced geodesics are the exception). Modern camp knives are designed to cut through airplane doors, not slice through salami and pine. And camp axes built since World War II are awful! However, there are some bright stars on the horizon, and I've starred (*) them in the text.

Details and source information are in appendix 4.

I won't pretend this book is a complete treatise on wilderness canoeing and camping. No single book this size could be. I offer this work as a thorough introduction, with high hopes that you'll find worthwhile hints to smooth your outdoor experience and encourage smiles.

—Cliff Jacobson

Part I

Equipment

CHAPTER 1

The Wilderness Canoe—an Investment in Freedom

My love affair with canoeing began in 1966 when a friend invited me to join him on a float trip down a small Indiana stream. It sounded like fun and rekindled memories of the good times I'd had on trips taken as a Boy Scout. It was a glorious day for a river float: warm, bright, and with a persistent breeze. The river was pleasant but not spectacular, and the canoe was a badly made fiberglass model that weighed at least 90 pounds. But no matter—the gentle beauty of the experience captured my heart. From then on I vowed to never be without a canoe of some sort.

Within the year I purchased my first canoe: a 15-foot fiberglass cheapie very much like my friend's. I pinched pennies for months to buy that boat and was paranoid about the possibility that it might be stolen. So when I camped out, I confidently chained it to a tree or the door of my car!

I paddled that canoe in blissful ignorance for more than a year before I purchased my first high-performance boat: a 17-foot, 9-inch, Sawyer Cruiser. After that came three aluminum Grummans of various lengths and weights, another Sawyer, six Old Towns, five Mad Rivers, three Daggers, one Bell, and three cedar-strip canoes that I built myself. Ultimately I ran out of storage room in my garage and was forced to sell some off—a terribly painful experience for someone who loves canoes as much as I do. Fortunately, I now own two canoe trailers, so the possibility of adding to my ten canoes excites me.

As you can see, canoe fever is incurable. One remedy is to simply paddle at every opportunity. Millponds, lazy rivers, wilderness lakes—it makes no difference. That's the beauty of the canoe: It's the only craft I know that is as much at home on tiny creeks as it is on giant lakes and reservoirs. I've even paddled mine on the ocean with complete confidence!

Selecting the Wilderness Canoe

Wilderness canoes should be longer and deeper than those used for day-tripping. Long canoes are faster (and thus easier to paddle) than short canoes, and deep hulls provide a margin of safety on wind-lashed lakes and thrashing rapids. Choose a canoe at least 17 feet long, with a width (beam) of not less than 34 inches and a center depth of at least 13½ inches. The bows should have increasing flare so they'll have sufficient buoyancy to climb up over big waves without knifing dangerously through them.

The extreme ends (stems) should be beefy enough so they won't break when the canoe hits rocks. Because a canoe's ability to rise and fall easily with the waves depends upon its hull design and not the height of its ends, high bows and sterns serve little purpose other than to add weight to the canoe. Generally, ends should not be higher than the center depth of the canoe plus 10 inches. Thus, a canoe with a 13-inch depth should have a maximum end height of 23 inches. Ends that are too high act as sails, making canoe handling on windblown lakes difficult.

Keels: Friends or Fiends?

An external keel will make any canoe track (hold its course) better. However, it will also act as a cow-catcher in rapids: It will hang up on rocks and cause upsets. There's smug satisfaction in watching your friends spill when the keel of their canoe catches on the same rock that your keelless canoe easily slid over just moments before. Later, when your friends have dried out, you'll swear that your superiority in rapids is due to your impeccable paddling skill rather than to a smooth-bottomed canoe!

Let's not mince words. External keels are generally the sign of an inferior canoe design. A canoe that requires an afterthought tacked on below to make it paddle straight belongs back on the drawing board. Good tracking may be achieved simply by combining a round or V-bottom, narrow ends, a straight keel line (see the section on rocker below), and somewhat squarish stems (ends). Aluminum canoes are formed in two halves, so they need a keel to hold the halves together. But even here the keel could be mounted on the inside of the hull rather than the outside.

The real reason for keels is to stiffen a floppy bottom. The biggest, flattest canoe bottom can be strengthened considerably by hanging a piece of angled aluminum or a 1-by-2 along its length. Throw in a bunch of ribs and maybe a vertical strut or three and the most shapeless hull will become rigid.

My recommendation: Avoid canoes with keels. The exceptions are aluminum canoes, which don't come any other way. Some aluminum-canoe makers offer shallow-draft "shoe" keels on their heavyweight whitewater models. Shoe keels make a lot more sense than the standard T-grip rock grabbers.

Rocker

The fore and aft upward curve of the keel line of a canoe is called rocker. A canoe with lots of rocker (1½ inches is a lot) will turn easily in rapids and rise quickly to oncoming waves. But it will track poorly and be slower on the flats than a similar hull with no rocker.

Racers like a canoe with zero rocker—perhaps a hint of lift in the ends, that's all. Whitewater canoes should have severe rocker—3 or more inches is not uncommon. A wilderness tripper might fall somewhere in between—about 1 to 1½ inches. The important thing to consider is how the boat will be used. A canoe that tracks like a mountain cat when near empty will turn even more reluctantly when heavily loaded. A heavy load forces a canoe down into the water (acts like a keel) and so improves tracking. Wilderness canoes ordinarily are heavily loaded and therefore require some rocker. Conversely, it makes little sense to have lots of rocker in a minimally loaded day cruiser.

The amount of rocker a canoe needs depends largely on its length and hull configuration. Short hulls need less rocker than long ones, and flat-bottomed canoes turn more easily than round-bottomed ones. Very short canoes—14½ feet or less (solo boats)—with no rocker may be turned easily with minimal paddle effort by simply leaning them on their sides (you use the rocker in the sidewall). A rocker of more than 1½ inches is ridiculous in a true solo canoe unless, of course, it's a flat-out whitewater slalom boat.

My advice: Use a tape measure to determine the amount of rocker in a canoe before you buy it. Figure on zero rocker for a racer, maybe ½ inch for a day cruiser, and up to 1½ inches for a wilderness tripper. For all-out whitewater use, the more rocker, the merrier.

Tumblehome

The inward curve of the sides of a canoe above the waterline is called tumblehome. Some canoes have lots of tumblehome; others have none at all. Tumblehome is used for the following reasons:

- The craft can be made wide at the waterline for stability and narrow at the gunwales for ease of paddling (you don't have to reach so far over the side).

- Curved sidewalls are more rigid than broad, flat areas; thus a canoe with lots of tumblehome will be stiffer and require less bracing than a gently arched or radically flared boat.

Figure 1-1 The fore and aft upward curve of the keel line of a canoe is called rocker. Rockered canoes turn more easily than those without rocker.

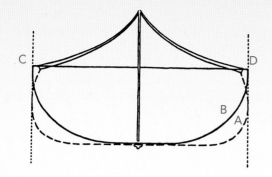

Figure 1-2 The inward curve of the sides of the canoe above the waterline is called tumblehome (canoe A). Canoe B has flared sides, which are much more seaworthy. Note that the maximum beam (C-D) is the same for both canoes.

The most seaworthy configuration of any watercraft consists of sides that flare boldly right to the gunwales, such as in a wild-river dory. Nonetheless, most of the best tripping canoes necessarily feature some tumblehome to maintain sidewall stiffness and reduce gunwale width. Given a choice, I'd choose a canoe with no tumblehome whatsoever. Unfortunately, a lot of very good canoes don't come this way. Moral? Moderation in all things. It couldn't be more true for that ol'debbil tumblehome!

Shouldered Tumblehome (figure 1-3)

Here's a slick variation on tumblehome: Dave Yost, whose forty-seven canoe designs are built by nine companies in four countries, discovered that by extending the canoe sides upward to a double-radiused shoulder, the canoe could be made narrow at the rails yet flared below. Voilà! "Shouldered tumblehome" was born.

Many of the world's best whitewater canoes have had shouldered tumblehome for years, but now it's being applied to good canoes everywhere. Higher manufacturing costs (you need a two-piece mold) are one reason for the delay. The untraditional look of the shoulder is another. But the advantages of a radiused hull go beyond improved seaworthiness to include:

- The rails or gunwales (gunnels) can be mounted perpendicular to the keel line and flush with thwarts and seats. This produces a stronger trim joint and a cleaner, more pleasing look.

- The shouldered curve functions like an I-beam and strengthens the sidewall below the rails. The result is that lighter gunwale stock can be used.

- Modern paddling techniques call for heeling canoes to enhance their turning ability. Traditionally tumblehomed canoes often capsize during these maneuvers. Fully flared craft with shouldered rails do not!

Flat or Round Bottom?

Many wilderness canoeing texts recommend flat-bottomed canoes over round-bottomed ones on the assumption that round-bottomed hulls lack stability. Yet the fact remains that accomplished canoeists prefer round- or even V-bottomed canoes for use on every type of water, from placid lakes to thundering rapids.

As far as stability is concerned, when it is loaded, a round-bottomed canoe feels nearly as stable as a flat-bottomed one, and in reality the round hull is far more stable in rough water because you can control the canoe with your body. The responsiveness of the round hull permits you to make small balance adjustments easily. You can ride the waves and rapids and

Figure 1-3 Shouldered tumblehome.

Side View

cross-section

feel every movement of the canoe—like a jockey on a well-trained racehorse. Should you broach (turn broadside to the waves), you can immediately transfer your weight to expose more of the side of the canoe to the oncoming waves. On the other hand, the sluggishness of a flat-bottomed canoe prevents much real control except for steering.

Because of their curved shape, round bottoms are stronger than flat bottoms. Thus, round-bottomed canoes do not usually require the additional reinforcement of keels. Keelless, flat-bottomed canoes commonly suffer from lack of hull rigidity and have difficulty retaining their bottom shape when paddled through the water.

Additionally, round-bottomed hulls are considerably faster than flat-bottomed ones. Although you many not be concerned with speed, the time may come when you will need to paddle many miles against the wind on a large lake. At this time you will be grateful for whatever speed your canoe possesses.

The Case for the Short Canoe

If your canoeing will be limited to small streams and rivers, a small, light canoe may be right for you. If you plan to do a lot of rock dodging in shallow rapids or to twist your way down narrow, mountain-fed streams like the ones in North Carolina, Vermont, and West Virginia, a 16-foot, deep-hulled canoe would be a good choice. Short canoes generally turn quickly and are light and easy to handle on portages.

Carrying long canoes through brushy areas, between trees, and up and down steep banks can be very frustrating. It is in these areas that the short canoe excels. And if you prefer to paddle alone (see chapter 11, Solo Canoeing Is Different), you will find a lightly loaded, narrow 13- to 16-foot canoe to be fast, responsive, and easily maneuvered.

Tandem (two-person) canoes that are shorter than 16 feet generally respond sluggishly to the paddle and have poor directional stability. With the exception of specialized whitewater craft, such canoes are better adapted to portaging than paddling. There is little sense in buying, paddling, or carrying more canoe than you need. However, to attempt a rough-water voyage with a canoe that is too small is to invite disaster!

Carrying Capacity and Freeboard

Carrying capacity is the amount of weight a canoe can safely carry. Manufacturers usually state this figure in "pounds to a 6-inch freeboard"—which is the distance from the waterline to the top of the gunwales. The greater the freeboard, the greater the ability of the canoe to handle rough water, assuming the canoe is well designed. While some experts recommend a minimum of 6 inches of freeboard, no serious canoeist I know would think of using any canoe so heavily loaded on anything but a mirror-calm lake. My own preference for tripping is a 9-inch minimum. A deep-hulled 17- to 18-foot canoe will easily ride that high if moderately loaded.

Manufacturer's capacity figures are largely a joke, though, because capacity figures tell you nothing about how a canoe will perform when loaded. For example, canoes 1 and 2 in figure 1-4 both have the

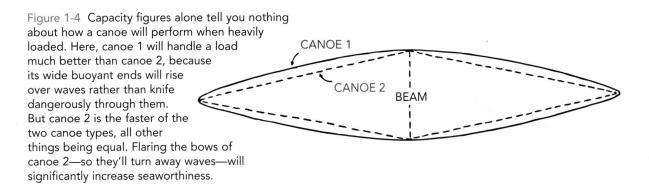

Figure 1-4 Capacity figures alone tell you nothing about how a canoe will perform when heavily loaded. Here, canoe 1 will handle a load much better than canoe 2, because its wide buoyant ends will rise over waves rather than knife dangerously through them. But canoe 2 is the faster of the two canoe types, all other things being equal. Flaring the bows of canoe 2—so they'll turn away waves—will significantly increase seaworthiness.

CANOE 1

CANOE 2

BEAM

same carrying capacity. Canoe 2 is faster than 1, but 1 will ride the waves and rapids better (run drier, that is).

If you want to increase capacity, you'll have to widen the beam or carry the existing beam farther forward. Do either and you'll lose speed. The solution is to lengthen the craft. Note that it is impossible to improve on one variable without changing the other.

Weight

Portaging is part of the daily routine in wilderness travel, so select a canoe you can carry for long distances. Fifty-five to 70 pounds is a reasonable weight for a high-volume, durable tripping canoe that will be used in rapids. For lake travel, select the lightest canoe you can find. Acceptably strong ultralight canoes are a reality. For example, the 18-foot family-sized We-no-nah Sundowner weighs just 42 pounds in ultralight Kevlar construction. The Sundowner is the most popular lightweight canoe in the Boundary Waters Canoe Area of Minnesota. You can rent one from a number of outfitters.

Speed and Ease of Paddling Are Not the Same

Canoes are displacement hulls; their maximum speed is a function of their length. The longer the canoe, the faster it will run. However, speed and ease of paddling are not the same! Some canoes feel fast but aren't. Others are quick but seem slow. At an easy cruising speed of around 3 miles an hour, a light 16-foot canoe will usually feel faster, and paddle more easily, than a heavier 18-footer. But push both boats hard and the

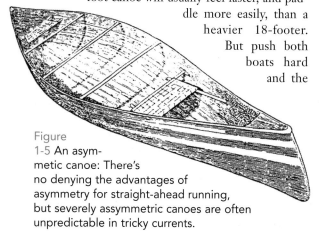

Figure 1-5 An asymmetic canoe: There's no denying the advantages of asymmetry for straight-ahead running, but severely assymetric canoes are often unpredictable in tricky currents.

shorter craft will bog down in its bow wave while the longer one slices easily along, still below its hull speed. The point is that a short, light canoe may be right for you if you pack light and paddle at a moderate pace.

Asymmetry

The displacement formula breaks down in shallow water because a hard-pushed canoe produces a substantial bow wave that is difficult to climb over. Racers refer to this phenomenon as climbing, and they counteract it by paddling canoes that have long narrow bows (to better cut the water) and fat buoyant sterns (for better flotation in the wave trough). This asymmetric hull shape (see figure 1-5) produces greater speed on any water, but especially on water less than 2 or 3 feet deep.

Severely asymmetric canoes are great for going fast, but they may be unpredictable in tricky currents. Some high-performance canoes built in the 1970s and '80s featured bizarre asymmetry that caused big problems in bad rapids. But times—and designs—have changed. Now nearly all the best canoes, including those designed for whitewater, are asymmetric. Old ideas die hard.

Some Serious Rules

1. All things being equal, the longer the canoe, the faster it will run. Short canoes usually turn more easily than long canoes. They also fit between waves better and so may be more seaworthy in rapids. If you want a fast canoe—especially in shallow water—choose an asymmetric hull shape.

2. Stability, ease of paddling, and seaworthiness are functions of hull shape. Except for fishing, the vote goes to round or V-bottoms for use on all types of water.

3. Tumblehome is a necessary evil. However, it should not be carried too far forward or aft, as in the case of aluminum canoes. Better to flare the ends so they'll deflect water away from the canoe, rather than provide a path into it. Shouldered tumblehome makes sense on any canoe.

4. Good canoes don't have keels. Period.

5. Manufacturers' capacity ratings are generally

meaningless. If you want a load carrier, opt for a shape that carries its beam well forward and aft. If you want speed, specify fine, hollowed ends and a relatively straight keel line. And if you want to maximize both variables, select a beamy 18½-foot canoe with fast lines!

Selecting a Store-Bought Canoe

Since you usually can't take a new canoe out and try it before you buy, here are some things to look for and some tests to perform right in the store:

1. Use a tape measure to determine length, width, and depth. Don't believe the manufacturer's specifications. Is the canoe big enough for rough water?

2. Place the canoe on grass, a carpet, or the showroom floor. Climb in. Can you kneel beneath each seat? This is important, because kneeling welds you to the craft in rough water and thereby increases stability. *Exception:* Some fine-lined canoes are too narrow in the bow for kneeling (you can't spread your knees wide for stability). In these boats it's better to have a low-mounted seat and to brace your feet solidly against the bow flotation tank or an improvised foot brace of some sort. Knees should be spread and braced against the sides of the canoe.

3. The manufacturer's listed canoe weight is almost always optimistic (I have never owned a canoe that weighed less than its advertised weight). Take a bathroom scale with you when you go canoe shopping!

4. Spin the canoe around on the ground. If it spins easily and is a keelless model, it probably has a fair amount of rocker and will turn easily. You can also look at the hull at ground level to see how much dead rise there is at the ends—or you can measure it precisely. But the spin test will approximate maneuverability if you compare several canoe models. Remember, you want a canoe that turns reasonably well when loaded.

5. You will probably carry a wilderness canoe almost as much as you will paddle it. The carrying yoke or center thwart should be installed at almost the exact center of the canoe. Have the salesperson help you place the canoe on your shoulders (just let the center thwart rest on your neck). Is the canoe balanced, or is one end much heavier than the other? If the canoe is out of balance, can the center thwart be easily moved?

6. Canoes built of nonbuoyant materials must have built-in flotation. Usually, this consists of Styrofoam blocks placed in sealed compartments in the ends. Make sure flotation does not interfere with front-leg room.

7. To prevent bottom wobble, a flat-bottomed canoe should have an inner or outer keel, or it should have its bottom reinforced with additional material.

As you look around for the ideal wilderness canoe, remember that novice canoeists buy small, short canoes because they are light and easy to handle and store. As a result, many manufacturers design their small canoes for an inexperienced market—with high bows and sterns, flotation under the seats, big keels, and so on. Experienced wilderness canoeists usually select the longest and deepest canoes they can carry; thus big canoes are usually designed to meet the needs of more knowledgeable paddlers.

Solo-Canoe Considerations

Solo canoes are not just for solitary purists. They are for everyone who feels the rhythms of nature and marvels at its beauty. Two words—elegant and precise—best describe the manner of solo canoes. Paddling down a twisty stream in a purebred solo canoe is like touring the back roads of America in a vintage sports car. These little canoes encourage smiles.

The traditional requirements for length, depth, and beam don't apply to solo canoes. Most variables (speed, tracking, turning, portability, seaworthiness, and general handiness) will be maximized in a canoe length of 14 to 16 feet, an outwale (outside edge of gunwale) beam of 26 to 29 inches, and a center depth of 11 to 12 inches. Except for use in severe whitewater, additional depth is unnecessary, since the paddler is located at the craft's fulcrum.

Tumblehome is less of an evil in solo canoes than in tandem ones because a lone paddler doesn't need to

coordinate movements with a partner. Many modern solo canoes have shouldered tumblehome and asymmetric hulls.

The lighter the solo canoe, the faster it will accelerate and the snappier it will feel. A lithe, well-built cruiser will weigh about 35 pounds. Except for rock-bashing whitewater, 45 pounds is the absolute limit for a true solo canoe. Ultralight Kevlar-composite canoes are worth the hundreds of extra dollars they cost. Compare a 32-pound Kevlar canoe to an identical 42-pound fiberglass one and you'll see why!

You'll find more information about these exciting little canoes in chapter 11, and in my book *Basic Essentials: Solo Canoeing* (Globe Pequot Press, 1999).

Building Materials: Aluminum

Aluminum canoes are inexpensive, strong, reasonably light, and maintenance-free. In the past most of the canoes used by professional outfitters were aluminum, but now craft built of Royalex and polyethylene are more popular.

Since the machinery that produces aluminum canoes is very expensive, there have been few design innovations. Most aluminum canoe designs are decades old—some date back to the 1940s. Few are very good. Invariably, 18-footers—which are designed for a more knowledgeable market—are best for wilderness travel. Look for hard-tempered aluminum and closely spaced flush rivets. Spot-welded members should be above the waterline.

The greatest drawback of aluminum is its tendency to cling to subsurface rocks—a characteristic that can be minimized by applying paste wax to the hull. Aluminum also dents, and try as you may, you will never remove the dents completely. Old aluminum canoes gradually take on the appearance of a high school shop ballpeen hammer project as they acquire dent upon dent!

Fiberglass

Fiberglass is the easiest of all canoe materials to repair. Of importance to manufacturers is that fiberglass can be formed into tight curves, which allows for very sophisticated hull designs. Fiberglass is not as durable as aluminum, Royalex, or polyethylene, but it's plenty strong enough for wilderness trips. Granted, Kevlar is considerably stronger than fiberglass, but possibly not enough to justify the hundreds of extra dollars that all-Kevlar construction commands. Buy Kevlar to save weight, not to gain strength!

Most good fiberglass canoes have some Kevlar in their laminations. It's mostly used to beef up delicate stems and abrasion-prone areas. You can't talk about fiberglass today without mentioning Kevlar in the same breath. See the Kevlar section later in this chapter for more information.

Construction Methods

There are so many ways to build fiberglass-composite canoes that it would require a full chapter to outline them all. To understand the most commonly used procedures, you should know some terminology.

Fiberglass cloth is composed of twisted strands of fiberglass that are woven at right angles to one another. Cloth yields the highest glass:resin ratio (about 1:1) of all the fiberglass fabrics and therefore has the greatest tensile strength. Most of the best all-fiberglass canoes are built of all-cloth laminates.

Fiberglass matt is composed of chopped cross-linked glass fibers that are held together with a dried resin binder. Matt has a glass:resin ratio of about 1:3, which means it's only about one-third as strong as woven cloth. Its main use is as a stiffening agent in canoe bilges and other places where extreme rigidity is desirable. Canoe hulls can also be stiffened with fiberglass cloth (some are), but this is more expensive, in terms of both labor and material costs.

Roving is a much coarser weave than cloth. Its glass:resin ratio is slightly less than that of cloth, but its impact resistance is greater. It is also used to help stiffen a hull.

Gel coat is a clear, abrasion-resistant, waterproof resin that's used on the outside of fiberglass/Kevlar composite canoes. An added pigment gives the canoe its color. Some fiberglass/Kevlar canoes are built without gel coat (called skin-coat construction) to save weight. Skin-coat canoes are more porous and not as durable as those with gel coat. Moisture that passes through the skin coat may produce a milky look. However, this does not affect the watertightness of the hull in any way.

Some gel coats weigh more than others. Clear (no added color) is naturally the lightest, followed by almond, then white. Dark colors like red and green tend to be heaviest, though there are exceptions. For example, a yellow Kevlar canoe is usually heavier than a red one, because more yellow pigment is needed to mask the gold Kevlar fibers. A handful of manufacturers are now using red Kevlar, and they don't even try to color it. They simply apply clear gel coat to the surface. The result is a light and strikingly beautiful canoe. The bad news is that unprotected Kevlar (gold or red) degrades in sunlight. A colored gel coat protects best; or you can apply a chemical, like 303 Protectant, that has an ultraviolet barrier.

As you've probably guessed, my favorite canoe colors are almond and white. These colors are light and they scratch white, so that scrapes with rocks don't show too boldly. White is also the easiest color to match when making cosmetic repairs—something every canoeist does every year.

Note: These color concerns apply only to gel coats that are used on fiberglass/Kevlar composite canoes. Different-colored Royalex, polyethylene, and wood-canvas canoes all weigh about the same.

Resins

There are polyester, vinylester, and epoxy resins—and dozens of formulations for each.

Polyester resin is the least strong, least expensive, and the standard of the canoe-building industry.

Vinylester resin may be the best compromise between cost and strength. Vinylester has low toxicity and it's relatively easy to work with. Many of the best Kevlar canoes are built with this resin.

Epoxy resin is the strongest of all resins. It is also expensive, difficult to work with, and frequently more toxic than polyester or vinylester. Epoxy is used on a regular basis by only a small number of custom canoe builders. Whether it has enough advantages over vinylester to warrant its higher cost is debatable.

How They're Built

Chopper-gun layup: A mixture of chopped strands of fiberglass and polyester resin is sprayed into a mold. The resulting canoe is very heavy, not very strong, and cheap. All the worst canoes are built this way. The telltale matrix of chopped fibers is visible on the inner walls of the craft. Chopper-gun canoes are no bargain at any price.

Hand layup: Glass cloth, and possibly roving and matt, is laid into a mold by hand, then saturated with resin and squeegeed out. All-cloth canoes are the toughest and most resilient of the breed; they are also the most expensive. You can tell hand layup at a glance—you can see the crisp outline of the glass weave in the inside of the hull.

Vacuum-bagging: A plastic vacuum bag is placed into the mold and the air is pumped out. This compresses the resin-soaked laminate and evenly distributes the resin, thus giving you the highest glass/Kevlar:resin ratio possible—all of which translates into a very light, very strong canoe. All the competitive racing canoes are built this way.

Foam cores: A canoe bottom that flexes due to water pressure won't maintain its shape and paddling efficiency. For this reason performance-minded canoeists prefer hulls that are as stiff as possible. The lightest, strongest way to stiffen a canoe is to sandwich a layer of closed-cell foam between the Kevlar or fiberglass laminates. Often, foam ribs are added to increase the torsional stiffness of the sidewalls. The entire boat is then vacuum-bagged to eliminate as much resin (and weight) as possible.

Vacuum-bagged foam-core hulls are extremely light. Some Kevlar racing models weigh under twenty-five pounds, and tripping boats of forty-five pounds are a reality. On the surface, you can make a very good case for this type of construction. However, the light, stiff hulls preferred by racers often break when they hit rocks. You need some flex in a wilderness canoe, even if it means sacrificing paddling performance. And because there's less fabric (fiberglass or Kevlar) in a foam-core boat than in an all-cloth one, the hull is more easily damaged. Once the foam core is cut through, cosmetic repairs become difficult. Replacing large sections of damaged foam has been described as similar to performing a lobotomy. Canoes with foam cores are ideal for racing, lazy waterways, or folks who can afford to repair or replace them when they become damaged.

Still, foam-core canoes have improved significantly in recent years, and well-built (but not ultralight) models hold up surprisingly well in moderate rapids. My wife, Susie, and I have paddled our old Kevlar/foam Mad River Slipper solo canoes on many

mean Ontario rivers, and they have never let go. There are lots of patches, but the boats are as solid as new.

Kevlar 49

Kevlar is a honey-gold-colored fabric manufactured by the DuPont Company. It looks much like fiberglass cloth (and it is used in the same way); only its properties and price are much different. Kevlar 49 composites have a tensile strength about 40 percent higher than epoxy/fiberglass and a specific gravity of 1.45 grams per cubic centimeter, versus 2.55 for glass. This means that canoes built of Kevlar are much stronger and lighter than equivalent glass models. Kevlar is widely used as tire cord fiber and as bulletproof material in flak vests—testimony to its incredible strength. Unfortunately, the fabric is very expensive and difficult to work with, so all-Kevlar canoes typically cost $400 to $800 more than identical fiberglass models.

Unlike fiberglass, Kevlar cannot be sanded. It just frizzes up like cotton candy—the canoe looks like it needs a haircut! Bash enough rocks with a Kevlar canoe and you're certain to expose the "hairy" fibers of the cloth. Repairing the mess requires painting on resin (epoxy, polyester, or vinylester) and cutting off the fibers while the resin is "green." The alternative—and the recommended procedure—is to cover the damaged area with a fiberglass patch, which can be sanded.

A composite layup with S-glass (an abrasion-resistant form of fiberglass) as the outer layer will be stiffer, more durable, easier to patch, nearly as strong, only a little heavier, and much less expensive than an all-Kevlar layup.

The trend today is away from single-laminate (all-Kevlar or all-fiberglass) construction. Top-line canoe manufacturers now blend canoe materials like steel alloys, taking advantage of today's knowledge of what works best, where. There are dozens (hundreds?) of proprietary layups that use E-glass, S-glass, Kevlar, nylon, Dacron, carbon fiber (graphite), closed-cell foams, and other materials in an array of dazzling configurations.

My preference? A vacuum-bagged epoxy or

vinylester Kevlar-composite canoe with an S-glass outer layer. Color? Almond or white, of course. I also like Kevlar/graphite composite canoes, even though black models show every scratch and don't photograph well.

Polyethylene

When the first polyethylene kayaks appeared, they received mixed reviews. Granted, they were strong—you could wrap one around a boulder and later retrieve it intact. But the boats were heavy, and state-of-the-art designs simply didn't exist.

Now that's old hat. Some of the best whitewater kayaks are currently rotationally molded from cross-linked polyethylene.

Given the success of polyethylene kayaks, it was only a matter of time before canoe companies got into the act. The first real success was the Coleman canoe—a less-than-daring, buff-bowed design with a network of interior aluminum tubes for stiffening. At the outset Coleman discovered that unsupported polyethylene sheet simply wouldn't hold its shape unless it was given a helping hand through internal struts, ribs, and keel. But the same metal framework that held the plastic in shape also kept it from giving when the boat smashed headlong into a rock. The result was that these canoes performed better on paper than in the maelstrom of a rocky rapid.

The problem is: How do you stiffen a polyethylene canoe without resorting to internal struts and ribs? Old Town Canoe Company* found an answer. In 1985 it sandwiched an expanded polyethylene core between two layers of rotationally molded cross-linked polyethylene. The result was a tough and rigid boat—one whose properties were similar to that of a sandwiched Royalex hull. And because of the stiffness imparted by the foam core, no internal bracing was necessary.

The attractiveness of cored cross-linked polyethylene centers around its strength, resistance to abrasion, stiffness, and relatively low cost. The finished canoe is still rather heavy, and the aesthetics of wood or fiberglass simply aren't there. Nevertheless, if you want a good, tough canoe at an attractive price, this is the route to go.

ABS (Acrylonitrile Butadiene Styrene) and ABS Royalex

Ribbed ABS plastic canoes appeared on the market in the 1960s with high hopes. Within two decades they disappeared without a trace. Good! These boats were neither light nor inexpensive and their designs were just short of dreadful. Even their strength was uncertain. In fact, commercial outfitters who tried conventional ABS canoes in the livery trade found that they literally came apart at the seams! Their one redeeming characteristic was good resistance to abrasion. No canoeist I know will mourn their passing.

However, when expanded to foam (Royalex, made by Uniroyal), ABS is an exceptional canoe material. Royalex differs from ordinary ABS plastic in that it is laminated and vacuum-formed under intense heat and pressure so that its central core contains many tiny air pockets. The resulting product, called thermoplastic laminate, is very strong, naturally buoyant, acceptably light, and fairly expensive.

Royalex canoes are nearly impossible to puncture, and they "snick" over subsurface rocks so easily that even a mediocre canoeist has little difficulty making it through a twisting rock garden. While paddlers of aluminum canoes are still pushing off rocks, Royalex owners are already hundreds of feet downstream. Unfortunately, Royalex is difficult to form into tight curves, which means that fine entry lines and other features that contribute to high performance are hard to obtain.

Still, Royalex is the choice for remote rivers and mean rapids, simply because no other material takes abuse so well. Here's why Royalex canoes and wild Canadian rivers go together:

- Your canoe is strapped to the struts of a chartered floatplane. The pilot winches the straps so tightly that they permanently dent your canoe.

- The river is rocky and shallow—you drag your canoe for miles. The bottom is a mass of deep gouges and scratches.

- You use ropes to lower your canoe around a waterfall. Gouges and dents develop as the craft bangs along the rocks.

- There's a 3-mile portage through a swamp. You save energy by hauling the canoe on a line, like a dog on a leash (a common practice on the Arctic tundra). Naturally, there are more scratches and dents.

- You return to your starting point by train. Your canoe is shoved into a railroad car, and gear is wedged inside the craft. Two more canoes are stacked on top and also filled with gear. The shapes of the canoes change before your eyes!

Do you really want to treat a $2,000 Kevlar canoe this way?

A Lighter Royalex

R84 Royalite is the newest and lightest form of Royalex. It has the same foam core and ABS substrate as conventional Royalex, but a weatherable plastic skin is used in place of the vinyl outer layer. The resultant R84 product is stiffer and about 10 percent lighter than conventional vinyl-covered Royalex. R84 canoes are almost as light as those built from fiberglass composites, but they are much less expensive. The exciting news is that this new, lighter Royalex lends itself to the manufacture of fairly sophisticated designs.

Cedar-Strip Canoes—The Ones That Win Races

Many of the canoes that win long-distance, flatwater races are hand-built of cedar or redwood strips, nailed to a form, glued together, and covered with fiberglass cloth and polyester or epoxy resin (the nails are removed prior to glassing). The result is a very beautiful, very light canoe. Since construction is entirely done by hand, the few companies that produce this style of canoe command high prices ($1,500 and up). Strip canoes, however, are easily built by anyone with power tools, basic woodworking know-how and patience. They are very inexpensive to make. Easy-to-follow plans for the construction of several excellent canoe models are available at low cost from the Minnesota Canoe Association.*

It is interesting to note that the greatest cross-continent canoe safari of the twentieth century was completed in a canoe built of Sitka spruce strips and fiberglass. In April 1971 Verlen Kruger of DeWitt, Michigan, and Clint Waddell of Saint Paul, Minnesota, launched a hand-built 21-foot strip canoe at Montreal's Lachine docks on the St. Lawrence River. The two men paddled 6,500 miles across some of the roughest waterways in North America and terminated their trip at the Bering Sea in Alaska just five months later. Vital canoe statistics were:

Length: 21 feet
Width measured 3 inches off the bottom: 27 inches
Width measured at the center thwart: 34 inches
Depth: 18 inches at the bow; 12½ inches rest of length
Weight: 85 pounds
Seats: Sawyer-molded fiberglass, bucket type
Yokes: Formfitted center yoke for one-man carry and a pad and yoke at each end for two-man carry
Cover: 8-ounce waterproof nylon snap-on for complete protection from spray

Experienced paddlers will recognize Kruger's hand-built canoe as a lengthened version of the standard Canadian racer. The Waddell-Kruger expedition to the Bering Sea is one of the most fantastic canoe voyages of our time—perhaps of any time. The fact that this trip was safely completed in a modern canoe of revolutionary design should do much to dispel the myth that canoes have changed little since the time of the Indian birch barks.

Wood-Canvas Canoes

Wood-canvas canoes are making a comeback! The world-famous Chestnut canoes are again being fabricated in Canada, and scores of smaller custom builders have taken up the banner. Prices are competitive with state-of-the-art Kevlar canoes.

A good wood-canvas canoe will weigh about the same as an all-cloth fiberglass one, will be nearly as strong, and, because its bottom flexes, will slide over rocks easily. Many canoeists feel that absolutely nothing paddles as well as a traditional wood-canvas canoe. Certainly few other canoes are as beautiful.

Folding Canoes

Mention folding canoes and rapids in the same

A 17-foot Pakboat (folding canoe) negotiates a rapid on the Horton River, Northwest Territories, Canada.

breath and you're apt to make experienced canoeists shudder. Too bad, because these canoes are quite amazing.

I first saw folding canoes in action in 1992, on the Hood River in Canada's Northwest Territories. The Hood is extremely remote—access is by charter floatplane, from Yellowknife, 300 air miles away. The Hood has scores of big rapids, some of which go on for miles. I was portaging my Royalex canoe around a particularly dicey Class III rapid (see the river rating scale on page 69) when I saw three forest green folding canoes head downriver. I just shook my head and said, "No way."

Seconds later, one canoe impaled a rock and began to fold around it. Suddenly, the hull let go and the craft continued on, literally twisting and bouncing off rocks as it snaked from channel to channel. I watched another canoe negotiate a 3-foot ledge, certain it would bite the bullet at the bottom. Wrong. It just bent upward (nearly in half) and climbed out of the wave trough. I don't think my Royalex canoe would have made it.

I put my pack down and watched the show. I was amazed at how capable these craft were in big water.

The crew put in below the rapid and we shared some tea and smiles. They were from Norway and though they had canoed other Arctic rivers, this was their first big trip with folding boats. Our crews continued to play tag downriver for two more days, and I watched them run more rapids we chose to portage around. I told them I would never again thumb my nose at folding canoes.

Pakboats/ScanSport, Inc.* is the major (only?) producer of folding canoes in North America. It made the Mad River Escape folding canoes (no longer manufactured) that you may be familiar with. Pakboats range in size from 14 to 17 feet; weights run 38 to 53 pounds. The hulls are formed by a reinforced PVC skin held under tension by an interlocking framework of tubular aluminum. Assembly takes about forty minutes. The seats are adjustable to support sitting or kneeling, and rocker can be tuned to suit different paddling conditions. The disassembled canoe stores in a 35- by 17- by 13-inch bag. Prices are slightly less than what you would pay for a state-of-the-art Kevlar canoe.

Folding canoes set you free to follow your star in a way no hard-shelled canoe can.

Ease of Repair

If you use your canoe hard in rocky whitewater, you will ultimately need to repair it. Canoes built of fiberglass and Kevlar are easiest to repair—a properly applied patch is hardly noticeable. Wood-strip canoes mend nicely, as do wood-canvas ones. It's possible to fix a Royalex ABS or aluminum canoe, but the patch will be a glaring reminder of the rock you hit. From the aesthetic viewpoint, polyethylene hulls cannot be repaired. Folding canoes are easily patched.

Despite what some canoe manufacturers say, no canoe material is indestructible. So consider the merits of a less durable canoe that is easily patched over a more durable one that is not.

Buying a Used Canoe

Now that you are familiar with canoe design and construction, you should have a pretty good idea of what you want in a canoe. The following guidelines will help you get the best deal on a good used canoe:

1. Know the retail value of the canoe before you talk to the owner. Figure on paying up to 80 percent of the current retail price for well-cared-for, top-line aluminum canoes and around 50 percent for lesser-known aluminum, fiberglass, and ABS cheapies. Quality-built fiberglass, Kevlar, and Royalex canoes are commonly 60 to 75 percent of their new retail cost, if they have been well kept.

2. If you are trying to save money, purchase a canoe with a hole in it. Contrary to popular belief, canoes are easily patched (see chapter 8, Canoe Rescue and Repair). Check with commercial outfitters, who often sell damaged canoes cheaply (shoddy equipment is bad for their image). With

ingenuity and the proper repair materials, you can often restore a canoe to nearly new condition.

3. Turn used canoes upside down and sight along the keel. Don't buy a canoe with a "hogged" (bent-in) keel. Once a keel is bent, it is almost impossible to straighten properly.

4. Carefully sight along each gunwale. It is very difficult to straighten heat-treated aluminum gunwales, although a hammer and a piece of 2-by-4 can be used to improve aesthetics somewhat. Plastic and wood gunwales that are cracked or broken must be completely replaced.

5. On aluminum canoes check for stressed or pulled rivets, which could cause leakage.

6. Check fiberglass canoes for signs of hull delamination. Home-built and factory prefabricated kit models especially should be carefully examined, as the quality of these canoes depends entirely upon the skill of the builder. This doesn't mean that hand-built canoes are bad. On the contrary, many canoe clubs own their own molds, and club members produce superb canoes at a fraction of the cost (and weight) of factory-built models. A well-constructed club-built canoe may be an excellent investment. Occasionally a racing enthusiast will offer a nearly new canoe for sale at little more than the original cost of the building materials, simply because he or she is displeased with the canoe's performance. Canoe clubs and canoe races are good places to frequent if you are looking for a good, inexpensive canoe.

In summary, select a canoe of adequate size and depth. Be certain that the keel line of the canoe is straight, and check for damaged fittings. Eliminate from consideration any fiberglass or Kevlar canoe that shows signs of hull delamination, and be knowledgeable of the canoe's value before you buy. Lastly, join a canoe club. Club membership will bring you into contact with skilled paddlers and canoe builders and will increase your chance of locating a good used canoe at a reasonable price.

CHAPTER 2

Low-Cost Ways to Improve the Performance of Your Canoe

If you want to learn the fine points of canoeing, attend a competitive race event. Flatwater, downriver, or whitewater slalom—it makes no difference. In every case the name of the game is winning. And the difference between winning and losing is often a matter of only seconds or tenths of a second. At the highest levels of competition, the performance edge is as much due to the right equipment as it is to the capabilities of the paddlers.

Between races check out the boats. But look beyond the basics of brand names and hull design. Examine instead how the canoes are tricked out—how they're "tuned." Study the seating arrangement: height and support of seats, type of sliding mechanism (if any), location of knee pads, toe blocks, thigh straps, and so forth. What about safety accessories like grab loops and flotation? It won't take you long to discover that these customized race machines are a far cry from what you can buy in the stores.

After the race engage in some friendly banter with the competitors. Artfully turn the subject from racing to fast touring and wilderness tripping. Do your new friends own cruising canoes? If so, what modifications have been performed to make them safer and more comfortable to paddle? Listen intently and bring a notepad. You'll discover a wealth of honestly useful ideas.

Here are some tips you might learn from your conversations with the masters. Emphasis is on low-cost modifications that you can perform on your own canoe.

Carrying Yoke

Canoes are usually carried by one person with the aid of a padded carrying yoke (an extra-cost item). Aluminum yokes are channeled to fit over the existing center thwart (an exception is the excellent Alumacraft yoke, which is supplied as standard equipment in lieu of a center thwart), while wooden yokes replace the thwart completely. Most manufacturers install the center thwart or yoke in a location determined by a formula, which is often subject to some error. For example, the yoke on one of my canoes was misplaced by 4 inches, making the craft so tail-heavy that it was impossible to carry.

The most satisfactory method of balancing a canoe is to try it on your shoulders. I like just enough weight in the tail that the bow will rise very slowly when the canoe is shouldered. I consider a canoe out of balance if more than gentle pressure is required to bring it back to a horizontal position. You can easily change the balance on your canoe by reinstalling the yoke in a new set of mounting holes drilled in the gunwales.

If you are very broad-shouldered, you will like the spacing of factory-made yoke pads; but if you're of average build, you will need to move the pads closer together and change their angle somewhat. Most people prefer pads mounted at right angles to the yoke bar, with a distance of 7½ inches between them. Bolt or clamp the shoulder pads to the yoke, as illus-

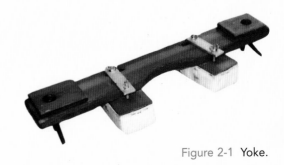

Figure 2-1 Yoke.

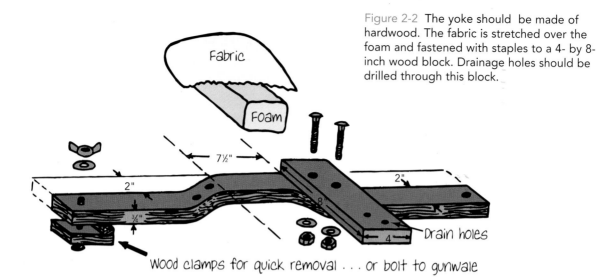

Figure 2-2 The yoke should be made of hardwood. The fabric is stretched over the foam and fastened with staples to a 4- by 8-inch wood block. Drainage holes should be drilled through this block.

trated in figure 2-2. I generally prefer the security of bolts; however, clamped pads can be more easily moved to fit the shoulders of different-sized people.

If you do much portaging, you'll want a wooden yoke. The springiness and warmth of wood against your neck makes for more comfort than the inflexibility and coldness of aluminum. Make your yoke from a good hardwood (ash or oak is best) and finish to ¼ by 2 inches to ensure adequate strength. Cut two 8- by 4-inch yoke pads from ¼-inch pine and pile polyurethane foam on each block (use pillow padding, available at any discount store). Compress each pad to about 2½ inches and cover with a light-colored Naugahyde to reflect heat. (I found the difference in surface temperature between a black pad and a white pad in strong sunlight to be 35 degrees!) Staple the Naugahyde into place and finish with upholstery tacks. Then drill a few ½-inch or ⅜-inch-diameter holes through the face of each yoke-pad block so water that accumulates in the foam (when you capsize) will drain out. Commercial yokes don't have drain holes, so moisture becomes trapped in the yoke pads and causes the wood blocks to rot.

Secure your yoke to the gunwales with stainless-steel bolts or use the simple clamp device illustrated. Clamp-in, removable yokes are the way to go if you

plan to carry a passenger—the yoke can be removed to provide more room for the rider.

Bourquin Boats* (Jeannie Bourquin) makes the best bolt-on yoke pads I've found; Empire Canvas Works* has the best clamp-on ones. Bell Canoe Works* and Old Town Canoe Company* can supply gunwale clamps for securing yokes to canoes. You'll find curved ash yoke bars (sans portage pads) for sale at most canoe shops.

Shock Cords and Rubber Ropes

On a trip down the flooded Groundhog River in northern Ontario, my partner and I inadvertently ran a 5-foot falls. When the bow of our 18-foot canoe punched through the big roller below, the canoe filled with several inches of water. We spun broadside in the rapids, swamping completely. Fortunately, our four watertight Duluth packs stayed put through the run, providing us with sufficient buoyancy to keep afloat. We retained enough freeboard to paddle cautiously ashore.

In whitewater you need the additional flotation provided by watertight packs, and you can only use this flotation if packs are well secured in the canoe. If your canoe is aluminum, drill a series of ⅜-inch-diameter holes along the gunwales about 4 inches apart. These holes will provide anchor points for cords and steel hooks to which heavy-duty rubber ropes are attached. If the gunwales of your canoe have water-drain slots (as on wood-canvas models), you can hook your cords or rubber ropes directly to them. The solid rails of most fiberglass and ABS boats, however, present more of a problem. Usually it is possible to drill small holes though the inwale or just below the gunwale. Short loops of parachute cord can then be run through these holes to provide attachment points for your security ropes.

Run at least two rubber ropes across each pack, and where very heavy-duty rapids will be encountered, add a length of nylon parachute cord. Tie the cord with a quick-release knot (see chapter 10, Tying It All Together) so you won't have difficulty salvaging your gear if you overturn. You can stuff your bailing sponge, fishing gear, and loose articles under the ropes to prevent loss in an upset. The parachute cords will prevent "pack-bob" (packs rising up in a water-filled canoe). Rubber ropes permit quick removal and replacement of packs when making portages. It is a real pain in the neck to constantly tie and untie a network of ropes.

Drill holes in thwarts and deck plates and install lightweight, fabric-covered shock cord (figure 2-3 shows the procedure). Wet clothes, maps, and oddities placed under the corded thwarts will stay put in high winds and on portages.

Some Thoughts about Tying in Packs

Many very good canoeists believe that packs should never be tied into a canoe, but should be free to float out in a capsize. Granted, there's no need to tie in gear if you're traveling in the company of other canoes on a "pool-drop" river—that is, one where rapids are short and there's a quiet pool below. Most Minnesota and Ontario rivers are like this. If you capsize in a short rapid, packs will float into the pool below where friends can rescue them.

There is also no need to tie in packs if you use a nylon spray cover on your canoe. A covered canoe usually turns bottom-up when it capsizes, and the cover and packs remain with the canoe. The twisting motion and susceptibility to abrasion of folding canoes also suggests that packs should not be tied in.

Finally, the Boundary Waters Canoe Area and surrounding lake country of Ontario demand a "no tie-in" approach. Boundary Waters lakes are small—often there's a portage every thirty minutes. It's a hassle to tie and untie packs at every portage, even if doing so offers some security afloat.

The place to tie in packs is on a big brawny river with rapids that run for miles. Capsize here and you'll be lucky to rescue your canoe, let alone packs that float out and are lost in the gathering flow. For example, the lower 150 miles of the Clearwater River in Alberta average at least 5 miles an hour. Some stretches run twice that speed. Two canoes in my crew capsized in a long rapid when we paddled this river in 1996. Both teams lost some expensive gear that wasn't tied in. Later, we found a lost paddle lodged in some brush 30 miles downstream!

Your skills, the nature of your route, your support team, and whether or not you have a covered canoe should determine whether or not you tie in packs. If there is an axiom here, it's that when you do tie in packs, tie them so securely that they double as flotation and absolutely, positively cannot escape from the canoe! The recommended combination of rubber ropes and quick-release parachute cords works well.

Painters

Painters, or end lines, should be attached as close to the waterline as possible. Where lines are secured to the deck of a canoe, the force of the water acting on the canoe is so distant from the point of attachment of the painters that a quick pull of a rope can, in some rapids or currents, overturn the canoe. Drill a hole below the deck plate and epoxy in a length of ½-inch-diameter PVC water pipe. The tube will keep water from leaking into the canoe when the bow plunges in rapids.

The best way to keep painters available and out of the way is to coil and stuff them under a loop of shock cord attached to the deck. Thus stored, they can be released by a simple tug of the end. They won't stream out independently if you capsize and will remain in place while portaging. Use bright-colored ⅛-inch polypropylene (it floats!) rope for painters.

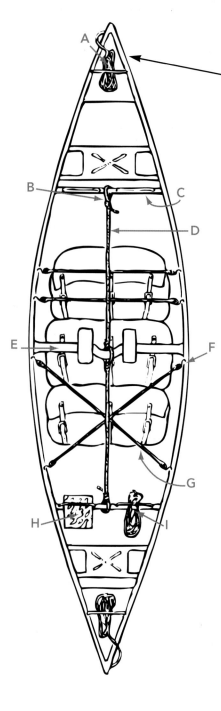

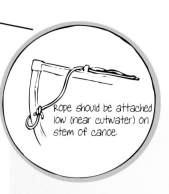

Rope should be attached low (near cutwater) on stem of canoe.

A. Painter secured under loop of shock cord.

B. Quick-release knot.

C. Shock cord strung through holes in thwart.

D. Light nylon rope prevents pack-bob if you upset in heavy rapids.

E. Yoke with padded shoulder pads may be bolted in or secured with quickly removable brackets, as illustrated in figure 2-1.

F. Steel hook snaps to hole in gunwale.

G. Heavy-duty rubber rope keeps packs secure if you capsize.

H. Map secured under shock cord.

I. Emergency throwing line—coiled and bound.

Figure 2-3 **A customized canoe protects your valuables.**

Grab Loops

Attach a loop of polyethylene rope to each end of the canoe. Should you swamp in rapids, you can quickly grab the loop, which may be more accessible than a painter. Grab loops are also convenient hand-holds for lifting the canoe.

Glare Reduction

Glare from the deck plate of an aluminum canoe can be hazardous. An easy solution is to paint deck plates flat black.

A Working Canoe Needs Five Thwarts

A typical ash thwart weighs a pound or two, so canoe makers like to use as few as possible. To save weight, many modern canoes have just one thwart in the center. Watch how these canoes flex when they are paddled through water: In time their hulls break down—fiberglass delaminates and Royalex goes soft. The canoe begins to creak as parts come loose. A working canoe should have five thwarts, positioned approximately as follows:

1. Yoke: installed just forward of the balance point of the canoe, as explained earlier.

2. Forward thwart: located a hand's width behind the bow seat.

3. Stern thwart: set 23 to 25 inches forward of the leading edge of the stern seat. This spacing provides room to set three number 3 Duluth packs (see Frameless Packs on page 25) or other large tripping packs side by side in the rear compartment of a typical 17-foot canoe.

4–5. A short thwart at each end of the canoe. Bow and stern thwarts should be installed just behind the deck plates, with enough space between to provide a convenient handhold for lifting the canoe. Don't dismiss the importance of these short thwarts—they tie the ends of the canoe together and take stress off the decks, which are simply screwed in place.

A lot of very good canoes don't have enough thwarts, or they have thwarts in the wrong places.

You can easily add or move thwarts. Every canoe shop has straight ash thwarts and curved yoke bars.

Double-Bolt the Yoke and Thwarts

The yokes and thwarts of most canoes are secured to the gunwales with a single bolt at each end. This is not strong enough for a working canoe. Two thin bolts are better than one thick one. Make whatever modifications you must, then tell the manufacturer. A courteous letter or phone call may encourage change.

Canoe Pockets

Verlen Kruger, who completed a three-year cross-continent canoe odyssey of some 28,000 (!) miles, was the probable inventor of canoe pockets. On an early safari of 6,500 miles (Montreal to the Bering Sea), Verlen installed plastic bicycle baskets in his canoe and used them to store sunglasses, bug dope, and such. The baskets provided no security for valuables in a capsize, but they were handy nonetheless.

A better solution is to sew up an envelope-style bag from waterproof nylon and tie it to a canoe thwart or gunwale. Or buy one of the many thwart bags that are commercially available.

Canoe Tumplines

A tumpline consists of a wide leather or canvas strap secured to a pack or bundle. Place this strap just above your forehead, grab the tumpline near your head, lean forward into the trace, and take off down the trail. The early voyageurs routinely carried 180 pounds across rugged portages using only this rig. If tumplines have a failing, it is that they exert tremendous pressure on neck muscles, and most modern voyageurs don't have strong-enough necks to tolerate this for very long. Consequently, many canoeists use a combination of tumpline and shoulder straps on their packs. By distributing the weight between tumpline and straps, you can carry very heavy loads for short distances in relative comfort.

For years canoeists have been trying to install tumplines on their canoes to make carrying easier. Unfortunately, conventional tumplines are too rigid. When the canoe bounces up, the tump comes off

Figure 2-4 A canoe tumpline that works.

Figure 2-5 A tumpline ingeniously designed by Ken Saelens.

your head and wraps around your neck. And when the canoe comes down, your head receives the full impact of the weight. Three decades ago I began to experiment with canoe tumplines. At the time I was anticipating an Arctic canoe trip with a 13-mile portage. Although I was excited about the trip, I began to have nightmares about carrying my 75-pound canoe across that portage. I figured that with a tumpline, somehow I could make it. I tried rigging one using shock cords, but that didn't work—the thing kept slipping off my head. So I posed the problem to an inventive friend of mine, Ken Saelens. Ken thought a while, then attached a 24-inch length of canvas beneath the yoke of the canoe with two heavy-duty rubber ropes (figure 2-5). The result was dramatic. The tumpline took about 50 percent of the weight off my shoulders, while the canvas eliminated the dangerous possibility of it coming loose and strangling me. In addition, the canvas was handy as a lunch tray and storage shelf for small items.

Foot Braces and/or Knee Pads

If you're familiar with the recent canoeing literature, you know that the modern way to paddle a canoe is to sit, not kneel, in it. Right? Not necessarily! Whether you sit or kneel—or alternate between the two—depends on the design of the canoe you're paddling and how you prefer to paddle.

If you have a high-volume Grumman/Marathon or Old Town Tripper with its high-mounted seats, you'll have to kneel in rapids. It's purely a matter of getting the CG (center of gravity) low enough for stability in the rough stuff. However, kneeling is practical only if the canoe you're piloting is wide enough at the bow to permit a comfortable kneeling stance (knees spread wide against the bilges). If it isn't—and most fine-lined cruisers are not—then you're best off to maintain your position on the low-mounted seat and brace your feet firmly against a bow flotation tank or improvised brace.

If foot braces are important in the bow of a skinny cruiser, they're even more important in the stern. The simplest brace consists of a pair of wood rails glassed to the floor or sidewalls of the boat. An aluminum tube, flattened at the ends, is screwed to the rails.

Figure 2-6 Foot braces lock you firmly into the canoe when you paddle from a sitting position. The simplest brace consists of a pair of wood rails glassed to the floor of the canoe. An aluminum tube, fastened at the ends, is screwed to the rails.

On the other hand, if your canoe is spacious enough up front for comfortable kneeling, you'll want to raise the seats to a comfortable 10- to 12-inch height (if they're not already set there) and install knee pads. You can purchase self-sticking neoprene pads or make your own from a closed-cell foam trail mattress. Glue knee pads into the hull with contact cement.

Most big tripping canoes provide for both sitting and kneeling options. You may want to install knee pads and foot braces in these boats.

Seat Height and Placement

I have yet to own a canoe whose seats were placed where I wanted them. Seats on fine-lined cruisers are generally mounted low for stability rather than high for efficiency and all-day comfort.

Many of the best canoes now come with sliding seats, which solves the trim problem when paddlers of different weights are aboard. But seat height is another matter. Most canoeists simply refuse to raise or lower their seats to a height that suits them, falsely believing that it's wrong to tamper with what was obviously ordained by God.

If you don't like the location of your canoe seats, change them, even if it means drilling new holes through the sidewalls of an expensive canoe!

Canoe Covers

Canoe covers are usually home-built affairs. They're constructed of waterproof nylon and have holes (skirts) for the paddlers. They attach to the canoe by snaps, velcro, or stainless-steel cable.

Some folks swear by canoe covers (I'm one of them). Others swear at them! There's no denying that they cut wind (as much as 50 percent), keep out rain and whitewater, and extend the versatility of low-volume canoes—you can use a small canoe in rough water if it's covered. However, covers can be extremely dangerous, especially if they come off in a capsize and entrap you, or if the spray skirt does not permit an easy exit.

The best setup I've used is a three-piece model of my own design. It has a belly section that expands or shrinks as the load height changes. The end caps can be rolled and tied—and may remain on the canoe—while portaging. For solo canoeing I prefer a two-piece cover that I also engineered. Step-by-step instructions for both these designs can be found in my book *Canoeing Wild Rivers* (Globe Pequot, 1989). Commercial versions are available from Cooke Custom Sewing.* Dan Cooke supplies a no-shrink Mylar template, which ensures a perfect fit on any canoe.

You don't need a full splash cover unless you're a whitewater fanatic or are canoeing the Canadian North. The one-piece expandable belly described on the next page provides enough protection for all but the most severe conditions. If you can sew a straight stitch you can make a belly cover in about three hours.

The belly section weighs about a pound and stuffs to football size. You can use it as a small sail or tablecloth, or as a rain cover for packs and firewood.

This belly section is generic—it will fit any canoe of roughly similar length if the snap positions on the canoes are identically placed. For example, the belly piece on my 17-foot Dagger Venture also fits my

Materials

1. Pattern: None! The canoe is your pattern.

2. Snaps: 24 brass snaps. Check 'em with a magnet to be sure they're not plated steel.

3. Waterproof nylon: 2½ ounces per square yard is strong enough for friendly waterways; 4- to 6-ounce stuff is best for the Arctic barrens.

4. One-inch-wide seam tape or nylon webbing: about 20 feet.

5. Extras: 2-inch-wide Velcro, 1-inch-wide pajama elastic.

Procedure

1. Pop-rivet snaps through the hull, 2 inches below the rails, 8 inches apart. Begin the snap line at the rear edge of the front seat and end it at the back thwart. Use an aluminum backup washer behind each rivet. You'll need about 12 snaps for each side of the canoe.

2. Cut a 60-inch-wide piece of fabric that reaches from the front edge of the bow seat to the rear thwart. Hem all sides, then sew seam tape to the inside hem. Next, fold over and sew the water deflector channels illustrated in figure 2-8. Thread pajama elastic through the channels and rear hem. Tighten the elastic slightly, then sew down the ends.

3. Set snaps through the hem to match those on the canoe. Nylon stretches when wet and shrinks when dry, so don't pull the material too tightly!

You can modify the belly to accept a passenger by installing a quick-release skirt in the center.

Figure 2-7 A three-piece canoe cover designed by the author. This model features a belly section that expands as the load height changes, and end caps that can be reefed while portaging.

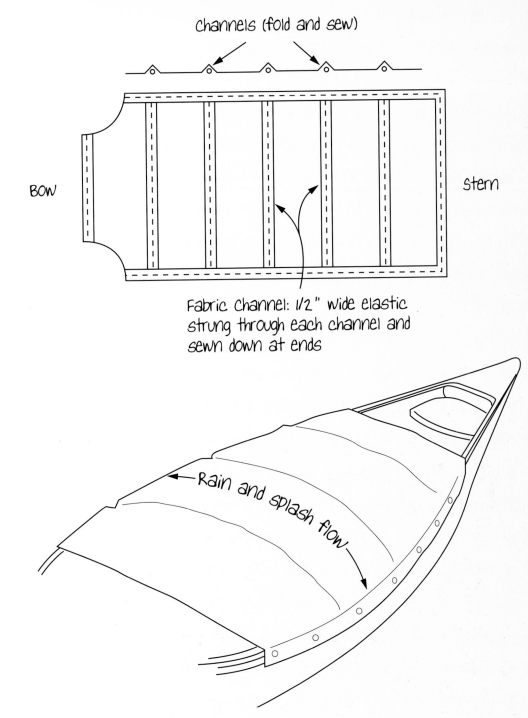

channels (fold and sew)

BOW

stern

Fabric channel: 1/2" wide elastic strung through each channel and sewn down at ends

Rain and splash flow

Figure 2-8 Belly section cover.

16-foot Dagger Legend and my 17-foot Old Town Tripper.

When the canoe is loaded with packs that come above the gunwales, the belly will rise up like a camel's hump to direct rain and splash toward the ends of the canoe. The elasticized channels will contain the runoff and deflect it sideways into the river, rather than into the skirts of the paddlers—a plus in rain and rapids.

Waterproof nylon, nylon webbing, nickel-plated brass snaps, and other canoe building materials are available by mail from Thrifty Outfitters* in Minneapolis.

CHAPTER 3

The Necessities

Packs and Substitutes

Frameless Packs

For short, close-to-home trips, just about any type of soft pack or duffel bag will do. But for trips of a more serious nature, you'll want to invest in authentic packsacks. The most popular and practical for canoeing is the venerable Duluth pack, which is traditionally constructed of 15- to 20-ounce-per-square-yard canvas. Straps are usually heavy leather and are secured with solid brass rivets and waxed thread. A stout tumpline (head strap) is sometimes provided. Duluth packs are extremely rugged and are commonly sized as follows:

Number 2: 24 inches wide by 28 inches deep
Number 3: 24 inches wide by 30 inches deep
Number 4: 28 inches wide by 30 inches deep, with a 6-inch sidewall (set out)

The most popular size is number 3, though some canoeists prefer the larger number 4 for lightweight, bulky items like sleeping bags and clothes.

Despite the advent of more modern packs, Duluth packs remain popular. Here's why:

- They have a huge capacity—there's always room to stuff one more thing in a Duluth pack.

- It's easy to waterproof the contents of these packs by inserting a nested pair of 6-mil plastic bags into them (see Waterproofing Your Outfit at the end of this chapter for the specific procedures).

- Duluth packs are designed to sit upright in a canoe instead of on their backs or bellies like packs of more conventional design. This stand-up feature has value when the canoe takes water in rapids or waves. The craft can fill with water and, as long as it remains upright, no water can enter

the mouth of the pack. This is because the weakest part of any waterproof bag is its closure, which is just beneath the flap of the erect Duluth pack—out of contact with accumulated water.

- Duluth packs fit easily into the unique contours of a canoe without wasting space.

- Despite their ominous reputation as instruments of torture, Duluth packs carry easily if you use a tumpline.

Figure 3-1 **The Duluth pack—still the best choice for canoe tripping.**

A tumpline consists of a wide leather or fabric strap that's secured to the "ears" (sides of the pack at shoulder level) of a packsack. Place this strap just above your forehead, grab the tumpline near your head, lean forward, and truck confidently down the trail. The tumpline should be adjusted so that nearly all of the pack weight is carried on your neck muscles. When you tire of the tumpstrap, simply brush it aside and transfer the weight to the shoulder straps. The early voyageurs carried hundreds of pounds of furs by this method, and packers in undeveloped countries still rely on this system.

Tumplines are most useful when ascending steep hills, as they take considerable weight off the pack straps. To make a tumpstrap for your pack, simply sew a well-reinforced D-ring to each side of your pack below shoulder height and mount the tumpline across them.

Place awkward bundles, like day packs, fishing rods, and canoe paddles under the tumpstrap in the hollow of your back, as illustrated in figure 3-2. When your neck and head begin to ache, cast off the tumpline and shift the load to the shoulder straps. Change back to the head strap when the pain is gone. Once you become accustomed to a tumpline (it takes only a few portages), you'll want one on all your trippingpacks.

The best testimonial for tumplines comes from Himalayan porters, who use them almost exclusively to carry heavy loads for tourists. If hip belts helped with uphill loads, native Himalayans would use them! You can prove this by carrying a heavy backpack up a staircase using the shoulder straps alone. Now attach a makeshift tumpline below the yoke of the pack and climb the stairs again. The stability provided by the tumpstrap will astound you.

Important: Take time to adjust the tumpline right! What works for one voyageur is wrong for another. Consider this before you give up on the grand idea.

The best way to rest muscles on a long, mean portage is to switch between tumpline, hip belt, and shoulder straps. No rule says your pack can't have all three! Traditional canvas Duluth packs with optional tumplines are available from Duluth Pack.* CLG Enterprises* and Cooke Custom Sewing* make excellent nylon versions.

State-of-the-Art Soft Packs

In recent years a number of state-of-the-art canoe packs have emerged. Most notable are those made by Grade VI,* Granite Gear,* Camp Trails,* Cooke Custom Sewing,* and Ostrom Outdoors.* These packs use straight-through construction (no compartments) and a sophisticated shoulder-harness/hip-belt system that is more comfortable than the standard Duluth design. Most are comfortable enough to double as full-fledged hiking packs, and they can be set upright in a canoe if you don't fill them too full. For the past ten years I've been using a Cooke Custom Sewing Pioneer pack, and it earns high marks. Naturally, I added a tumpline.

Fully Waterproof Packs

Rafting bags, like the SealLine models made by Cascade Designs,* appear attractive for canoeing because they are absolutely watertight, even when submerged in a pounding rapid. However, it's tedious to roll and seal the waterproof mouth every time you need to access pack contents, and there are no outside pockets, lash points, or pack flaps under which to store loose items.

Some rafting bags have hip belts. None have tumplines. Even the best rafting bags can't match the comfort of a well-packed, tumpline-equipped Duluth pack. Hard granite and sharp thorns take their toll on the PVC-coated material. When holes develop, you'll have to find and patch them—or sandwich pack your gear, as suggested in Waterproofing Your Outfit on page 35.

small Pack

Figure 3-2 Packing with a tumpline.

Packs with Frames

Packs with frames—external, internal, or in between—are awkward for canoeing. The frames may bend or break, or catch on seats and yokes during loading operations. Empty frame packs cannot be rolled and stuffed inside other packs to save space as the trip progresses.

Stick with canoeing long enough and frame packs will disappear from your gear closet. Exceptions: Some grizzled Arctic travelers include one frame pack per canoe for long-distance hiking. And a small internal-frame rucksack is useful for frequently used items like rain gear, sweaters, and optical equipment.

Rigid Packs and Wanigan Boxes

Yes, you can carry eggs and thermos bottles on a canoe trip without breaking them. All you need is a rigid pack of some sort. For centuries the traditional solution has been the woven ash pack basket, which is available from Duluth Pack* and L. L. Bean.*

I've worked with Duluth Pack to develop an enlarged cruiser pack that will accommodate a standard 18-inch-high pack basket. The Cliff Jacobson version has an extended flap, a double canvas bottom, and two side pockets that run the length of the pack. Each side pocket will accept two MSR or Sigg aluminum fuel bottles. There's enough room under the extra long closing flap to stuff "one more thing." Be sure to order this combo with a tumpline.

I nest my pack basket inside two heavy rubberized army clothes bags (available at military surplus stores), which then go inside the CJ cruiser pack. A loop of shock cord (permanently tied to each bag) secures each bag independently. This is a very sturdy waterproof unit, and one that packs well in a canoe.

I'm also fond of the Wanigan Canoe Pack & Pantry made by Stormy Bay.* This tough plastic box is portable and watertight, and it will fit crosswise in the belly of a narrow tandem canoe. The Stormy Bay wanigan has padded shoulder straps and fast, foolproof latches. Optional accessories include a plastic dishpan—which takes up no space in the pack—and shelves. You can easily attach a tumpline. The box is strong enough to sit or stand upon.

Figure 3-3 The Maine pack basket: Items that are breakable or that might be uncomfortable in a conventional soft pack are placed in the pack basket. To make a watertight unit, the basket is first placed in a waterproof army clothes bag.

The Hard Pack—a molded polyethylene box made by CLG Enterprises*—is another option. It's sized to fit inside a number 3 Duluth pack, or you can use the optional carrying harness. The Hard Pack loads from the top like a pack basket and is similar to the no-longer-manufactured plastic Rec-Pac, which was popular in the 1970s. A snug-fitting lid and rubber gasket make the unit reasonably waterproof.

Or you can follow the lead of Canadian canoeists

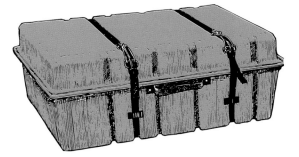

Figure 3-4 The Stormy Bay wanigan: A tough Norel plastic box that's portable and watertight. The wanigan has padded shoulder straps and a 5,200-cubic-inch capacity (about the same as a number 3 Duluth pack).

and place hard items in plastic olive jars or pickle barrels. Three or four 15-inch-diameter olive jars will fit in a number 3 Duluth pack. Twenty-four-inch-high plastic barrels can be purchased from western rafting companies. Uncomfortable carrying harnesses are available from some Canadian outfitters.

Here are two do-it-yourself alternatives to commercial hard packs:

1. Varnish a large cardboard box inside and out and place it inside your soft pack. For greater longevity, apply fiberglass instead of varnish.

2. Next time you go discount-store shopping, take your Duluth pack with you. When you pass the housewares section, locate a plastic trash can liner that fits inside the pack. The cheaper cans tend to be flimsier and so conform better to your bony contours than do more expensive rigid models.

Tip: To waterproof the mouth of the plastic trash can, insert the trash can inside a tough plastic bag. This will prevent sharp objects inside the pack from puncturing the delicate waterproof liner. Then insert the whole combo into your Duluth pack.

Points to Consider Before You Commit to Any Pack

1. Portaging a few hundred yards several times a day (the typical trip scenario) is not the same as hiking 15 miles along a mountain trail. You don't need serious hiking gear for short carries. You do need equipment that stacks well in canoes!

2. A tumpline takes the weight off your back and so negates the value of sophisticated suspension systems.

3. Sophisticated features don't come cheap. State-of-the-art backpacks cost much more than common Duluth packs. A serious backpacker needs just one pack; a wilderness canoeist needs three or more per canoe.

4. After a rain or capsize, you may have some wet, bulky gear that won't fit inside your pack. Be sure the closing flap of your pack is long enough to accommodate these items. A general rule is that the flap

should roughly equal the length of the pack. There's no such thing as a pack flap that is too long!

Waterproof Camera Bags and Dry Boxes

I bemoan the passing of the wonderful military amphibious assault gas mask bags. No modern camera-sized bag is as watertight. Most camera buffs use military ammo boxes or plastic Pelican* boxes (they are the best), which are available at outdoor stores.

I've seen a lot of dry boxes fail on canoe trips. A blade of grass, a plant seed, dirt, or other foreign material may break the seal and cause it to fail. If you are very meticulous about keeping seals clean, good dry boxes—like the recommended Pelican—work fine. Unfortunately, the rigor of canoe trips demands compromises, and attention to seals is not always a priority. For this reason I cannot commit my heart to "waterproof" boxes.

Here's how I pack my optical and communications gear:

- Camera: I have an ancient amphibious assault gas mask bag that is still sound. If and when it fails, I will switch to a small Cascade Designs* SealLine bag. The beauty of a bag over a dry box is that a small amount of foreign matter won't corrupt the roll-down seal.

- GPS: I keep my GPS in a small foam-lined Tupperware box packed inside a transparent Cascade Designs See Bag. This setup is rugged and waterproof. Yes, it has survived a capsize.

- VHF Radio: In an emergency (only!) I'll use my telephone-sized VHF transceiver to contact overhead aircraft. I keep the radio in a foam-lined Pelican* case stored near the bottom of my pack basket.

Tents

You can be a bit lavish when selecting a canoe tent. After all, the longest portage in most canoe country is seldom more than a mile—hardly a backbreaking distance to transport a tent of reasonable weight. What's reasonable depends, of course, on your perspective, though most canoeists would agree that 12 pounds is about maximum for a tent that will be used by two people.

Size

It works out that each camper needs a space of around 7 feet by 2½ feet just to stretch out and store gear. Increase the area to 8 feet by 3 feet and you enter the realm of comfort. Widen it another 6 inches and ahh . . . pure luxury. A floor plan of 7 feet by 8 feet and enough room to sit fully upright is ideal for two. Evidently most canoeists agree, for nearly all the tents you see on canoe trails are technically classified as four-person models, even though they're commonly (and wisely) occupied by just two.

Sleeping two in a tent built for four may seem like needless pampering, until:

- You encounter a storm. Then extra space is essential, not just for sanity but to keep your bedding dry. Even the best tents will deform some in high winds, and if you're snuggled against a sidewall, water is sure to condense on your sleeping bag. And if your tent has a "cap" fly (a three-quarter-length fly that doesn't extend to the ground), wind-driven mist might blow in through the breathable nylon canopy. Now, if you can just put some distance between the tent sidewall and your sleeping gear. . . .

- You become wind- or bug-bound and have to eat, relax, and make repairs to equipment inside your tent.

- Your neighbor's tent destructs in a high wind. Thank God you have a four-person tent and can handle the overload!

Fabrics

The only suitable tent material is nylon. Cotton tents are too heavy, they gain weight when wet, and they mildew. When you buy a nylon tent, make sure you specify two-ply construction. This means that the tent consists of two layers of fabric. The main tent body is built of a porous nylon or mosquito net, to let body-produced water vapor out. To keep the rain from getting in, a chemically coated waterproof fly is suspended a few inches over the inner tent. The result is a shelter that is completely watertight, breathable, and lightweight. You can pitch the tent without the fly on clear nights, or you can remove the rainfly and use it separately as your only shelter for camping in the fall, when bugs are no problem (some of the best canoe tents have integral flies that cannot be removed).

Bulk

Bulk is more important than weight. You can live with a few extra pounds, even on a go-light canoe journey, but not with a tent that won't fit in your pack. The culprit is usually the length of the poles—sections longer than 23 inches simply won't fit crosswise in most packs without protruding from under the closing flap. And anything that's secured by friction alone can work free and be lost.

A good canoe tent should pack small enough to fit completely inside the waterproof confines of your packsack. Unfortunately, some otherwise outstanding canoe tents do not.

Here's how to pack a tent with obnoxiously long poles:

1. Stuff or roll the tent without the poles or pegs. Pack the tent inside your pack.

2. Place poles and pegs in a sturdy nylon bag with drawstring closure. Sew a loop of nylon webbing to each end of the bag and attach lengths of parachute cord to the loops.

3. Pack the pole set under the pack flap and snake the closing straps though loops in the cord ends. Now your pole bag can't possibly fall out of your pack. Figure 3-8 shows the procedure.

Geometry

You'll pay more for sophisticated geometry—geodesic domes and tunnels—than for simple-to-sew but reliable A-frame tents. Be aware that price does not necessarily indicate foul-weather performance, nor how easy (or difficult) it is to pitch the tent.

The best and worst canoe tents are domes. The truly great ones—like the North Face VE series—are frightfully expensive and possibly overkill for the kind of forest camping most people do. Cheap domes are worse than a well-pitched tarp. Spend one rainy

Figure 3-5 Eureka A-frame and dome tents.

night in a discount-store dome and you'll know for sure that the designers never did! Check these features of a good canoe tent:

1. The waterproof fly should stake right to the ground. Wind can whip under a short cap fly and tear the fly right off the tent! Failing this, the fly must cover every canopy seam and zipper. Tents that have exposed seams or zippers will leak in rain.

2. Every door and window needs a protective overhang that the wind can't blow aside.

3. Extra-large self-healing coil zippers should be used throughout. The sliders should be made of nickel-plated metal, not plastic. Zippers need a secure weather flap.

4. Check the vulnerable corners of the tent, where seams and zippers come together. Are they all completely covered by the waterproof fly?

5. Poles should be made of tempered aluminum. There is no such thing as a good plastic or fiberglass pole!

6. Pretend your hands are wind and perform these tests: First, push hard against the center sidewall. It should deform then immediately return to shape when you remove your hand. Then shake each pole hard. The tent should rustle quietly—not flutter violently—and return to its taut shape when you let go. Don't buy any tent that won't stay drum-tight.

7. A second door provides flow-through ventilation and is handy if a door zipper goes bad.

8. The bug screen should be colored black so you can see through it. And it should be mounted outside the door so you can zip the door without reaching through the net.

Every serious canoe tent should meet these minimal requirements, though most don't. Old-fashioned A-frame tents—like the popular Eureka Timberline and its derivatives—are excellent canoe tents, and they're not too pricey. Chapter 17 presents some practical ways to stormproof tents. And my book *Camping's Top Secrets* (Globe Pequot Press, 1998) suggests more ideas.

Sleeping Bag

Average canoe-country temperatures seldom drop below freezing, and in this climate a sleeping bag filled with 20 ounces of good down or 2 pounds of quality synthetic is quite adequate. In fact, I would rule out as too warm any closely fitting bag with more filler than this.

A real advantage of Quallofil, Primaloft, and Polarguard is that these synthetic materials, unlike down, stubbornly refuse to absorb water. If a Quallofil or Polarguard bag gets wet, it can be wrung out and will retain a good share of its warmth. Down, on the other hand, possesses almost no insulating value when water-soaked.

However, as I've already pointed out, there's no excuse for getting your sleeping bag—or anything else—wet on a canoe trip. If you don't know how to waterproof your gear or stormproof your tent, you need to learn the basic waterproofing skills outlined at the end of this chapter.

Trail Mattress

A good trail mattress should smooth out the lumps and insulate your body from the cold, damp ground. It should also be lightweight, compact, and reliable.

Air mattresses are pretty much a thing of the past for deep-woods camping. And for good reason: They are a hassle to inflate and they're cold on chilly nights. An old solution is to place a thin closed-cell foam sleeping pad on top of an air mattress. This combination is warm and comfortable, even in below-freezing temperatures.

Today's knowledgeable campers rely almost exclusively on self-inflating air/foam pads, like the popular Therm-a-Rest trail mattress. Every camping shop has them.

Any air-filled mattress will eventually fail, so if reliability is a concern, you may want to stick with an all-foam product. *Tip:* Make a breathable cotton flannel cover for your self-inflating air/foam or open-cell foam pad. Nylon covers are hot and sticky against bare skin, and they wander all over the tent floor. A cotton cover will add years to the life of your trail mattress.

Cooking Gear

See chapter 16, for a discussion of essential cooking gear.

Stoves

There are gasoline, kerosene, multifuel (burns any liquid fuel), propane, butane, and wood-burning stoves. For canoeing, gasoline stoves make the most sense. Propane stoves are too heavy, butane models don't put out enough heat, and kerosene stoves are smelly and must be primed. Multifuel stoves are ported to burn a variety of liquid fuels, so they are much less efficient than gasoline models. Gasoline stoves run more efficiently on naphtha (Coleman and Blazo brand fuels) than on white gasoline. *Warning:* Do not use unleaded automotive fuel in a stove that is designed to burn white gasoline. Impurities in automotive unleaded gas may create a dangerous condition or cause some stoves to malfunction.

A low-profile gasoline stove with a pressure pump that puts out around 8,500 Btu per hour is best. Store gas in 1-liter aluminum bottles or the original metal

Stove Tricks

- Empty the fuel from your stove after each outing and burn the tank dry at the end of the camping season. Residue from fuel left in stoves is the major reason for stove failure.

- Mix a capful (no more) of carburetor cleaner with half a tank of gas and burn this mixture in your stove at the end of the season to clean out damaging gums and varnishes.

- Keep leather pump washers lubricated with high-grade gun oil. Avoid vegetable oils, which can gum up stove parts.

- Replace the rubber gasket inside the stove filler cap at least once every two years. Gaskets harden with age and leak air—a major cause of stove failure.

can. I allow 2 liters of gas per week for a party of four people (not including the original stove-tank filling).

One wood-burning stove, the Super Sierra, shows promise. This compact stainless-steel unit is powered by a small fan that runs on a single A-cell battery. The stove has a mechanical damper and weighs just 1 pound. Heat output at peak efficiency is a remarkable 15,000 Btu per hour. A windscreen, grill, and pot set are available. For details write ZZ Corporation, 10806 Kaylor Street, Los Alamitos, CA 90720.

Cutlery

Knives

For day-tripping any good jackknife will do, but for more adventuresome canoeing you'll want a blade that's long enough to produce kindling, slice sausage, and reach to the bottom of the peanut butter jar.

My vote goes to a sheath knife with a 4- to 5-inch-long blade. A thin (no wider than ⅛ inch across the spine), flat-ground blade is better for slicing and spreading than one with a hollow ground (concave) or saber-ground blade. High-grade tool steel takes a keener edge and is much easier to sharpen than stainless.

Here are two of my favorite sheath knives:

1. Idaho Knife Works* Cliff Knife: Custom knife-smith Mike Mann and I designed this practical camp knife along the lines of the wonderful old Gerber Shorty—which, unfortunately, is no longer produced. The Cliff Knife has a 4.3-inch, flat-ground blade, made from 0.078-inch-thick L6 bandsaw steel. I have no affiliation with Idaho Knife Works. I recommend the Cliff Knife to you simply because it works so well for me.

2. Grohmann* #1 and #2 (4-inch elliptical blades) Camp Models: Russell/Grohmann knives have won numerous international design awards. In 1997 I encouraged Grohmann to offer flat-ground versions of these superb knives. You'll find an assortment of stainless-steel models in good camping stores. Duluth Pack* has a small inventory of carbon steel blades.

Much as I love my sheath knife, I wouldn't be without a Swiss Army knife and Leatherman. These tools are too practical to leave at home.

Ax and Saw

You need an ax for splitting kindling, driving stubborn tent stakes, setting rivets in torn pack straps, and repairing bent hardware on canoes. An ax provides the edge you need to make a cheery campfire when the woods are soaked from rain. You don't need a big one: Saw your wood into 12-inch lengths and you'll have no trouble splitting them using the safe procedure illustrated on page 110.

For years, I carried an all-steel Estwing hand ax on my canoe trips. Then in 1998 my friend Dick Person, who lives in a log cabin in the Yukon, gave me a Gransfors* Small Forest Ax, which has a 19-inch hickory handle and a 1½-pound head. The hand-forged blade is hardened to R57C, which is harder than conventional axes and as hard as most good knives! The ax came from the factory shaving-sharp (really). An excellent sheath is provided. If you want the best ax on the planet, Gransfors is it. Prices are very reasonable—you won't have to sell the farm.

Gransfors axes can be mail-ordered from Duluth Pack.*

Most sheaths that come with cutlery are too thin. To make your own sheath, obtain some heavy sole leather and soak it in water for a few minutes until it's flexible. While the leather is wet, mold and cut it to the shape of the tool (you should make a paper pattern first). When the leather is reasonably dry, glue the sheath together with contact cement and seal the edges with brass rivets. Use the procedure illustrated in figure 3-6 to keep your ax keen and free of nicks.

Folding Saw

You'll need a saw to maintain a fire on a rainy day. Triangular-shaped metal saws are flimsy, and they won't cut big logs. Three folding camp saws I can recommend are:

1. The Fast Bucksaw. This beautiful hard-maple saw has an easily replaced 21-inch blade (refills are available at hardware stores). When assembled, it's so rigid that you'd swear it was a one-piece model. Mail-order only from Fast Bucksaw, Inc.*

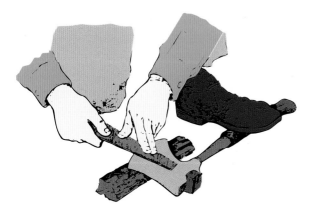

Figure 3-6 Here's the best way to sharpen an ax in the field. When using this method, care must be taken to prevent the file from going too far forward (a bad cut could result). For the utmost in safety, equip your file with a handle and guard (impractical accessories on extended canoe trips).

2. The tubular aluminum TrailBlazer* is a full-stroke rectangular saw in the old bucksaw tradition. It comes with two blades—one for wood, one for bone or metal.

3. When it comes to lightweight saws, the Sawvivor can't be beat. Its rectangular aluminum frame assembles in seconds and locks tight, with no play whatsoever. The saw weighs just 10½ ounces, complete with a 15-inch blade. The Sawvivor is an official saw of the U.S. Army.

Tips: Keep your disassembled folding saw in a nylon bag. This will keep the parts cleaner and speed assembly time.

Occasionally spray saw blades with WD-40. This will improve cutting performance and resist rust.

Shovel

A foot-long piece of aluminum tubing with one end smashed flat makes an excellent ultralight shovel.

Signaling Equipment

Don't leave home without these items:

Personal Gear

- Whistle—The pealess, blaze-orange, Fox 40 is the loudest and most reliable wilderness whistle you can buy. I keep my Fox 40 attached to a zipper pull on my life jacket.

- Heliograph mirror—some years ago, in the Boundary Waters Canoe Area, I encountered a teenage girl who had appendicitis. Miraculously, there was a Forest Service float plane flying overhead. I used the sighting mirror on my Silva Ranger compass to bring the floatplane down. The girl was flown to the hospital in Grand Marais, Minnesota, and her appendix was safely removed. A genuine heliograph mirror (the type with a sighting hole in the center) is easier to use than a standard mirror.

Group Safety Items

Search and rescue operations are usually daytime affairs, so flares don't have much value on a canoe trip. Colored smoke, however, is very useful. On two occasions, I've used orange smoke to signal my floatplane pilot. In both cases, the pilot never saw our bright red canoes and yellow tents. It was the orange smoke that brought him down.

Orange smoke signals are available at every sailing shop and marina. Smokes, flares, mirrors, and complete (lightweight) signal kits are available by mail from Orion Safety Products (Appendix 4).

Footwear

- Leather boots get wet and stay that way. For serious canoeing, choose from the following:

- Rubber boot with steel shanks and 16-inch-high tops. These are preferred mostly by Canadian bush travelers, who often wade icy rivers.

- Rubber-bottom-leather-top shoe-pacs of the L. L. Bean* type—popular with canoeists who want more support, comfort, and breathability than provided by all-rubber boots.

- Inexpensive tennis shoes and wool socks. For chilly March whitewater, wear neoprene wet-suit socks inside oversized sneakers.

- River sandals are fine for wading warm streams as long as there are no pebbles that can catch underfoot. You may need to wear thick wool socks to prevent mosquitoes and blackflies from nipping your toes. *Tip:* Buckles and laces hold much better than Velcro. In all, sandals are better for rafting than canoeing.

- Reef-runners are flexible nylon moccasins that slip on and secure with Velcro or elastic. Designed for surfboarding and sailing, they work well for warm-water canoeing where there are no portages—or pebbles.

- Knee-high Tingley rubber overshoes roll to fist-sized, and their soft rubber soles won't slip on wet rocks. Wear wool socks and sneakers inside Tingleys and you're set for both summer sun and an Arctic adventure. Most big hardware chains (like Fleet Farm) carry Tingley boots. They are very inexpensive.

For wilderness canoeing you need an extra pair of boots or shoes. I wear 12-inch Bean boots for most of my paddling and switch to supple, high-top canvas sneakers for wading and relaxing.

Personal Clothing

For one- or two-day trips, bring a complete change of clothes. For outings longer than two days, add two changes of underwear and three or four pairs of socks. Be sure to take a medium-weight wool jacshirt or fleece sweater and nylon windbreaker. Canoe-country temperatures seldom drop below freezing, so there really is no need to take additional clothing.

Regardless of the clothing you select, it should be nonrestrictive to allow freedom for paddling. Shirts and jackets should be comfortable to wear under a life jacket. For this reason bulky down and fiberfill jackets are not recommended. Your canoeing wardrobe should consist almost exclusively of wool, polypropylene, or fleece for warmth and quick-drying nylon for wind and water protection. Cotton is acceptable only for wind parkas or for use in very warm weather.

Long Johns

For chilly spring canoe trips, long johns are a must. Polypropylene, fleece, Dacron, and wool all work well, and differences among these fabrics are less pronounced than manufacturers will admit. *Warning:* Some fabrics (notably polypropylene and certain Dacron blends) absorb body odors and smell awful in a short time. And insect repellents dissolve some synthetics instantly.

Rain Gear

The best rain gear is a two-piece coated nylon rain suit. Avoid ponchos and below-the-knee rain shirts; these can make swimming difficult if you capsize.

If you want a reliable, inexpensive rain suit, check out the ones at industrial-supply stores—the same places

Reef Runner

Tingley Rubber Overshoe with Sneaker Inside

River Sandal

Old Tennis Shoe

16" High Rubber Boot—best for cold water and bad portages

Figure 3-7 Footwear.

where construction workers shop. The new industrial rain suits are very light and are constructed of fabrics that are similar to those used on the best foul-weather suits. But because there are no pockets, formfitted hoods, or other niceties, they cost much less.

At the far end of the cost spectrum are PVC and neoprene-coated foul-weather sailing suits—they won't let you down no matter how bad it rains. They are worth every penny if you need them and can afford them.

Early Gore-Tex garments often leaked when they became soiled, but the new-generation stuff is reliable, even when dirty. Be sure to specify rainwear-without-compromise (RWC) construction on all Gore-Tex foul-weather gear. Garments that do not have the RWC tag may leak in prolonged rain.

Buy what you can afford, but don't waste your money on frills you don't need. And get your outfit large enough to fit over baggy trousers and a life vest. Rains are frequently sporadic in canoe country; stripping off a life jacket every time you want to put on or take off your rain gear is a hassle. Incidentally, some rain trousers are equipped with snaps or Velcro at the ankle, which severely restricts ventilation. Rain trousers should hang straight and "pump" air with every move you make.

Finally, be aware that even the best rain gear will develop holes if you wear it all the time. So wear rain clothes only when it rains and switch to a lightweight, breathable nylon shell for protection from wind.

See appendix 2 for a checklist of essential personal and community gear.

Waterproofing Your Outfit

If money is no object, you can buy state-of-the-art neoprene or PVC-coated packsacks that are guaranteed not to leak—at least when new. And you can patch, glue, and ultimately replace them after a few dozen mean portages. That's because no matter how substantial a pack fabric is, it will ultimately succumb to the effects of abrasion. For example, how long will the best PVC-coated pack last when it's loaded with 60 pounds of gear and dragged solidly across sharp granite or slammed hard onto a pebble beach? These are the harsh realities of wilderness canoe travel.

The inner fabric of a packsack is also subject to considerable abrasion. Every time you stuff a pair of sneakers, hand ax, or sleeping bag deep inside the pack, you rub off a microthin layer of its waterproof coating. Eventually, the bag will leak and you'll need to repair it. Far better to devise a waterproof system that can be maintained at low cost—one that will keep water out and provide the abrasion protection you need.

The key to the system is to sandwich inexpensive plastic bags between layers of abrasion-resistant material. For example, to waterproof your sleeping bag, first stuff the bag into its nylon sack (which need not be watertight), then set the sack inside a 4-mil-thick plastic bag. Pleat and twist the end of the bag, fold it over, and secure it with a loop of shock cord. Then place this unit into an oversized nylon sack (again, it doesn't have to be waterproof). Note that the delicate plastic liner—which is the only real water barrier—is protected from abrasion on both sides!

If you line your nylon stuff sack with a plastic bag, then stuff your sleeping bag into it as advised by some authorities, you'll abrade and eventually tear the plastic liner. The method I've suggested creates a waterproof seal and eliminates the damage caused by the most careful stuffing.

How to Waterproof Your Portage Pack

1. Insert a 36- by 48-inch, 6-mil-thick, plastic bag into the packsack. You'll find these huge bags at canoe shops, or you can mail-order them from Duluth Pack.* This is the waterproof layer of your packing system.

2. Place a second 6-mil plastic bag—or one sewn from nylon, canvas, or polyethylene—inside the first. This is your abrasion liner.

Guidelines for Waterproofing Your Gear

- Pack in the reverse order that you'll need things. For example, you'll erect shelter before you prepare meals, so pack your tent above your food. If possible, try to position critical items near the bottom of your packsack. Rationale: Water must filter through the contents of the pack to wet what's on the bottom.

- Pack in horizontal layers. Thus, sleeping bag, foam pad, tent, and so on, are placed sideways, not straight up and down. Rationale: Your pack won't fill out with a degree of "spinal curve" to match the contour of your back if you insert unyielding uprights.

- Best use of space results when items are matched to the pack's internal dimensions. So make your stuff sacks long and thin rather than short and fat.

- Poles longer than about 20 inches won't fit crosswise in a pack, and if you set them vertically, you'll foul up the whole packing system. So place poles and stakes in a secure bag to keep them separate from the tent. Figure 3-8 shows how to pack poles and stakes so they won't be lost in a capsize.

Packing Out

You'll need three large, soft packs for a one- to two-week canoe trip. My preference is one number 3 Duluth pack, one Cooke* Pioneer pack, and the 18-inch-high pack basket/Duluth cruiser combination that I mentioned on page 25. Don't use number 4 Duluth packs—they are hard to handle and they don't fit well in a canoe. Each canoeist should bring a small day pack or fanny pack for frequently used items like rain gear, sweater, gloves, binoculars, and snacks.

How to Pack Your Gear

1. Divide your food bags (see chapter 16) equally among all members of your crew. Place your share of the food on the bottom of your pack.

2. Place your sandwich-bagged sleeping bag on top of your food bags. Your foam sleeping pad goes next.

3. Each canoeist should have his or her own clothes bag. This is a pillow-sized nylon stuff sack that holds clothes and personal gear. Set your clothes bag on top of your foam pad.

4. Hug the pack to exhaust air, then tightly pleat and roll down the inner plastic abrasion liner.

5. Place the tent (minus poles and stakes) horizontally on top of the abrasion liner, inside the unsealed waterproof liner. The tent should fit snugly, like a cork in a bottle.

6. Tightly roll down the outer waterproof liner.

7. Place tent poles—in their secure bag—just under the pack flap, as illustrated in figure 3-8. Run the pack straps through the security loops and cinch them down. The poles will stay put if you capsize. You now have a completely watertight unit that will withstand long-term submersion.

Note: The tent is often damp or muddy, so it's placed between the abrasion liner and waterproof liner to separate it from the dry pack contents below. And it won't get wet if you capsize! Limited pack space dictates that if you carry a tent, you should carry less food.

At this point, traditionalists are probably shaking their heads in disbelief that I would suggest packing food and personal gear together. Doesn't this encourage bears?

No! On the contrary, putting all your food in one pack—like they do in the Boundary Waters Canoe Area of Minnesota—can be unwise if you're a long

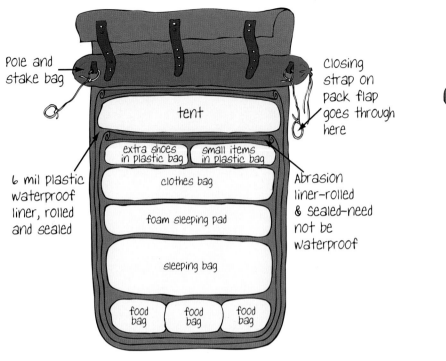

Duluth-style pack

Pole and stake bag

Closing strap on pack flap goes through here

6 mil plastic waterproof liner, rolled and sealed

Abrasion liner—rolled & sealed—need not be waterproof

tent

extra shoes in plastic bag

small items in plastic bag

clothes bag

foam sleeping pad

sleeping bag

food bag

food bag

food bag

Figure 3-8 A waterproof system of packing your gear.

way from help and a bear gets the pack that contains all your food. Better to distribute your "eggs" among many "baskets"—and develop a sound plan. Chapter 18 presents one that hasn't failed me yet.

Pack basket. Place hard items—cook kit, stove, fuel bottles, first-aid kit, and other items that might gouge your back—into the pack basket. Separately seal the two waterproof liners and cinch down the pack flap.

Packing the Canoe

The important thing is to have a low, well-balanced load, with most of the weight as close to the middle of the canoe as possible. Packs can be stacked one behind the other, or sideways, parallel to the gunwales—whichever is convenient. If possible, set packs

upright so their mouths won't be submerged in bilgewater. Box-sided packs that are too long to be set upright can be placed belly-down or on their sides. Side loading uses space better and simplifies handling at portages. Don't lay packs belly-up in the canoe—the backs and shoulder straps will absorb bilge-water and soak your shirt when you portage.

You can check a canoe's trim by pouring some water into the hull. It should pool below the yoke. Some serious paddlers paint a waterline on the sides of their canoe. Others just ask an onlooker how they're trimmed—a good plan as long as you remember that the bows of modern canoes are often several inches higher than the sterns. But the best plan is just adding water, as noted. Water doesn't lie!

Over the Portage and Through the Woods

The standard procedure for portaging is as follows: Each person takes a pack and a paddle and strikes out across the portage. While walking, both canoeists look for shortcuts back to the river or lake ahead, as well as obstacles that will have to be circuited when the canoe is brought over the trail. Packs are dropped at the end of the portage, and the pair returns. On the second trip one person carries the canoe and the other takes the last pack and any remaining items. Usually the person with the pack leads so that when the canoe carrier becomes tired, he or she can call to the person ahead to look for a suitable stopping place—like a jutting tree limb where the bow of the canoe can be set. When such a limb is found, the canoe carrier sets the bow in place and steps from beneath the yoke to rest. This procedure requires much less energy than setting a canoe on the ground and later lifting it to the shoulders.

In heavily traveled wilderness areas, wooden rests are often provided to prevent people from jamming canoe ends into tree branches. Although such rests spoil the primitive nature of the portage, they are essential to minimize environmental damage to foliage. In parklike areas where portages are known to be clear and in good condition, the canoe is sometimes carried over the trail first—primarily because it is the heaviest load and requires the greatest expenditure of energy.

Doublepacking!

Part II

Canoe Skills

CHAPTER 4

Portaging the Canoe

Every canoe trip includes some sort of portage—be it the innocent task of loading the canoe onto the family station wagon, carrying it to and from the launching site, or lifting it over fallen trees, dams, and other obstacles in a local stream. And if you're off to the wilds of Canada, portaging is part of the daily routine.

Although canoes, equipment, and paddling methods have changed considerably during the past century, the technique of portaging has remained the same. I say "technique" because portaging is as much an art as it is a feat of physical strength. I've seen 90-pound girls single-handedly lift 70-pound canoes and carry them nonstop over very rough trails for more than ¼ mile. And I've known 200-pound men who couldn't carry the same canoe more than 200 feet without dropping it on the nearest boulder. A canoe on land is out of its native habitat, and in the hands of a careless person it can suffer great damage.

The trickiest part of portaging is getting the canoe from the ground to your shoulders. Even old-timers who've sweated under the yoke for more miles than they can recall appreciate a helping hand here. Nonetheless, with a bit of practice, shouldering a 75-pound canoe is easy. In fact, once you get the mechanics down pat, you may prefer to loft it yourself rather than trust the outcome to a well-meaning friend who is not familiar with the process.

Surprisingly, it's almost always easier to carry a canoe alone than with a friend, because partners can rarely coordinate their movements. When one person bounces, the other jounces—all of which makes for a terribly awkward and painful experience. Two-person carries are only efficient on groomed trails, and then only when the canoe is

outfitted with a yoke at each end.

Except in wind, a healthy adult can usually manage a canoe of reasonable weight (up to 85 pounds) without help if he or she has a good yoke and knows the proven lift-and-carry procedures.

One-Person Lift and Carry

On wilderness trips I seldom pick up a canoe by myself. It just takes too much effort, and I would rather save my energy for the portage trail. However, there will be many times when you will need to lift a canoe to your shoulders alone, so you should become proficient in the one-person lift and carry.

Procedure

If you're right-handed, stand at the center left side of the canoe, facing it. Pull the canoe up by the near gunwale and grasp the center of the yoke with your right hand (figure 4-1). Keeping your legs well apart, flip the canoe onto your thighs with a quick pull of your right arm. As the canoe comes up, grab the far gunwale with your left hand just forward of the yoke (the canoe should now be almost wholly supported by your thighs). Next, transfer your right-hand position to just in back of the yoke on the gunwale (figure 4-2). Thus, your left hand is forward of the yoke on the top gunwale and your right hand is just behind it on the bottom gunwale.

The next part is the hardest. With a quick upward push from your right knee, snap the canoe up and around, over your head (figure 4-3), and settle the yoke pads on your shoulders (figure 4-4). Many beginners have difficulty here because they are fearful of getting their necks twisted up in the yoke. In reality this almost never occurs. It's sort

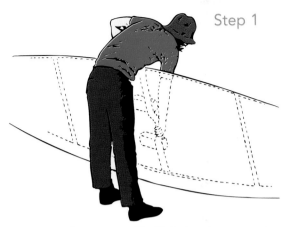

Figure 4-1 One-person lift: Right hand grasps yoke center and canoe is spun to thighs.

Figure 4-2 Left hand grasps top gunwales forward of the yoke and canoe is balanced on thighs. Note location of right hand.

Figure 4-3 With a quick upward push from your right knee, snap the canoe up and around.

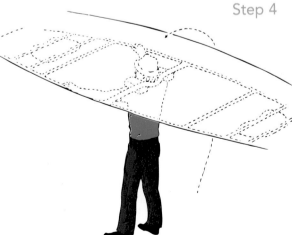

Figure 4-4 Settle yoke pads on your shoulders and . . . relax!

of like closing both eyes and touching your nose with a fist. Just as you always seem to successfully locate your nose, so too will you always find the portage yoke when then canoe comes up.

The keys to lifting the canoe are determination and a quick snap. You would have to be very strong to pick up even a light canoe slowly, whereas a person of small stature will have little difficulty raising canoes weight up to 90 pounds if he or she is snappy about it. When teaching this lift to new canoeists, I often tell them to remember right, left, right to ensure that their hands will be properly positioned during the pickup sequence. Thus, the right hand grasps the yoke center and the canoe is spun to the thighs, the left hand grasps the top gunwale forward of the yoke; the right hand grasps the lower gunwale just in back of the yoke, and the canoe is snapped to the shoulders.

The key to carrying a canoe is not strength at all; rather, it's learning to relax under the portage yoke. In order to accomplish this successfully, it is best that you have one or two friends help you position the canoe on your shoulders. When the yoke pads settle into place, stand perfectly straight and reach forward with your hands to grasp the gunwales. Place your fingers on the shelflike lip of the gunwales and your thumbs on the opposite side. If the canoe is properly balanced (slightly tail-heavy), light pressure from your fingers will bring the bow down to a horizontal position. The canoe is now ready for portaging. To get used to the yoke, stand in place and drop your left arm to your side. Most of the canoe's weight will now rest on your right shoulder. Repeat, dropping the other arm. You will become less tired on portages if you continually change the weight from shoulder to shoulder.

Two- or Three-Person Lift, One-Person Carry

The two-person lift is identical to the one-person lift except that your helper stands next to you, behind the yoke, and you stand slightly in front of it. The canoe should be supported on the thighs of both you and your partner prior to raising it into position. Your hands will be forward of the yoke

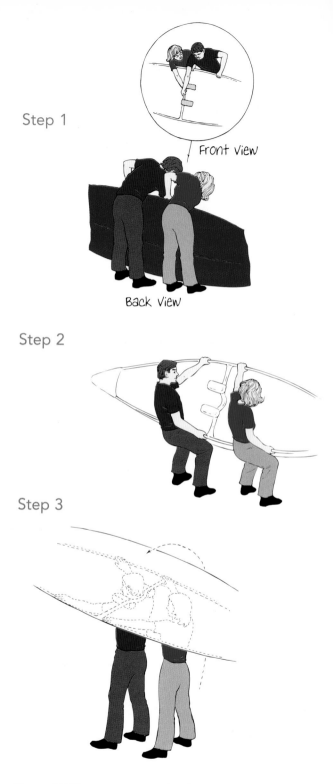

Step 1

Front View

Back View

Step 2

Step 3

Figure 4-5 The two-person side lift.

and your partner's will be behind it. At a mutually agreed-upon signal, flip the canoe, with the help of your partner, up onto your shoulders.

For a completely effortless pickup, try the three-person lift. This is identical to the two-person lift except that you have an additional person. Position yourself at the yoke and have one helper stand at the bow thwart, the other helper at the stern thwart. Again, you should all be on the same side of the canoe. All lift together. Nothing could be simpler.

End Lift

The end lift is an easy way for one or two people to get a heavy canoe up. Stand at the right rear of the canoe, facing the stern. Reach across with your right hand and grasp the left gunwale near the stern seat. Grasp the right gunwale with your left hand (figure 4-6, step 1). Now just roll the canoe over on its front end (step 2) and lift the tail in the air (step 3). While holding the canoe high, bow on the ground, shuffle yourself forward into the yoke. If you have a helper, let him or her hold the canoe up while you snuggle into the yoke.

The end pickup is popular with people who for one reason or another don't feel confident using the standard side lift. Although lifting a canoe by one end is accepted practice, it is not good canoeing technique, mainly because the end in contact with the ground gets chewed up. I would never use this method with a wood-trimmed canoe!

Racing Carry

Each paddler places his or her end of the canoe (usually right-side up) on a shoulder and cradles an arm around it for support. Once the canoe is in position, racers take off at a run and make very good time over short distances.

Where's the Portage?

Much of North America's canoe country consists of a maze of lakes connected by waterfalls, rapids, and meandering streams. In some cases you can run the rapids or walk the streams. Often, you will

Step 1

Step 2

Step 3

Figure 4-6 End lift.

have no recourse but to pack your canoe and gear over rugged portage trails.

In frequently traveled areas a portage may be marked by a sign, blazed tree, jutting pole, or small opening in the forest. On isolated routes there may be nothing to mark the way, yet a route around impassable water often exists. Most portages are trampled into place by large animals like moose and bears, which, like you, need to get around rapids and falls. It remains for you to find these trails.

Portages are most often located on the inside curves of rivers, and this is where you should look first. When you hear the roar of rapids and see the white plumes of dancing horse tails leaping high into the air, immediately get to the inside bend and paddle ashore. Then get out of your canoe and start looking. Walk the rapids to see if they are safe to run. Sometimes a single hidden ledge can make a rapid unnavigable, and you may not be able to see the ledge until it is too late!

The absence of a portage does not mean that the rapid is safe to run. Unusually high water may flood existing portages, making them impossible to find, and very low water can change channel characteristics so completely that you may paddle right by the portage without seeing it.

In some areas, especially those near James and Hudson Bays, portages are so overgrown with vegetation that you may have to hack your way through a maze of brush to reach safer water at the end of the trail. Cutting paths through the bush is not in keeping with the modern wilderness ethic (leave only footprints, take only pictures), but occasionally, for reason of safety, you may have no other choice. Fortunately for the environment, the scrubby trees you destroy will quickly grow back.

Never underestimate the power of rapids, especially if the water is high. The rule of thumb in the wilderness is: If in doubt, portage! Develop your whitewater skills at home, not on an isolated canoe trip where a single error can be fatal.

C H A P T E R 5

Paddle Power

Equipment First—The Canoe Paddle

Auto buffs know that the easiest way to improve the performance of a car is to put on good tires. Granted, hot wheels won't turn a Buick into a BMW, but they will make it more fun to drive. Paddles are the wheels of your canoe—good ones will smooth the ride. Here's how to tell a great paddle from a shaved down 2-by-4.

First Consideration—The Right Length

Any prescription for paddle length must take into account the kind of canoe (whitewater tripper, flatwater cruiser, racer, and so on) you are paddling, the height of the seats, the length of your torso, the reach of your arms, your own strength, and how you prefer to paddle—dynamic racing/switch style, slow-paced North Woods J-stroke, or the like. For these reasons experienced canoeists often own a shed full of paddles, each designed for a specific purpose and paddling style.

These variables influence paddle length:

- **Height of your canoe seat:** The higher you sit, the longer your paddle must be to reach the water. Seats on the typical high-volume Royalex or aluminum canoe are set relatively high (11 to 13 inches off the floor) for comfort, while those on modern fine-lined cruisers are strung low (7 to 9 inches) for stability. What works best in a high-seated canoe is awkward in a low-seated one.

- **Length of arms and torso, and strength:** Long-armed folks who sit tall in the saddle can wield longer paddles than those with short arms and torsos. Strong arms can handle long paddles better than weak arms. And so it goes. Blend all these variables and things become mightily confusing. Table 5-1 suggests some good starting points for length without resorting to scientific measurements.

Here's the paddle-sizing procedure if you want to get technical:

1. Set your canoe in the water and climb aboard.

Table 5-1 **Suggested Straight-Paddle Lengths for Use in the Following Canoes***

	High-Volume Tandem Canoes		Solo Canoes	
People with...	Aluminum and Royalex canoes	Sleek Fast Cruisers	Racers and fast cruisers	Freestyle and white-water canoes
Short torsos and arms	54"	52"	52"	56"
Average-length torsos and arms	56"	54"	54"	58"
Long torsos and arms	58"	56"	56"	60"

Note: These are guidelines. They are not engraved in stone! Bent-shaft paddles (see discussion on page 46) should be about 2 inches shorter.

2. Measure the distance from your nose (height of the grip) to the water. That's the shaft length. To this add the length of the blade (20 to 25 inches, depending on paddle style). That's the correct paddle length for you. Note that the overall length of the paddle is in part programmed by the blade length.

If you want to get more scientific, you can add in another variable—the weight of your tripping outfit. The more gear you pile into the hull, the lower it will set in the water, and the shorter your paddle must be.

Nonetheless, unless you're a masochist with figures, your original estimate—or the suggested length I've listed—will get you around in fine style.

To size a paddle without a canoe, stack up some books to equal the height of your canoe seat. Now sit down and measure from the floor to your chin. This would be the correct shaft length if your canoe rode on top of the water. Now decrease the measured shaft length by an amount equal to the expected draft of your canoe.

Straight-shaft flatwater slalom and whitewater paddles may be 2 to 4 inches longer than the formula measurement.

Paddle length is also a function of how you choose to paddle. Couple a fast cadence with a side switch (HUT!) every six strokes, and you'll want a short paddle. For carving effective turns, you'll want the extra reach of a long paddle. You'll also find that steering, via the conventional J-stroke, is easier with a long paddle.

Gripping the Paddle

Most people hog down on the shaft when they should be choking up. There should be 2 to 3 hands of distance (roughly equal to the freeboard of your canoe) between your lower hand and the paddle throat. Choking up reduces leverage, but it significantly increases reach.

Straight or Bent Paddle?

Bent-shaft paddles are best when you want to go quickly from A to B. Straight paddles are better for messing around in rapids and on local ponds.

Bent paddles are more efficient than straight paddles because they don't lift water at the end of the stroke and slow the canoe. Figure 5-1 shows you why. Fourteen-degree bends were most popular a decade ago; now, the trend is to 12-degree bends because they encourage better control and a higher, more relaxed sitting position. Bends of less than 10 degrees don't offer much advantage over a straight shaft.

There are reasons to select a bent blade besides blistering speed. Foremost is that straight paddles are largely levered through the water with your arms, while bent blades are pushed down with your shoulders and upper body. This makes better use of muscle groups and seems to reduce paddling injuries. For example, many canoeists report that they no longer get "paddler's elbow" (tennis elbow) and "sleeping hand" (tingling fingers) syndromes now that they've switched to bent blades. The physical advantages of bent paddles are real.

What about turns and correctional strokes? On a

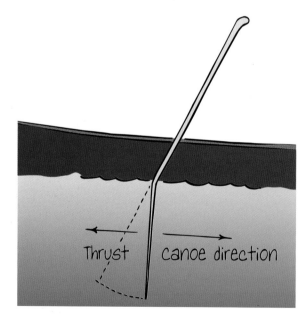

Figure 5-1 **Why the bent paddle is more efficient.**

straight paddle, one blade face is the same as the other, so you can link a series of strokes without changing your grip or reversing the blade. Watch how the stern paddler in a whitewater boat leans and low-braces as the canoe crosses an eddy line. Try this with the backside of a bent blade and you're apt to swim! A straight paddle is also the right tool when you want to sneak up on wildlife. The silent underwater stroke is all but impossible with a bent-shaft paddle.

But with practice comes perfection, and soon turns and steering strokes will come easier. In time, you may even come to prefer your bent paddle for everything.

In summary, bent-shaft paddles are about power and efficiency; straight paddles are about control and quiet. The idea is to match the paddle to the task. Every canoeist needs at least two paddles, so one might as well be bent.

Blade Style

Paddles, like canoes, are designed for a specific purpose, and each blade style has its place. The six shapes outlined in figure 5-2 pretty much cover the gamut of canoeing possibilities:

1. **Sugar Island:** A modification of the beavertail, the Sugar Island has its greatest width at the tip, which makes it better for use in shallow and aerated water (rapids). The Sugar Island style is favored by some of the best freestyle canoeists. It's probably the best all-around working design for a straight paddle.

2. **Beavertail:** Most ancient of the blade shapes, the beavertail took its form as the most efficient shape that can be cut from a 6-inch-wide board. When good waterproof glues were developed, the modern laminated paddle evolved and largely replaced the beavertail.

   However, the beavertail paddle is making a comeback among traditional paddlers. Its long, narrow, somewhat whippy blade makes subtle steering, à la the J-stroke, remarkably easy. A good solid ash beavertail paddle is strong (there are no corners to break), beautiful, and more efficient than modern canoeists like to admit.

3. **Ottertail:** This traditional lake paddle is even smoother and quieter than a beavertail. It's good for deep-water touring and messing around on ponds.

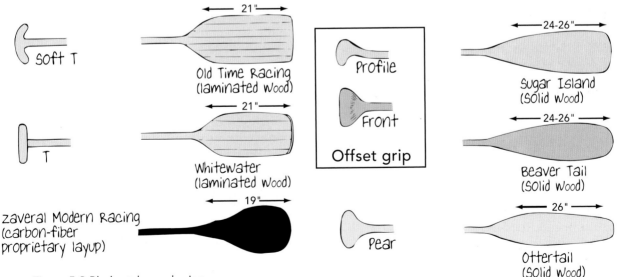

Figure 5-2 Blade styles and grips.

Figure 5-3 Zaveral paddle—paddles don't get better than this!

4. **Old-time racing:** The wide tip provides plenty of surface area in shallow rivers (where you can't submerge the whole blade), and the tapered shoulders allow you to bring the blade very close to the canoe for greater power and less frequent directional correction. The short blade also means less weight, thus faster recovery at the end of the stroke.

5. **Modern racing (Zaveral design):** This bizarre but superbly efficient shape is the brainchild of Bob Zaveral.* The medium-wide (8½-inch) blade provides power in shallow water, while the reduced shoulders encourage the blade to work close to the canoe. The symmetrical, silent-running blade tapers to a knife-thin edge all around. Almost all the top racers in North America use Zaveral graphite paddles. How do they work for all-around cruising? In a word, superb.

6. **Whitewater:** The short, wide blade and rounded edges provide good purchase in aerated water. A stiff blade and shaft encourage reliable braces (see the next chapter). Whitewater paddles are relatively heavy.

A Summary of Factors That Influence Paddle Performance

- Short, wide blades are for shallow water; long, narrow blades are for deep water. Narrow blades are quieter and easier to control than wide blades, and they produce less torque steer. Big blades are best suited to slow-cadence maneuvers and aerated water (rapids). Pick a blade size that won't tire you at the PDM (paddle strokes per minute) rate you prefer to paddle. Eight inches is a good width for an all-around cruising paddle.

- Paddle tips should have well-rounded corners. Square tips aren't very durable and they produce torque steer. Beginners will find them a handful.

- Both paddle faces should be identical (symmetrical), and without reinforcing splines. If one face is flat and the other cambered or splined, the paddle will arc (and possibly gurgle noisily) when pulled sideways through the water. A novice won't notice, but an expert will!

- Blade edges (all around) should taper to a ruler-thin edge. Thick edges may be more durable than thin ones, but they are noisier. Whitewater paddles need some beef for durability.

- Stiff paddles are best for bracing in aerated water; flexible paddles are better for cruising. You want some flex, but not too much.

- Durable edging: Old-time paddles were tipped with metal or fiberglass. Today's best blades are protected by tough resin.

- Solid wood or laminate? Laminates are lighter, stiffer, and stronger than some solid woods. But if you like the traditional look of a solid wood paddle, go for it. Sitka spruce, basswood, and cherry are strong enough to spoon the pond, and American white ash will stand up to any rapid.

Ultralight Carbon Fiber Paddles

The lighter the paddle, the better! Good wood paddles weigh 18 to 24 ounces—a half pound lighter than most hardware-store sticks. But if you think that's light, check out the ultralight carbon fiber bent blades that weigh 8 to 14 ounces! I'd feel undressed on any canoe trip without my 10-ounce graphite Zaveral* paddle.

Shaft Shape

The shafts of good paddles are planed to a long oval that runs at a right angle to the blade. This design is much more comfortable than the round shafts found on cheap paddles. A shaft that's too thick may tire your hands; one that's too thin may cramp them. Paddle makers don't plane their shafts to standard dimensions, so what fits one set of hands won't fit all.

A Good Grip

There are T-grips, pear grips, and offset grips.

- T-grips provide precise control of the blade angle, so they're best for rapids.
- Pear grips: Good ones feel like an extension of your hand and are the clear choice for all types of paddling, except the meanest rapids. Bad pear grips—like those on hardware-store paddles—don't encourage smiles.
- Offset grips are best for bent paddles, as they put the center of your hand in line with the force of the stroke. All good bent-shaft paddles have offset grips. It is a disadvantage to have an offset grip on a ruler-straight paddle.

Balance

Bad paddles are usually blade-heavy. Good ones transmit a feeling of unawareness of the blade.

The density of wood varies, so identical paddles may not feel the same. Good balance is probably more important than light weight.

Function Before Beauty

Some exotically beautiful and expensive paddles are too heavy and poorly balanced for serious paddling. More money doesn't always buy a better blade. Knowledgeable canoeists always choose function over beauty!

Care

Paddles may warp if they are stored flat or stacked in a barrel. Your best plan is to loop a cord around the grip and hang the cord from a nail. And no good paddle should ever be thrown carelessly into a car trunk when traveling. A fabric paddle bag (you can make or buy one) is your best protection on the road.

Paddles have come a long way since the days of oiled white ash. Canoe a mile with a 2-pound plastic paddle then switch to a 10-ounce graphite one. Summarize your experience in a word. If you said *wow*, you're a real canoeist!

Paddle Strokes

The Bow, or Forward, Stroke

To make the forward stroke most effective, reach as far forward as you can, but don't lunge. Put the paddle into the water at least 2 feet in front of your body. At the start of the stroke, the top arm is bent

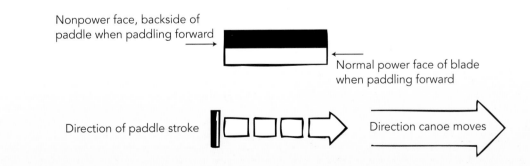

Figure 5-4 Diagrams in this book will use this identification system.

and the lower arm is straight. At the end of the stroke the positions are reversed. Keep your top hand low—below your eyes—and push. Most of the power in the stroke should come from pushing with the top hand, not from pulling with the bottom. The stroke is smooth and powerful, and the control is in the top hand. Paddle parallel to the keel, as close to the canoe as possible, and don't bring your lower hand beyond your hip. Bringing the paddle farther back than necessary wastes energy and power, and in fact actually slows the canoe, because the paddle lifts water rather than pushing it straight back.

At the end of the stroke, "feather" (blade face parallel to the keel line) your paddle forward to the starting point so the wind won't catch it and slow you down.

Solo adaptations: When straight-ahead power is applied to one side of a solo canoe, it will veer away from the paddling side. Two or three strokes (perhaps as many as four in a purebred solo racing canoe) is about maximum before the boat turns off course. To correct for this, traditionalists will use the solo-C, a variation of the J-stroke (described on page 52)—or a highly pitched version of the forward stroke. The alternative is to simply power ahead and switch sides when the need arises—a procedure best adapted to the short bent paddle.

The Back Stroke

Most canoeists pick up the back stroke out of necessity when a large rock looms ahead and they need to avoid it. Other names given to this stroke are "help!", "good grief!", and "@##&**!" It is the exact opposite of the forward stroke, and all comments made about that stroke apply here.

If you're serious about whitewater, you'll want to learn the back draw—an alternate form of the back stroke. The back draw is identical to the draw stroke explained below, except the power is applied parallel to the keel line of the canoe instead of at a right angle to it.

Procedure: Rotate your torso nearly 180 degrees (you're looking straight back toward the stern of the canoe) and draw. The canoe will move smartly backward. Though not necessarily more powerful than the conventional back stroke, the back draw allows you to turn your body and look backward in the direction you are paddling. It also permits instant transfer to the draw stroke without sacrificing control—a must when executing the back ferry, which is explained in chapter 6.

Solo adaptations: Here again the problem is keeping the solo canoe on course when power is applied to one side. Straight-line backing is best

Figure 5-5 Forward stroke: Put your paddle in the water at least 2 feet in front of your body. Keep your top hand low below your eyes.

accomplished by using a reverse-C (see page 60)—a slightly modified version of the J-stroke done in reverse. In tricky currents an accomplished solo paddler will often alternate between this stroke and a diagonal draw (a conventional draw applied at a 45-degree angle to the canoe).

The Draw Stroke

The draw stroke is the most important turning stroke. A powerful draw makes the bow person an active navigator rather than just a horsepower machine (figure 5-6).

For maximum power the draw should be executed from a kneeling position. Reach out as far from the gunwale as you can—don't be afraid to lean the canoe. Keep your top hand high and draw the paddle quickly and powerfully toward you. When the paddle reaches within 6 inches of the canoe, slice it out and draw again.

It is important to realize that the force of the water under the canoe has a righting effect on the canoe, so you can lean way out on this stroke and apply power with your whole body. The canoe will not tip over. The righting effect ceases, however, when the paddle is no longer in motion, so you must recenter your weight the moment you take the power off the paddle. The modern trend of running rapids is to run them as slowly as possible, as this gives you time to respond correctly and results in less damage to your canoe if it strikes a rock. Rudder motions are useful for turning only if you have forward speed, which is why the draw is so important. Although commonly used by both paddlers, the draw is most effective in the bow. It is not uncommon on whitewater streams to hear off in the distance a desperate stern paddler screaming, "Draw . . . draw!" to a frustrated partner.

Solo adaptations: Identical to the tandem draw. Net movement of the canoe is sideways, in the direction of the stroke. By varying the angle of the draw (to the diagonal), a variety of intriguing moves are possible.

The Pryaway (Pry) Stroke

The pryaway (figure 5-7) is used for moving the canoe away from your paddling side. It's a modern version of the old pushover stroke, though considerably more powerful. Slice the paddle into the

Figure 5-6 **Draw stroke.**

Figure 5-7 **Pryaway.**

water as far under the canoe as possible and with a deft, powerful motion, pry the paddle over the bilge. After some practice you'll find that it's easier and faster to use an underwater rather than an aerial recovery for your paddle. The mechanics of this will come naturally after a short time.

Unlike the draw, the pryaway has no righting effect, so you must keep your weight centered throughout the stroke. Since the pryaway is very powerful, it should not be used in shallow water where the paddle might catch on a rock and overturn the canoe. In shallow water the bow person should use a cross draw.

Solo adaptations: The pryaway is best at home in heavy water (powerful waves) where you need a quick lateral move plus the stability (bracing action) of a paddle that's always in the water. It is an essential stroke in the solo whitewater canoe.

The Cross Draw

The cross draw, as the name implies, is a draw stroke crossed over to the other side of the canoe. It is used in water too shallow to effect a proper pryaway.

Pivot at the waist, swing the paddle over the bow (the stroke cannot be done in the stern), and draw!

Figure 5-8 **Cross draw: This is your most powerful stroke for turning to the off side in a solo canoe.**

Don't change your grip on the paddle. Angle the paddle forward so it is nearly parallel to the water. Force water under and in front of the bow. As with the pryaway, keep your weight centered, because the cross draw has no stabilizing effect on the canoe.

Solo adaptations: This is *the* stroke for turning to the off side in a solo canoe. It is extremely powerful and, if properly applied and coupled with a strong lean, will snap even a straight-keeled solo canoe around quicker than a cat's wink. Older canoe books recommend the sweep stroke for off-side turns, but the cross draw is more effective, especially when the canoe has forward motion. Even professional canoe racers who never use crossover maneuvers occasionally cheat and cross-draw.

The J-Stroke

A canoe moving forward has a tendency to veer away from the side on which the stern person is paddling. When paddling backward, the reverse is true. The J-stroke is used to keep a canoe on a straight course. It is the stern person's stroke when paddling forward, and a reverse form of it (the reverse-J) is used by the bow paddler when moving backward.

Begin the J like a typical forward stroke, but shortly after the paddle enters the water, start changing its pitch ever so slightly by turning the thumb of your top hand down and away from your body. As the paddle is pushed forward through the water, continue to increase the pitch progressively. At the completion of the stroke, the thumb of the top hand should be pointing straight down, placing the paddle in a rudder position. If at the end of the stroke additional correction is needed, force the paddle out from the canoe in a prying fashion. If no further correction is necessary, take the paddle out of the water and repeat the stroke.

There are many variations of the J-stroke, and each canoeist develops a style that suits him or her best. Many very good paddlers finish the stroke by prying the paddle shaft off the gunwales or their thighs. Completing the stroke with a pry is frowned upon in some circles since it abuses pad-

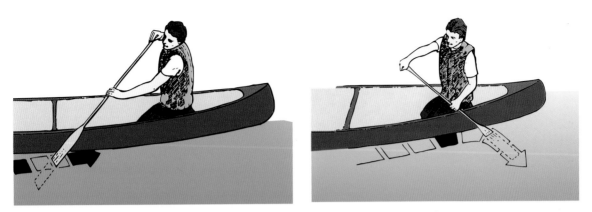

Figure 5-9 J-stroke, start (left) and J-stroke, finish. At finish, note that thumb of top hand is turned down.

dles (and gunwales). However, it is a very efficient form of the J, and most whitewater canoeists use it. Another variation of the J, used almost exclusively by paddlers of decked slalom canoes, is the thumbs-up J. This stroke is begun as a powerful forward stroke; upon completion the thumb of the top hand is turned quickly, snapping the paddle into a rudder position. A fast pry off the gunwales straightens the canoe. The result is a very powerful and relaxing stroke that permits you to paddle long distances without tiring. Some veteran canoeists scoff at this stroke, because they believe the mark of a good paddler is the ability to keep a canoe traveling on a straight course without veering. Both the thumbs-up and pry form of the J cause the canoe to veer slightly back and forth as it is paddled.

Many champion whitewater canoeists use the thumbs-up J for paddling their skittish, decked fiberglass boats. When gliding quietly among the lily pads, the traditional J is best. But in heavy rapids and waves, the newer, more efficient variations are often better.

Solo adaptations: The traditional J doesn't provide enough leverage to keep a solo canoe on course. You'll have to use the solo-C (see page 60) instead.

The Sweep Strokes

Sweep strokes are used to turn the canoe in a wide arc, either toward or away from your paddling side. Both the draw and pryaway are more efficient, especially in currents, and if you've mastered these, you will probably reserve the sweeps for quiet-water maneuvers.

Solo adaptations: The sweep and reverse sweep are essential strokes in the solo canoe and may be used to advantage in currents and heavy water. Use the full sweep in the solo canoe.

Figure 5-10 Bow sweep stroke.

Figure 5-11 Solo sweep: Canoe will pivot on its mid-point and turn clockwise.

Figure 5-12 Stern sweep: Canoe will accelerate and turn toward paddler's left.

The Stern Pry

The stern pry is a powerful stroke for turning the canoe toward the stern person's paddle side. It is similar to the reverse stern sweep except that only the outward portion of the arc is completed. Start the paddle near the tail of the canoe and push it smartly outward. For maximum power pry the paddle shaft off the gunwale or your thigh. Combine this stroke with a well-executed cross draw at the bow and the canoe will literally pivot on its midpoint. Use a draw at the bow instead, and the craft will slip sideways (no forward motion) in the direction of the draw. The pivot and side slip and pivot illustrated in figures 5-13 and 5-14 are essential whitewater maneuvers.

Note: Because of its long lever arm, the stern pry

is more powerful than the pryaway. It is also better in shallow water, because the paddle can't catch on rocks and upset the canoe.

The Sculling Draw

The sculling draw is an impressive-looking stroke. It is not one that you need to learn right away, as you can use the draw to perform the same function. However, it is a nice stroke in its place, and that place is in landing parallel to a shoreline in water too shallow to get a good draw.

Place the paddle in the water in a draw position at a comfortable distance from the canoe. Turn the leading edge of the paddle about 45 degrees away from the canoe, and while holding this blade angle pull the paddle backward through the water for a

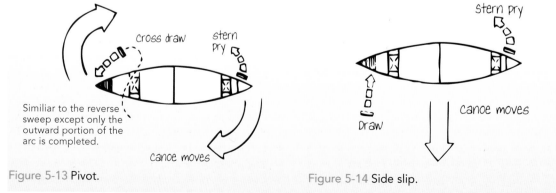

Figure 5-13 Pivot.

Figure 5-14 Side slip.

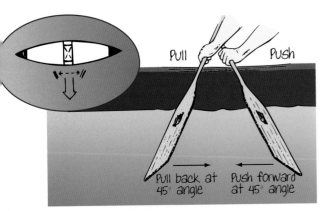

Figure 5-15 **Sculling draw.**

distance of about 2 feet. Then reverse the angle of the leading edge 90 degrees from the previous direction and, while holding this new blade angle, push the paddle forward about 2 feet to complete the stroke. The sculling draw is sometimes called the figure-8 stroke because the paddle appears to describe an 8 in the water. This is not really accurate, however, since the paddle is pulled straight fore and aft, and only the blade angle is changed.

Power-Paddling (the Minnesota Switch)

The term power-paddling was coined by Harry Roberts, former editor of *Wilderness Camping* magazine and *Canoesport Journal*. The name describes the dynamic technique in which canoeists paddle powerfully ahead and, on signal, switch sides to maintain a straight course.

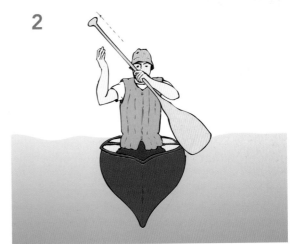

About fifty years ago some professional Minnesota racers tried the switching technique in competition. The results were dramatic. Not only could a canoe be paddled faster by switching sides every six strokes or so, but it could be paddled farther, since the paddlers became less tired. Over the years the Minnesotas witch grew in popularity, and today all professional racers use it instead of the J-stroke.

To an old-school canoeist, the Minnesota switch is a prime example of poor technique, mostly because the canoe does not travel a straight-line course. But it is efficient, especially on wilderness trips when you want to make good time against big

Figure 5-16 **Minnesota switch: Switching sides is easy as 1, 2, 3. If correctly done, only a split second is lost.**

Figure 5-17 As you gain solo experience you'll develop a repertoire of special strokes. Here, Charlie Wilson braces into a turn in his Bell Flashfire canoe.

oncoming rollers on a windswept lake. Kruger and Waddell used the Minnesota switch almost exclusively on their voyage to the Bering Sea. Their cadence was approximately sixty strokes per minute, with a switch after each six to eight strokes.

Procedure: Paddlers sit low in the canoe with feet braced (foot braces are desirable) firmly ahead. After a half-dozen or so strokes, the stern paddler—who can best see the course of the canoe—shouts "HUT" or some other agreed-upon signal. Paddlers then switch sides in unison (see figure 5-16) and without missing a beat, continue to power-paddle ahead. This is a precise, snappy maneuver, one that requires more finesse and coordination than you might guess. If done correctly, only a split second is lost; if improperly executed in a strong current, a capsize is possible.

Experienced racing teams do all their paddling this way, with bent-shaft paddles. To maneuver, they draw or switch sides and draw—or the bow person uses a post, which is basically a high brace (figure 5-19). As mentioned, racers occasionally cheat and cross-draw at the bow to effect turns. But mostly, they power-paddle ahead and switch sides to maneuver.

Some traditional canoeists maintain that you sacrifice canoe control when you adhere to power-paddling techniques. Until I paddled with the racers, I believed this too. But it simply isn't so. What onlookers often perceive as loss of control in tight turns is in reality the maneuvering limits of a racing canoe at speed. Race boats are straight-keeled; at best they turn poorly even when piloted by expert teams. It's doubtful that experienced whitewater folk could make these canoes sing any more beautifully on a twisted course.

However, there's no denying that kneeling paddlers who use long, straight paddles (long paddles have more leverage than shorter ones) and whitewater slalom strokes in their highly rockered canoes enjoy the greatest control in difficult waters. For this reason the complete canoeist should know—and appreciate—both styles of paddling.

The Braces

Low brace. The low brace functions as an outrigger—it's not really a paddling stroke. Its purpose is to stabilize the canoe in turns and to keep it from capsizing in big waves.

To execute the stroke, reach far out, paddle laid nearly flat on the water—or at a slight climbing angle to the current—palm of the top hand up. Put your weight solidly on the paddle—a halfhearted effort isn't good enough. If you're capsizing, a powerful downward push will right you. The push should be lightning fast and smooth; don't slap the water with your paddle.

The low brace is essential for turning into or out of eddies (see chapter 6, On the Water) and any-place the stern person needs to check a strong inside turn. Canoe teams frequently run heavy waves in a "ready brace," or motionless outrigger position. Then, if an unusually high "haystack" (standing wave) threatens to unhorse them, the paddler on the tipping side can instantly brace to offset the dangerous lean.

Solo adaptations: Solo canoes are skittish, and they depend on strong leans and braces to keep them from capsizing in rough water.

You can use the low brace effectively on calm water too. Get up a full head of steam, reach back at about a 30-degree angle, and brace hard, power face of the paddle at a strong climbing angle to the water. The canoe will spin right around your paddle, in effect executing an inside wheelie, or "static axle." Wahoo! Pure fun. The low brace is one of the most important (and spectacular) strokes for playing on quiet water.

High brace. There are times when you need a strong brace, a draw, and a canoe lean all at the same time. Enter the high brace. Basically, the high brace is nothing more than a stationary draw with the power face of the paddle held against the current or at a strong climbing angle to it. The success of the stroke depends on speed—either paddling or current—and a strong lean to offset the pull of the moving water. The high brace blends easily to the draw—an essential stroke for pulling into an eddy and for making sharp turns.

Solo adaptations: When you find yourself capsizing to your off side (side opposite your paddle), reach far out on a high brace and put your weight and trust on your paddle. You cannot do eddy turns or maintain stability in rough water without the high brace!

How to Paddle a Tandem Canoe Alone

Many people prefer to solo a tandem canoe from the stern seat because the canoe is so narrow there. But this knocks the canoe way out of trim. The bow rides high while the stern sinks low; in effect, you're paddling a 7-foot canoe with a 10-foot overhang! The slightest breeze will unhorse you.

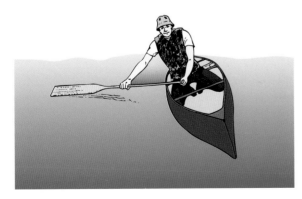

Figure 5-18 **Low brace.**

Figure 5-19 **High brace.**

A good procedure is to kneel just behind the center thwart or carrying yoke. If the canoe is too wide here for comfort, scoot sideways and place both knees close together in the bilge. The canoe will heel over smartly and sit firmly on its chine. Your center of gravity is very low—you won't tip over! This classic Canadian position (figure 5-20) provides acrobatic control on quiet water, but it's tiring and precarious in rapids.

Rapids and Wind

Level trim is the rule for running rapids, which means you must pilot the canoe from its center. Remove the center thwart and install a narrow seat or wide kneeling thwart 18 inches behind center and 10 to 12 inches off the floor. You may need extra-long bolts to drop the thwart to the suggested height. The leading edge of the thwart should pitch downward about 30 degrees so it doesn't jab your derriere when you kneel. Your yoke must be removable so it won't interfere with your centralized position.

If you don't want to modify your canoe, try this procedure on reasonably calm water: Turn around on the front seat and paddle the canoe backward. The stern is now your bow. If there's a thwart next to the bow seat, remove it so it won't interfere with sitting. Place your gear forward of the yoke to trim the canoe.

When the weather gets rough, shuffle forward to the center thwart and kneel just behind it. The thwart should barely touch your chest. You'll have to move your gear to level the craft. Wind and rapids may keep you on your knees for some time, so be sure you have padding. The strap-on pads that gardeners wear provide good grip.

Paddling a big tandem canoe alone in wind (even a gentle breeze) can be a bear. Your best plan is to weight the windward end about 2 inches down so the craft will weather-vane, as shown in figure 5-21. On the other hand, it's usually best to run heavily loaded tandem canoes dead level under all conditions. Chapter 6 will tell you why.

Paddles

Your solo paddle should be about 3 inches longer than your favorite tandem paddle to provide leverage for maneuvering. A 7-inch-wide blade conserves energy and has enough bite to make snappy turns.

You can really blast across a lake if you use a double-blade paddle that's around 9 feet long. To make one, cut off the aluminum shafts on two

Figure 5-20 **Becky Mason** demonstrates the Canadian style of solo canoeing.

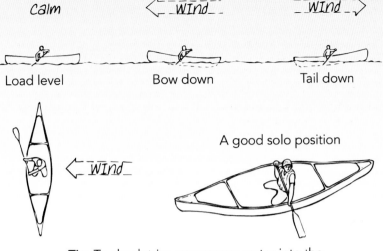

Calm   ⟵ _Wind_   _Wind_ ⟶

Load level   Bow down   Tail down

A good solo position

⟵ _Wind_

Tip: To check trim, pour some water into the canoe and see which way it flows

Figure 5-21 **Paddling in wind.**

identical aluminum or plastic paddles and install a locking sleeve.

Warning: Many accomplished canoeists feel that double blades are for kayaks and plastic flitter boats, and for canoers who don't want to learn the art of soloing! So be ready for some serious flak if you use twin blades in your open canoe.

Poles are an interesting alternative to paddles. With one, you can go easily upstream or down, through deep or shallow water. Windmill your pole and you'll rocket across the water faster than most tandem teams. And you can turn and stop instantly. Experienced polers confidently ascend and descend rapids that are the common domain of experienced paddlers. And they do it alone in their canoes, while standing!

Modern polers favor a strong, lightweight 6060-T6 aluminum pole about 12 feet long. Sturdy take-down poles are available. Poling is serious sport. If you're interested, join the American Canoe Association,* which provides instruction. And get Harry Rock's excellent book, The *Basic Essentials of Canoe Poling* (Globe Pequot Press, 1992). Harry has won every major ACA poling

competition since the early 1980s. Some years ago, I had the privilege of taking a poling lesson from him.

Safety Concerns

Capsizing on open water is your only real concern. Without a support crew, you'll have to swim your outfit to shore—reason enough to always wear your life jacket. Be sure your canoe has enough flotation so it won't sink. Flotation foam adds about 4 pounds to a canoe, so minimal amounts are often used on high-performance craft.

Secure your gear to the canoe so it won't drift away if you capsize. The canoe must have a bow line so you can tow it to shore. Carry a sheath knife in case you have to cut yourself free of a tangled rope.

Getting water out of swamped canoe isn't hard. However, climbing back aboard in waves is! In rough water you'll probably have to swim, so you'd best be prepared for it.

If you love paddling alone (which doesn't necessarily mean going alone), you'll want to get a

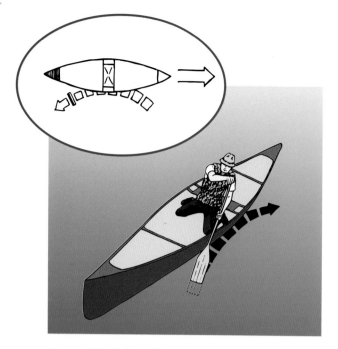

Figure 5-22 Solo-C. The reverse-C (above) is done the opposite of the forward-C.

downsized canoe that's built for the purpose. Chapter 11 will tell you all about them.

Purebred Solo Strokes

As you've probably already discovered, all the typical tandem strokes can be used with varying success in the solo canoe. There are, however, a number of strokes and techniques that are unique to the solo canoe, and these you'll find detailed in my book *Basic Essentials: Solo Canoeing* (Globe Pequot Press, 1999).

The solo-C (figure 5-22) is the one purebred solo stroke that you'll want to learn right now. It is nothing more than a refined J-stroke with a diagonal draw component added at the start.

To watch an accomplished soloist C-stroking along, canoe running true and quiet, is a rare treat.

Mastery of the solo-C represents canoe technique at its pinnacle!

Leaning the Canoe

It would be unfair to leave the subject of paddling without mentioning the technique of leaning the canoe to make a turn. To make a gradual turn with the canoe under power, lean the canoe (an inch or two is sufficient) to the outside of the turn (the reverse of what you would do on a bicycle). If you hold the lean, the canoe will cut a nice arc in the opposite direction of the lean. Professional racers accomplish much of their turning by this method, and lone paddlers of decked slalom canoes often use a counterlean to help keep their skittish boats from turning away from their paddling side. *Caution:* Don't use this technique for quick turns in rapids—you'll upset the canoe!

Standing in the Canoe

The procedures discussed in this chapter naturally assume that you will either sit or kneel in your canoe. But what about standing? Is it a viable position? Older canoe books suggest that it is, while modern texts dismiss the idea with a simple snicker and an admonition that you should never stand in a canoe.

Hogwash! There are two times when you may want to stand in your canoe:

1. Just before entering a rapid—to check the course from a higher vantage point.

2. In calm water when you want to stretch your legs.

Those who suggest that standing in a canoe is unsafe simply don't know the limits of their craft. It is, in fact, possible to stand in almost any canoe—even a skittish solo one—if you brace your feet wide apart and maintain balance on the centerline.

CHAPTER 6

On the Water

Once, along the Hood River in the Northwest Territories of Canada, my partner and I entered what appeared to be a relatively simple rapid, only to discover that the waves and hydraulics were much worse than we had bargained for. It required all our strength and skill just to maintain alignment with the powerful current—to keep from capsizing in the frothy water. The waves grew to monster proportions, and ultimately they completely engulfed the canoe and blotted my bowman from sight. But the tough nylon spray cover held, and the big Royalex canoe plunged confidently on through.

The run was a long one, perhaps ¼ mile. There was no time to question the route, only react. Finally, it was over and we drifted aimlessly into the pool of ice-blue water below, our faces beaming with smiles, our bodies pumped high with the excitement of a successful run. Granted, we had stepped beyond safe bounds, but we had made it, and through it all we had retained perfect control of our craft (or so we thought). But our friends on shore had quite a different perspective. They laid into us with vociferous threats, unrepeatable expletives, and gave fair warning that we better never, never pull a dumb stunt like that again! Repeated attempts to clear ourselves by suggesting that the run was easy were not enough. It was evident to everyone that God had directed our descent. We humbly apologized and vowed to show better judgment next time.

As you have just observed, luck will occasionally get you through a difficult whitewater passage or across a dangerous running sea, but more often than not a lucky paddler is a good paddler. Unfortunately, in the process of becoming good, a spill or three is inevitable. Although competent canoeists question those who tip frequently, they also wonder about those who have never tipped at all. Your safety on a canoe trip depends in large measure on your ability to respond correctly—and automatically—in dangerous situations. Proper responses can only be learned from practice. "Upsetting experiences" have educational value, and your survival in rapids may well depend on your whitewater education.

Loading the Canoe for Rough-Water Travel

Canoes should be loaded in the water, not on land. Standing in or placing heavy loads in canoes half out of water can bend aluminum and break wood and fiberglass bottoms. Admittedly, there are times when you may have to bridge your canoe while loading it. Just be careful, and don't make a practice of this procedure.

A canoe almost always handles better when loaded dead level. Neither the bow nor the stern should be higher. If an uneven distribution of weight is unavoidable, the lesser of two evils is to lighten the bow. But a light bow will give you problems in a headwind—you'll have difficulty keeping on course (the canoe will try to weather-vane into the wind). On the other hand, a weighted stern will provide better directional control in a following sea, although if the tail is too low, big waves may pour right in! In rapids directional control will be reduced by burying one end. With the front end high, you may successfully negotiate large, standing waves, but you'll lose this advantage when you pile up on a rock because you can't maneuver. So load dead level whenever possible and keep the weight as close to the center and as low as possible in the canoe.

As I noted in the last chapter, the exception to level trim is when you're running a lightly loaded canoe in wind. Rebalance your canoe only if you absolutely, positively cannot hold your course. Frankly, advice about retrimming a canoe in wind is largely academic.

You'll have your hands full in big waves—you'd better make adjustments before you leave the quiet eddy!

Chapter 7 (Common Canoeing Hazards) outlines the dangers of surfing in a following sea and beating upwind.

Catamaraned Canoes

For greater stability on rough water or while sailing, some authorities recommend that you "catamaran" a pair of similar canoes. To prevent water buildup between the two craft, you are generally advised to use strong poles to separate the canoes about 4 feet at the bow and 6 feet at the stern. If poles are securely lashed to the canoes and a large square sail is hoisted, the rig will make reasonably good time in a strong tailwind. However, running at an angle to the wind (tacking) is nearly impossible with such an outfit, and any degree of maneuverability is out of the question. Moreover, an important advantage of the single canoe over more stable, paired craft is its ability to roll with the side thrust of waves—an ability that is completely negated by the rigid, unyielding design of the catamaran. In short, paired canoes respond poorly to the pitch of a rough sea and consequently tend to ship water readily.

An additional concern is the danger of a rope lashing or wood crossbrace breaking, and if this happens in a good blow, a dunking is inevitable. I have used paired canoes for casual downwind sailing and for placid-water recreational paddling, but I consider them downright dangerous for general rough-water use, with or without sails. A well-designed canoe will weather out 6-foot waves if paddled by a team of experts. Catamaran-rigged canoes, on the other hand, even if securely braced and tied, are almost sure to break apart under these conditions.

When a sudden squall blows up and the waves grow to impressive heights, you will do best to put your faith in proper canoeing techniques. If this fails, hang on to your swamped canoe and trust your life jacket.

Canoe Sailing

On a trip to James Bay, we fought wind and driving rain for ten straight days without a break. At one point in the trip, we covered only 12 miles in three

days without a break. On another day sixteen hours of strenuous, continuous paddling were required to cross 20-mile-long Mattagami Lake, just south of Smoky Falls, Ontario. When we finally entered the very large Moose River, we knew we would have to fight the prevailing north wind for more than 100 miles to reach James Bay. Then a miraculous change of weather occurred. The wind shifted completely to the south, providing us with a steady tailwind of perhaps 20 knots. We quickly fashioned sails and put out to sea, easily covering the 100-mile distance to Moosonee in just fifteen hours! Shortly after we arrived at our destination, the wind reversed itself again. Our sail had given us the edge to play the weather odds and win.

The best and easiest way to rig a sail for a wilderness canoe is to use two paddles or poles and a rainfly or poncho. Roll the fly or poncho around the paddles as you would a scroll (figure 6-1). In practice the bow person holds the rig against the gunwales and supports the paddle blades (or pole bases) with his or her thighs or feet. By opening and closing the scroll-like sail to catch the wind, you can control the speed of the canoe. You can also change the direction of the sail somewhat, allowing you to tack slightly.

It is not a good idea to tie makeshift sails in place on loaded wilderness canoes. A heavily loaded canoe can

Figure 6-1 Two paddles and a rainfly or poncho is an easy way to rig a sail.

easily get out of control in a high wind and capsize, throwing you overboard while it keeps on plowing down the lake. You may find yourself not only in the water in a running sea but canoeless as well. Handheld sails work well enough for most situations. If you prefer a sturdier, more permanent arrangement, install a mast step and bar and do it right.

Evasive Tactics

Assume you are canoeing on a river with a strong current. Directly in front of your canoe is a large rock. If you try to steer around the rock, you are likely to get caught broadside and possibly destroy your canoe. Back-paddling is not the answer, for that will merely postpone the inevitable. You require a tactic that will slow the canoe down and move it sideways at the same time—you need a back ferry.

The back ferry makes use of two directional forces: the forward velocity of the river and the back-paddling speed of your canoe. In figure 6-2 the stern person is paddling on the left and begins the back ferry with a powerful stern pry. The pry is repeated until the proper angle to the current (usually about 30 degrees) is attained. The stern paddler then joins the bow person in paddling vigorously backward. The

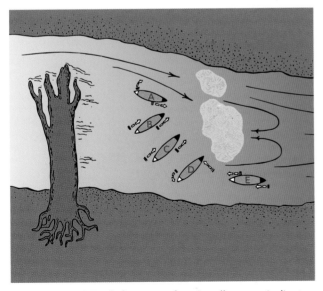

Figure 6-2 Back-ferry to safety (small arrows indicate direction of paddle movement).

net movement, as illustrated, will be nearly sideways. The faster the river speed, the smaller the ferry angle, and vice versa. Only experience will tell you what angle is best. You can easily increase or decrease the ferry angle by drawing or prying as needed.

On powerful, fast-flowing rivers getting to shore quickly can be important, especially if there is a bad rapid or bouldery falls ahead. Begin the back ferry by angling your stern in the direction you want to go. Maintain the proper angle and paddle backward until your stern barely touches the shore. Then pull the bow around (using a draw or pry, whichever is appropriate) until the canoe is parallel to the land.

Landing stern-first is a good habit to get into. In very swift currents bow landings can be dangerous, because a river is slowest near its edges and fastest near its center. When you nose into the slow water at the shoreline, the faster main current grabs your stern and spins it downstream. If there is a sufficient current differential, you can be spun around so rapidly that you may lose your balance and possibly overturn the canoe.

Another evasive tactic based on the principle of vectors is the forward ferry. It is identical to the back ferry except that you spin the canoe 180 degrees and paddle forward instead of backward. This technique is used mostly by paddlers of kayaks and canoes that can turn quickly. Since the forward ferry is considerably more powerful than its backward counterpart, you can use a steeper angle to the current. You can also paddle longer distances without tiring.

On a recent Canadian river trip, my partner and I put ashore just above a bouldery falls. After about an hour of scouting we concluded that portaging was out of the question because a high rock bluff ran for several hundred yards along the river's edge. It was apparent that a portage, if one existed, was on the other bank of the 100-yard-wide river. Somehow we would have to cross to the other side. We were within 50 feet of the falls, and the current was moving at perhaps 5 miles per hour. Paddling straight across was out of the question. We decided to use a very shallow-angled forward ferry to test the current. Encountering no difficulty at the outset of our crossing, we steepened the angle considerably as we approached the enter. We landed almost directly

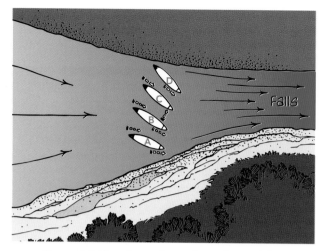

Figure 6-3 Crossing a river using a forward ferry (arrows indicate direction of paddle movement).

opposite our starting point on the other side of the river. I don't know what we would have done if this method had been unknown to us.

Although there are other whitewater techniques, wilderness canoes are usually heavily loaded and thus respond very sluggishly to the paddle. You can't effectively draw a heavy canoe sideways very far to avoid obstacles. Ferrying will be one of your most useful river tactics.

River Features

River Bends

Whenever possible, stay on the inside of bends. Rivers run fastest and deepest at the outside of bends, and because of this most of the debris usually piles up there. Should you overturn and get your life jacket or clothing caught in the branches of a half-submerged tree, it could be impossible to work your way free. You may be lucky to escape with your life! For this reason you should seek the outside of a bend only when the water is low or the current sluggish.

The safest way to negotiate bends is by ferrying. For crossing wide expanses of water, the forward ferry is preferred; otherwise, the back ferry is best. To begin the back ferry as you approach a curve, tuck your tail to the inside of the bend and back-paddle. Although going around a bend sideways appears dan-

gerous, it is in fact quite safe, for your canoe is almost perfectly aligned with the current. A slight pry or draw will quickly spin the bow downstream, putting you back on course. When you hear the thunder of rapids ahead but a curve prevents your seeing the telltale haystacks, get to the inside of the bend and cautiously back-ferry, keeping your stern just a few feet from shore. Should the rapid prove unrunnable, a few paddle strokes will bring you to the safety of the riverbank.

In 1982 friends and I experienced a polar gale along the remote Hood River in Canada's Northwest Territories. For three days we were confined to our tents by 55-mile-per-hour winds and unrelenting rain. When the weather cleared, we were greeted by a silt-choked river in flood stage, the hydraulics of which were unbelievable. There were uprooted dwarf willows and debris everywhere in the river, and they all piled up on the outside curves. The powerful current, which we estimated at more than 10 miles an hour, produced human-sized waves at the outside of every bend. In many places the river was more than ¼ mile wide!

Getting downstream that day was a matter of staying tight on the inside bends, away from the debris and engulfing whitewater. First we would ferry furiously to reach the right bank, only to ferry back across the channel when the river curved left. It was

Figure 6-4 Ferrying around a sharp bend: Keep away from the outside of the bend, except in low water (arrows indicate direction of the paddle movement).

a continuous and exhausting battle to stay on the inside of curves. And it would have been impossible without well-practiced ferries. Indeed, I doubt if we could have gotten downriver without them!

A final note on ferrying: Early in this chapter I emphatically suggested that canoes should always be trimmed dead level. Ferrying is an exception. Here, the downstream end is best trimmed slightly down. Since it's usually impractical to lighten one end of the canoe before the start of the ferry, your best bet is to always load dead level!

Eddies Are a Canoeist's Friend

If you have ever thrown a stick just beyond a large rock or bridge piling in a river with a good current, you have probably observed that the stick floats back upstream in the lazy current below the obstacle. This is an eddy. Paddling long stretches of difficult rapids can be exceedingly nerve racking. The quiet water of an eddy is a convenient stopping place to rest and collect your thoughts. Polers commonly travel upstream by hopping from eddy to eddy. If the water is sufficiently deep, paddlers can also successfully use this technique.

Since the movement of water within an eddy is opposite to that of the river's flow, there is a current differential at the eddy's edge. This is the eddy line, and crossing it in strong currents can be dangerous if you are not prepared for the consequences. If you cautiously poke your bow into the slow upstream current, the main flow of the river will catch your stern and spin it quickly downstream. The result is a possible dunking. To enter an eddy bow-first, you must drive powerfully forward across the eddy line. As the stern swings downstream, lean the canoe upstream to prevent upsetting. In figure 6-5 the bow person "hangs on" to the calm water of the eddy with a strong high brace and severe lean, while the stern person—who has not yet crossed the eddy line—also leans to the right to offset the centrifugal force of the current. As soon as the canoe completes the turn (which takes only a split second), the pair paddles forcefully up to the rock.

If, however, the bow person were paddling on the left (figure 6-6) and the stern person on the right, the roles—but not the canoe lean—would be reversed.

Both paddlers would drive the canoe forward until it crossed the eddy line; then, at that moment, the stern person would lean far out on a low brace while the bow person sliced forward into the eddy, completing the maneuver with a pry and a forward drive. Whew!

Whenever possible, I prefer to "eddy in" with the bow paddle on the inside of the turn, as illustrated in figure 6-5. The procedure is less tricky and seems to result in greater control, due to the powerful stabilizing effect of the high brace up front.

Any eddy turn from a fast current is exciting and sure to produce a dunking if you aren't well-practiced in the technique. The most common error is failure to apply a strong upstream lean as the eddy line is crossed. Another mistake is that of judgment—entering the eddy too late. It won't take you long to discover that you'll miss the eddy by a wide margin unless you enter it just below the rock. The current carries you downstream, remember?

The safest way to enter an eddy is by back-ferrying. Begin the ferry as you approach the eddy line. Set the stern into the quiet water and paddle back to safety. When you have rested sufficiently, leave the eddy at its weak lower end. If the upstream current is very strong, this may be impossible, in which case you'll have to use a fast forward ferry combined with a strong downstream lean—a sophisticated tactic called the peel-out.

To do a peel-out, the canoe is angled at least 45 degrees to the current (a somewhat steeper angle than is used for ferrying) and forward power applied. As the bow crosses the eddy line, the bow person reaches far out on a high brace and leans the canoe downstream (figure 6-7). The stern supports the lean and sweeps the canoe around. As the boat realigns with the current, the pair recenters the weight and resumes normal paddling.

In the alternate method (figure 6-8) the bow person paddles on the left and the stern person on the right. As the bow crosses the eddy line, both partners lean downstream; the bow person pries or cross-draws while the stern person applies a low brace.

Here again I prefer the former practice (high brace on the inside of the turn), because it seems to provide greater stability as the bow crosses the eddy line. But

Figure 6-5 An eddy turn with a high brace in the inside: Canoe must be leaned upstream when the bow crosses the eddy line.

Figure 6-6 An eddy turn with a low brace on the inside: Bow person may use a pry, as illustrated (preferred) or a cross draw to turn the canoe into the eddy.

Figure 6-7 Peel-out: Canoe enters the current at about a 45-degree angle. Bow paddler uses a high brace and leans the canoe downstream as the bow crosses the eddy line.

Figure 6-8 Peel-out: Using a low brace on the downstream side, the bow paddler stabilizes the canoe with a pry (illustrated) or a cross draw as the current spins it downstream.

perhaps I'm simply more experienced in the procedure.

When paddling difficult rapids, you should proceed from eddy to eddy. At each new stopping place, you can survey the conditions ahead and determine the safest course. Eddies can be used to your advantage only if you can perform competent ferries, so the importance of these tactics cannot be overemphasized.

Chutes

When the river narrows sufficiently for its flow to be severely restricted, a chute of whitewater is formed. When the fast water racing through the chute reaches the calmer water below, its energy dissipates in the form of nearly erect standing waves called haystacks. A series of uniform haystacks indicates deep water and safe canoeing—that is, if they are not so large as to swamp the canoe. To help the bow lift over the large haystacks, you can slow the canoe's speed by back-paddling, or you can quarter into the waves at a slight angle. You can also lighten the front end by putting the bow paddler behind the seat. Running a chute with large standing waves below is one of the few times when you may wish to stop and rearrange the load in your canoe.

Falls and Dams

Low falls can be successfully run if there is sufficient water flowing over them and if they are not so steep as to produce a heavy back roller at their base. If after checking a falls you decide it is safe to run, pick the point of strongest water flow, align the canoe, and proceed at river speed over the falls. Upon reaching the base of the falls, dig your paddles hard and deep to climb out of the trough below.

It is almost always unsafe to run a dam—any dam, even a low one—unless, of course, part of it has broken away. The trouble with dams is not the lack of flow over them or even the steepness of their drops. Rather, the danger lies in the well-formed back rollers at their bases. The back roller is actually an extremely powerful eddy, and the upstream current of this eddy can stop you dead in your tracks. Your canoe can be flipped broadside to the current and may spin over and over like a rolling cigar, perhaps to remain trapped until a period of drought lowers the volume of the river. Because some ledges and falls produce the same effects as dams, they should be considered extremely dangerous until proven otherwise.

Broaching at the base of a dam may mean certain death. Your only recourse in an upset may be to abandon the craft and your life jacket, and swim down under the eddy to the current beneath—a frightening maneuver that calls for calm nerves and a realization of what's happening.

Choosing a Safe Course through Rapids

Negotiating a complex rapid without incident requires skill, cool determination, an accurate appraisal of the dangers, and a good partner! Here are the rules for safe passage:

1. An upstream V indicates the location of rocks (figure 6-9); a downstream V is the safe approach.

2. You can't steer around obstacles in a fast-moving river. Rely instead on ferry techniques or sideslip maneuvers (the bow person draws while the stern person pries, or vice versa).

3. Scout the rapids from shore before you run them, and view everything from a downstream vantage point. Often, a substantial drop (ledge) that is

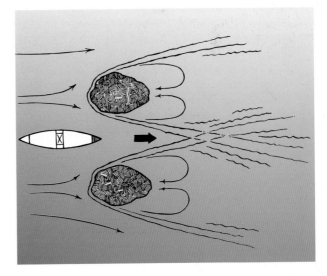

Figure 6-9 Choose a safe downstream V when entering a rapid.

Figure 6-10 Souse hole: the air-filled back roller of a souse hole can swamp a canoe and trap it. To escape you must swim out the side of the hole or shed your life vest and dive below the foam into the bottom current—procedures that require skill and determination. Souse holes are no place for open canoes.

invisible from above will be immediately evident from below. A binocular (not a monocular!) is useful for checking questionable spots.

4. Proceed downstream slowly—back-paddle to reduce speed. Maintain control with effective draws, pries, cross draws, and ferry techniques.

5. Take advantage of eddies to recover your strength and plan your strategy for the water ahead.

After years of teaching whitewater skills, I remain unconvinced that you can learn to read whitewater—to choose a safe course through rapids—from reading books. Certainly, you can learn the important paddle strokes and procedures, but that's not enough. Studying whitewater tactics on a printed page is akin to poring over a map of Great Slave Lake, only to discover its harsh realities from the seat of your canoe. If you want to become proficient at reading and running whitewater, you'll have to paddle in it—or more accurately, play in it. A weekend of on-the-water practice in the company of paddlers who understand the ways of running water will teach you more about choosing a safe course through rapids than a winter of fireside reading.

A Word about Your Partner

Some canoeists are lucky enough to paddle with the same partner all the time. Others are less fortunate; they have to adjust to the ways and incompetencies of a new person on every trip they take. Whitewater training sessions? Are you kidding? Learning comes out of necessity in the course of the canoe trip! By trip's end the new man or woman is "trained." Too bad that we may never seem him or her again! All of which bring us to the ultimate bottom line: *Whitewater tactics are for practiced whitewater teams. If in doubt about your partner's ability, portage, portage, portage!*

Early in my paddling career, I discovered that the best way to train a new partner was to make all route decisions (and shout commands) from my position in the stern—a practice complicated by the fact that the person up front is closer to the obstacles and can therefore see them much better. So I developed the habit of angling the canoe about 45 degrees to the current whenever I ran rapids. This improved visibility tremendously and enabled me to make more accurate judgments. A quick draw or pry instantly put the canoe back in alignment with the flow. Drifting at an angle to the current had another advantage: the boat was correctly set up for an immediate back ferry. To avoid a rock dead ahead, I'd simply call, "Back," and the canoe would respond with sideways motion.

Running angled also has the net effect of shortening the waterline of the canoe, which, like quartering lake waves, translates into a drier ride. Negotiating rapids out of alignment to the current is common practice among the experienced North Woods guides, although the value of the technique is seldom expounded in the canoeing literature.

Heavy Water

Heavy water is defined as rapids that generally rate high Class III or better (see the AWA river rating scale below). Here, waves rise to impressive heights with deep canoe-engulfing troughs below. Where large volumes of water flow over big surface rocks, a "hydraulic jump," or eddy set on edge, appears. This is the souse hole—a playground for decked whitewater canoes manned by expert paddlers, but no place for open canoes, no matter how skilled their occupants. (Amazingly, souse holes have been negotiated by skilled paddlers in open canoes.)

Negotiating huge waves, powerful currents, and boiling eddies calls for skill, iron-tough nerves, specialized equipment, a good partner, and a philosophy different from that of the cautious slower-than-the-current (back-ferrying and back-paddling) procedures I've outlined. When waves grow to human size and the tough below threatens to swallow you up, you must shift into high gear—paddle forward with gusto so as to have sufficient momentum to climb the faces of the big waves. Even then a swamping may be inevitable unless your canoe has plenty of speed and a fabric splash cover.

Heavy water is something you should look at, reverently photograph, then confidently portage around!

Many of the new guidebooks rate rapids according to the AWA (American Whitewater Affiliation) International River Rating Scale. This is most handy, as it allows you to plan a trip with confidence. In guidebooks where this rating scale has not been followed, you must rely on the individual judgment of the writer, which may be considerably different than your own. The International River Rating Scale is the great equalizer.

AWA International River Rating Scale

Water Classes and Characteristics

I. **Easy:** Bends without difficulty, small rapids with waves regular and low. Obstacles like fallen trees, bridge pilings, and so on. River speed less than hard back-paddling speed.

II. **Medium:** Fairly frequent but unobstructed rapids with regular waves and low ledges. River speed occasionally exceeding hard back-paddling speed.

III. **Difficult:** Small falls; large, regular waves covering boat. Expert maneuvering required. Course not always easily recognizable. Current speed usually less than fast forward-paddling speed. (Splash cover useful.)

IV. **Very difficult:** High, powerful waves and difficult eddies. Abrupt bends and difficult broken water. Powerful and precise maneuvering mandatory. (Splash cover essential.)

V. **Exceedingly difficult:** Very fast eddies, violent current, steep drops.

VI. **Limit of navigability:** Navigable only at select water conditions by teams of experts. Cannot be attempted without risk of life.

For all practical purposes a loaded wilderness canoe should not be taken into rapids of a higher classification than II. The risks are just too great. You should realize that a heavy spring rain can turn mild Class I rapids into wild Class II or III, and an early-fall drought can tame a Class III to where you can walk right down the middle of it. Water levels are extremely important in sizing up rapids. Where gauging stations exist, interpretive information can be secured from the administrative unit responsible for the gauge. This is usually the U.S. Army Corps of Engineers, the U.S. Weather Bureau, or your state's department of natural resources or conservation.

Your most accurate information, however, will be available from local canoe clubs that maintain their own gauges. These can be anything from a paint mark on a bridge piling to a rusted pipe. Primitive though they are, club gauges reflect the needs of canoeist and thus are most useful.

Lining and Tracking

One morning after some two hours of leisurely paddling down Ontario's Moose River, my partner suddenly realized that he had left his $300 camera at our last campsite. Somewhat begrudgingly and with unrepeatable expletives, I grabbed a painter and helped him tow the canoe 7 miles upstream to our

Preparing to line around a ledge.

The opposite of tracking is lining. This procedure is considerably more common than upstream work and is widely used to get around small falls, ledges, and other obstacles in the river. Some authorities recommend attaching lines to keep the upstream end of the canoe raised. They also advise attaching the bow line to a gunwale near the seat. I have found it best to leave lines attached to their customary rings at the bow and stern (which should be located close to the waterline). Often, while lining, you will be working above the canoe, possibly, hopping from rock to rock, or sometimes pulling from different sides of the canoe. If, for example, you let the canoe down a chute and for some reason need to pull it back up to realign it with the main current, you will be at a serious disadvantage if your lines are attached anywhere other than at the ends.

Canoeing texts make lining sound easy. It isn't. Controlling the path of a heavily loaded canoe in the powerful side-wall of a rock-studded passage requires practice. And agility! The recommended procedure is to use lines at both bow and stern. However, coordinating two ropes—and two people—requires much more skill than you might believe. Even the smallest miscalculation can send the canoe reeling sideways, where it may fill with water and wrap neatly around a rock or be broken nicely in two. For this reason many experienced canoeists prefer to line their canoe alone, with a single tail rope, even though it results in some loss of control.

Whitewater Safety

Despite some dangers inherent in the sport of canoeing, it is essentially a safe pastime. Whitewater clubs take to the rivers as soon as the ice melts, and although the water temperature is very cold (sometimes just a few degrees above freezing), we seldom hear of a drowning. This is because experienced paddlers respect rivers and are well prepared for upsets. Herein lies the key to whitewater safety: *Be prepared for an upset!*

Life Jackets

Many beginners assume that being a good swimmer is the most important safety consideration. While swimming ability is important, a life jacket and a cool

island campsite of the night before. I doubt that we could have paddled that distance very easily.

Upstream tracking is useful not only for retrieving lost cameras but also for getting around rapids when a portage is difficult or impossible to make. For best results while tracking, the upstream end of the canoe should be kept up. If your towing link or ring is located very far above the waterline, you will have to disconnect the bow rope and rig a towing harness. You want the line pulling right from the keel, if possible. The stern line is less important and can remain at its usual place of attachment.

Upstream tracking is just like ferrying. By keeping the canoe at a slight angle to the current (bow out, stern toward shore) while towing, you can walk upstream along the bank, and the wash of the current will carry the canoe out to the center of the river. Changing the angle of the canoe while pulling on the ropes will return it to shore. Obviously, tracking is impossible if shorelines are too brushy or rugged to walk along.

head are more so. Except in unusually calm conditions, you should wear your life jacket at all times. On a wilderness trip, especially, you are burdened with the extra weight of heavy clothes and boots. An upset in even a moderate rapid or mildly choppy lake can be hazardous. Lack of a life preserver has accompanied almost every canoeing fatality.

In 1974 a canoeist lost his life on the Coppermine River in the Northwest Territories of Canada. The man was a good swimmer and an experienced whitewater paddler. He and his partner put ashore just above a difficult rapid known as Rocky Defile. After considerable scouting, the pair decided to run the rapid. As soon as they started downstream, the canoeist realized that he was not wearing his life jacket. He had taken it off while checking the rapids and had neglected to put it back on. But it was too late. The canoe nosed into a heavy roller and began to climb. When it reached the top of the large wave, it teetered and flipped over on its side, throwing both paddlers out of the canoe. Four weeks later the body of the unfortunate canoeist was found. His partner, who wore a life jacket, survived and completed the remaining 200 miles of the journey alone. It is ironic that in the many miles these experts had paddled together, this was the first time that either had neglected to wear his life jacket. It was not incompetence that cost the life of this canoeist; rather, it was an oversight—a simple procedural omission—like forgetting to buckle your seat belt before you drive. Wilderness rivers bear no malice toward unprepared paddlers; neither, however, do they grant immunity from error.

Because your life jacket is so important, you should select a model that you can wear comfortably all the time. Eliminate from consideration the bulky orange horse-collar type—they are too confining and chafe the neck badly. Choose instead a vertical-ribbed or panel-style vest filled with closed-cell foam. And don't choose a personal flotation device (PFD) on the strength of Coast Guard approval tags alone. The life jacket requirements of whitewater paddlers are not the same as those of powerboaters. For example, the proper procedure for swimming in rapids is as follows: Lie on your back, feet pointing downstream. Keep your feet high to prevent somersaulting in the current, and use your feet and canoe paddle to ward

Lining a rapid on the Kopka River, Ontario.

off rocks (figure 6-11). Swim on your back or side, at an angle to the current, to reach shore. This technique is similar to the canoeist's back ferry.

To do this, you need as much floatation on your back as on your chest, and the bulky horse collars offer virtually no back flotation. Horse collars are

Figure 6-11 **Safest way to swim a rapid:** Keep your feet high to prevent somersaulting in the current, and use your feet and paddle to ward off rocks.

Figure 6-12 Type III life jacket (vertical ribbed): Get a life jacket that does not interfere with swimming!

designed to float the wearer head-up for extended periods of time—at the expense of maneuverability. You are seldom in the water for more than five minutes in a typical canoe upset. In order to avoid obstacles, you need a jacket that does not interfere with swimming. Fortunately, the Coast Guard now realizes that the needs of canoeists are best met with Type III floatation devices, which are comfortable to wear for long periods of time. Here's how to test the fit of a life vest that catches your fancy:

Figure 6-13 Type III life jacket (panel style).

- **Ride-up:** Grasp the jacket by the shoulders and lift it upward until the fabric jams under your armpits. This simulates performance in water. Now turn your head right and left. You should be looking over your shoulder, not at fabric-encased foam. Does the V-neck of the vest crunch against your chin? If so, keep shopping. PFDs that force the chin up may have a more positive righting movement than those that don't, but they hinder maneuverability in water—exactly what you don't want when you have to swim a rapid!

- **Arm function:** Take a seat. This test won't work while standing or kneeling. Now work your arms vigorously in a paddling motion. Any vest that chafes under the armpits will be intolerable to wear over the long haul.

- **Flexibility:** Hold your arms chest-high and draw them smartly inward as far as possible. Does the vest bunch up in front and cramp arm motion? If so, keep looking!

As you shop around for the ideal life vest, you'll learn that sizing, cut, and flexibility vary widely from manufacturer to manufacturer. For this reason it's best *not* to buy a PFD by mail. The above tests are your best indication of good performance in water and a fit you can live with.

It is interesting to note that there is little relationship between your weight out of water and your weight in water. Prospective buyers of life jackets assume that a 250-pound man needs more flotation than a 130-pound teenager. If the man is overweight and the teenager is mostly muscle, quite the opposite may be true. It is not uncommon for children to need as much flotation as their parents. Manufacturers have done an excellent job providing properly sized life jackets. The important thing, however, is to realize that the buoyancy rating of the jacket may or may not meet your requirements. You should test your life jacket in both calm water and rapids to assure that it will adequately support you.

Keeping Warm

Most canoeists rely on polypropylene, fleece, or wool garments for warmth. These fabrics won't substitute for a wet suit in near-freezing water, but they will keep you cozy in an all-day rain. As table 6-1 shows, your body will remain functional in cold water for only a short time. Even this doesn't tell the whole story, because the initial shock of cold water on your chest saps much of your energy. A waterproof paddling shirt can reduce this shock somewhat, but only a wet suit can eliminate it completely. Many canoeists compute the chill index of a river by taking the temperature of the air and water. If the sum of the two numbers is less than 100, a wet suit or dry suit is absolutely essential!

Although your body may remain functional for several minutes in cold water, you can die from immersion hypothermia after you've been rescued. Hypothermia occurs when body temperature drops below 95 degrees. As blood is rushed to the vital organs, chilling spreads throughout the body. This is accompanied by clumsiness, slurred speech, and loss of judgment. Coma and death may occur within a few hours if body temperature is not raised.

Field treatment for someone who has fallen into ice-cold water consists of warming the victim as quickly as possible. If a fire is available, use it! If not, place the naked (skin-to-skin contact) victim into a sleeping bag with one or two people.

If the victim is conscious and can swallow, you may give hot chocolate or soup as a psychological boost. Do not administer stimulants such as coffee or tea.

If hypothermia results from slow chilling over time, the victim should be warmed gradually. Apply radiant heat from a fire slowly, or use the classic sleeping bag treatment. Through it all, handle the victim gently, as roughhousing may initiate ventricular fibrillation of the heart . . . and death could result!

A final note: victims of hypothermia are almost always unaware of the seriousness of their situation. They will continually proclaim, "I'm okay!" It's up to you to diagnose the problem—and treat it quickly.

In 1980 I led a group of teenagers on a trip into the Boundary Waters Canoe Area. There was an icy drizzle and light wind on Saganaga Lake when we put in that morning—nothing serious, just fair warning to dress warm and wear rain clothes. Within the hour the rain picked up. But the kids were all singing and having a grand time, so I saw no reason to put ashore.

As we rounded a point, we overtook another group that was paddling in dead silence. "How's it goin'?" I called encouragingly. Groans of displeasure followed. I paddled alongside the lead canoe and struck up a conversation with the leader.

"Some of these kids don't have good rain gear," he commented. "But they're tough; they can hack it. Besides, we'll be in camp within the hour."

"I dunno," I responded. "Your passenger [a teenage girl] doesn't look so good."

"How ya doin', Linda?" he questioned. "You wanna go ashore and change clothes?"

"I'm okay," she whimpered softly. "I can make it till we camp."

The youngster didn't look very well at all. Her lips were blue and she shivered constantly. She had no seat cushion to protect her from the cold, wet bottom of the aluminum canoe. It was a perfect setup for hypothermia.

"I think we'd better get those clothes changed now," I quipped. "C'mon, let's put ashore on that point."

Table 6–1

Water Temperature	Amount of Time Body Will Remain Functional
Less than 40 degrees F	Less than 10 minutes
40 to 50 degrees F	15 to 20 minutes
50 to 60 degrees F	15 to 40 minutes
60 degrees F and above	One or more hours

There was another round of "I can make it" from the girl and "These kids are tough" from the leader, but I was insistent, so he finally routed the crew to shore.

The seriousness of the situation became evident when the leader observed that Linda could not get out of the canoe without help. Her legs simply refused to support her body! While we set up the tent and pulled sleeping bags and dry clothing from packs, the kids crowded around the girl and hugged her to provide as much warmth as possible. Then two girls ushered her into the tent and administered the classic sleeping bag treatment.

Within the hour Linda was revitalized. But the group decided to remain ashore for the remainder of the day—a wise decision, as hypothermia is a very draining experience, one that requires plenty of rest to fully recover from.

You don't need to paddle a remote wilderness to encounter an episode of hypothermia. People have died while canoeing familiar streams near their home! You have a moral responsibility to use your knowledge of hypothermia to help others you meet in the wilderness. It is not bad manners to strongly suggest that a group bivouac because one member is too cold or too tired to go on. The most inexcusable act you can commit in the outdoors is to say and do nothing when you know there's a possibility that another human being may become injured or die. A human life is an unfair price to pay for ignorance!

Basic Precautions

When you are canoeing whitewater, avoid long coats, ponchos, or anything dangling around your neck on a string. Should you overturn, these items are likely to be caught on submerged tree limbs or between rocks.

Also, avoid heavy boots, and never wear waders while paddling. Water-filled waders can make swimming in even a moderate current impossible.

If you overturn, your best life preserver is the canoe, and you should stay with it unless doing so will endanger your life. Upon upsetting, swim immediately to the upstream end of the canoe. A water-filled canoe weighs more than a ton, and should you get between it and a rock, you will be crushed. Hang on to the grab loop or stern painter and try to swim the canoe to shore. The canoe-over-canoe rescue touted by the Red Cross and Scouts works well on calm lakes with empty canoes, but cannot be done with loaded canoes on fast water. Unfortunately, this is where most canoe upsets occur.

If the water is very cold and there is no support crew to come to your rescue, your best bet is to leave the canoe immediately and strike out for shore. Hanging hopefully to a canoe in near-freezing water when there is no chance of rescue only hastens your early demise. Contrary to popular belief, and the writings of some canoe authorities, it is not easy to swim a swamped canoe to shore. And if you rely on the action of wind or currents to bring the craft (and you) to land, you're in for a much longer wait than you can afford!

C H A P T E R 7

Common Canoeing Hazards

Everyone has heard grim tales about paddlers who drowned when they capsized in ice-cold water or a powerful rapid, paddled over a dam, or were struck by lightning.

People who don't canoe react with horror to these stories and solemnly agree that canoeing must be a very dangerous pastime. Experienced canoeists know better. In fact, most knowledgeable paddlers canoe their whole life without ever being involved in a life-threatening incident. Certainly, occasional upsets are par for the sport, but death-defying encounters with power dams, waterfalls, strainers (downed trees that block a river), and icy water are not. Competent paddlers respect the power of running water and have a proven battle plan to escape its dangers. They also have the skills to execute their plan.

Herein lies the secret of safe canoeing: *Learn to paddle well enough so you can carry out your battle plan!*

What follows are some of the most common paddling hazards. I'll begin with not-so-serious (sometimes humorous) situations that are easy to avoid and end with scary predicaments that I hope you'll never encounter.

Losing Your Keys and Money

Scenario: You park your car in a dimly lit area at the trailhead and paddle off for a weekend of fun. You lock your billfold in the car, fearful you'll lose it in a capsize. The next day you return to find your car has been broken into. Your money is gone!

This scenario is repeated so frequently that it merits inclusion as a common paddling hazard. The rule here is simple: Don't leave anything of value in your car! Expensive cartop carriers will be stolen. Canoe racks should be locked on the roof or removed and stored inside the vehicle.

The most secure way to carry keys and money on a canoe trip is on your body. Money and credit cards are best bagged in a Ziploc, placed in a pants pocket, and secured with a heavy diaper pin. Put your key ring in a pants pocket and secure it to your belt with a length of nylon cord. Then stuff a large handkerchief over your keys so they won't fall out of your pocket if you capsize. Pocketknife and change go in another pocket, immobilized by another hankie.

Of course, you can also place these items inside packsacks. However, you are far more likely to lose a pack in a capsize than your pants!

Stuck in the Mud

An unimproved dirt road that leads to a put-in can become a quagmire if it rains hard while you're on the river. If someone in your party has a four-wheel drive vehicle and tow cable, you can put aside concerns. Otherwise, you'd best leave the vehicle on high ground, away from the river's floodplain. At the very least, turn the rig around so you'll be facing in an escape direction.

Always carry a tow strap, jumper cables, and simple tools in your car or truck. Vehicles that are stuck or won't start are among the most common paddling "hazards."

Embedded Fishhook/Bug in the Eye

A treble hook in the face can end a canoe trip immediately, so establish rules—like on which side of the boat you plan to cast—before you fish. If you leave lures attached to lines while you paddle, secure them to the rod with Velcro covers. Every bait shop has them. A capsize and an unsheathed treble hook can cause a serious wound. Absolutely never leave unguarded fishing lures in your canoe! Figure 7-1 shows a painless (really!) way to remove an embedded fishhook.

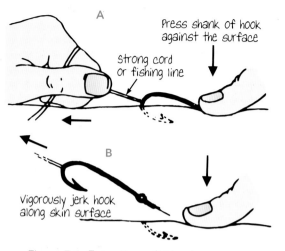

A

Press shank of hook against the surface

strong cord or fishing line

B

Vigorously jerk hook along skin surface

Figure 7-1 Extracting a fishhook.

Perhaps the most common serious medical problem you are likely to encounter on a canoe trip is a scratched cornea or foreign object (usually an insect) in the eye.

Some years ago a woman in my whitewater canoeing class got sand beneath her contact lenses when she capsized. The pain was unbearable. I gently lifted each eyelid and flushed out the particles with generous quantities of Eye Stream, a sterile irrigation solution. Then I applied a ribbon of Polysporin ophthalmic ointment (yellow oxide of mercury, ophthalmic 2 percent, is the non-Rx alternative) inside each lower lid and immobilized the eyes with oval eye patches and microfoam tape. Finally, I administered Tylenol.

The woman said the pain ceased shortly after I applied the ointment. The next day she called to report that her doctor was so pleased with the treatment that he had simply applied more ointment and replaced the bandages. Naturally, I was thrilled I had done things right.

Of all the medications in my kit, Polysporin ophthalmic ointment and large, oval eye patches have been the most useful. I've used these several times to treat eye infections and scratched corneas.

Tip: Eye patches are great for patching blisters!

Poor Judgment

Most canoeing accidents are the result of bad judgment. For example, an easy riffle abruptly turns into a respectable rapid. Suddenly, there's a ledge ahead. To avoid the ledge you must angle your canoe about 30 degrees to the current and paddle backward. You are familiar with the back-ferry technique, but you haven't practiced it in heavy currents. Panic ensues; you miss your cue and capsize!

The best way to avoid this scenario is to scout every drop and blind curve before you commit. When you see dancing water ahead, put ashore immediately. Walk the entire rapid and discuss it with your partner. Go with your gut feelings. Resist pressure from friends, defer to caution, and you won't get in over your head.

Fences

Perhaps the most dangerous obstacle a canoeist can encounter is a barbed-wire fence that crosses a river. Fences are extremely difficult to spot from the seat of a canoe, especially when the river is high. Livestock fences generally bridge rivers in shallow areas where there are few rapids, so you can usually avoid them with a powerful back ferry.

It's interesting to note that accomplished whitewater paddlers almost never back ferry because they can turn their short, responsive boats about face instantly and power forward (forward ferry) out of harm's way. For this reason many expert boaters dismiss the back ferry as a knee-jerk response. Don't believe any whitewater "expert" who suggests that forward ferries are a better plan. Tripping canoes are sluggish trucks; whitewater slalom canoes are hot sports cars. Master the back ferry. Stick with canoeing long enough and it will save your life!

Strainers (Also Called Sweepers)

A strainer results when the river flows between the branches of a submerged tree. If you get sucked into one, there may be no escape, especially if you're wearing loose clothing or a bulky life vest that catches in the debris.

Strainers are every bit as dangerous as dams—

maybe more so, because they don't look very ominous from above. They're most difficult to avoid on small, tight rivers that have lots of curves. Back ferry around blind corners—with the tail of the canoe nearly touching the inside shore.

Unzipped Life Jacket

Scenario: It's a hot, sunny day and you're broiling from the heat of your life jacket. You're tempted to remove the sweaty PFD, but you know better. As a compromise, you loosen the side straps and peel open the zipper to let in air. Ahhh . . . cool at last.

The river curves right and a downed tree looms into view. "Back!" you call boldly. But it's too late. Seconds later you've capsized and are swept into the branches of the partially submerged tree. The "wings" of your unsecured PFD wag in the water and an armhole catches a tree branch. You stop with a jerk and momentarily are held underwater. Thank God you're able to get free! Next time you go canoeing you'll keep your life jacket zipped up tight.

This situation is so frightening that whitewater instructors make a fetish out of berating clients who don't zip up. On the heels of this advice comes proper adjustment of your PFD. The rules for fitting a PFD on page 72 are written in stone!

Wearing High-Top Shoes While Canoeing a Raging Rapid

You have capsized in a shallow, powerful rapid and are thrown clear of the canoe. Instead of turning on your back, feet-up (the rapid swimming position— see figure 6-11), you instinctively drop your legs and attempt to walk. Seconds later a foot becomes lodged between rocks and the current mows you down. Luckily, you're wearing low quarter sneakers that you can kick off.

Hear are the rules:

1. Never attempt to stand in fast-moving water that is over knee-deep.

2. Wear low-cut, quick-drying shoes.

3. Carry a fixed-blade knife or fast-opening folder so you can cut shoelaces away if necessary.

Not Treating Life Jackets as Lifesaving Equipment

No one wants to wear a life jacket that is wet or torn. Do not sit on your life vest or leave it out in the rain when you're ashore. I always take my life vest into my tent at night. It makes a good pillow and a warm garment.

Paddling Barefoot

Sharp rocks, sticks, broken glass, and tin cans in the water can cause nasty wounds on bare feet. Protective footwear is a must if you have to step out of your canoe.

No Security Strap for Your Eyeglasses

You will lose your eyeglasses in a capsize if you don't have a security strap!

Hiding the Spare Paddle

You're canoeing a rapid when your paddle breaks. You reach for the spare but it's tied to thwarts or buried under a mound of camping gear. Suddenly, a rock appears ahead. Bang! And capsize!

Rule: Keep your spare paddle available. I'd rather leave it loose in the canoe, where it can float free and be lost in a capsize, than slow accessibility by tying it to thwarts.

No Sponge and Bailer

Removing accumulated water from your canoe is easy if you have a sponge and bleach-jug bailer. Bailers are essential for canoeing serious rapids, but for casual river paddling, an absorbent sponge is all the bailing equipment you need. The voyageurs carried in their 36-foot Montreal canoes a huge natural sponge that would absorb up to 2 quarts of water.

No Polaroid Sunglasses

It's a canoeing axiom that the most difficult drops are always paddled into the sun. Polaroid sunglasses—the kind that let you see rocks deep in the water—are an essential part of river canoeing.

Sitting through a Rapid When You Should Be Kneeling

Some folks are naturally lucky. A friend of mine is a very competent whitewater paddler, yet he seldom kneels in rapids. His excuse is that in the excitement of the pitch, he simply forgets. I've watched Tom handily run some spectacular Class III drops from the seat of his Dagger Venture. I've never seen him capsize or strike an awkward pose.

Perhaps my friend is more athletic than me. Maybe he's just luckier. Kneeling in difficult water has less to do with lowering the center of gravity than with boat control. Well-anchored, wide-spread knees provide pressure points from which you can heel the hull right or left, or brace far out with confidence. Don't be fooled by the success of downriver racers who never kneel in their long, skittish canoes. As I mentioned in chapter 2, seats of racing canoes are slung too low for kneeling, and the bows are too narrow to assume a wide kneeling stance.

Lightning

First scenario: You're paddling along a lakeshore when a storm blows up. Soon, wind-whipped waves send you scurrying along at what seems to be phenomenal speed. No problem . . . yet. Then you see it—wisps of lightning dancing in the sky. Better get to shore fast! A canoe on open water is no place to be in an electrical storm. The problem is that huge boulders line the shore as far as you can see. Dash into those boulders and you'll pack your canoe home in pieces. The alternative is to keep on paddling and take your chances on being targeted by a million volts of electricity.

As you can see, the off-quoted advice to get off the water when lightning strikes is sound only if the shoreline provides both an easy landing and a safe haven from the storm. In our scenario it does neither. Better to stay on open water, relatively close to land. Here's why: A lightning-protected zone extends from the tops of the tallest trees (or other topographic features) outward about 45 degrees in all directions. Paddle within this safe "cone of protection," but not so close to its center that lightning may jump from a tree to you. Lightning can easily breach 10 or 20 feet,

so—except in unusual circumstances—two or three canoe lengths offshore is the safest place to be.

Second scenario: You're canoeing a small river when the electrical activity begins. Should you head for shore or take your chances on the water? Here again, your choice should depend on the nature of the adjacent shoreline. For example, south-facing slopes encourage the growth of fast-growing shade-intolerant trees over slower-growing ones that can live in the shade. This means that some of the tallest trees may stand near the waterway. Holding hopefully to a tall tree is not the safest place to be in a lightning storm! I saw a classic example of this on a small Ontario river some years ago.

The storm began with heavy rain, punctuated by unrelenting lightning. I gathered my teenage crew around me and told them to hang tight and stay well out in the river. As I was explaining the rationale, I saw my colleague's red canoe disappear into the supposed safety of the alder-choked shoreline. Above my friend's head the top of a tall birch was aflame. The red canoe reversed power just as the burning top came crashing down.

As you can see, a tall shoreline tree is no place to be when lightning strikes all around. It is far safer to take your chances on the water, within the cone of protection.

Note: There's a misconception that wood and fiberglass canoes are safer than aluminum ones in a lightning storm. No way! A lightning strike may generate millions of volts of electricity—enough to fry anything in its path. The fact is that aluminum canoes may actually dissipate current better than nonmetal ones (the charge may be conducted around the hull, into the water). This is all scientific conjecture, you understand.

Surfing in a Following Sea

For a while you are powered along by a gently following breeze. Simply rudder and go with the flow. Then the wind intensifies and you pick up speed. Now the canoe feels lightheaded and out of control, like a monkey on a rubber band. Suddenly, there's a surge of power as the craft peaks a wave and begins to surf. Back-paddle and you'll capsize for sure.

Continue to rudder and you may do the same. On the other hand, if you can get up enough forward speed to climb off the wave face, the surf may pass you by. At any rate, it's worth a try.

Fortunately, canoes seldom surf very well for very long. Invariably, the wave passes and the stern falls into the trough behind. Whether or not the boat fills with water from the following wave depends on your prowess in climbing up out of the hole. (Just keep paddling and you'll do fine!) Surfing only becomes serious when a rocky shore looms ahead. Then you must get off the wave immediately or be tossed headlong into the boulder line.

To break the surf, get up a full head of steam, then make a snappy, well-braced turn into the wave trough. Lean the canoe smartly away from the oncoming wave. If you pull off the maneuver, you'll gulp some water and stall sideways in the wave trough. If you goof—or lean the wrong way—you'll enjoy a pleasant swim to shore. Once in the trough, simply turn upwind and paddle ashore.

Working Upwind

Working upwind is far safer than going with the flow. All you need to do is keep from taking on water as you knife into the oncoming waves.

Canoeing experts advise you to quarter the waves at an approximate 30-degree angle as the bow beats upwind. This procedure shortens the canoe's waterline, making it easier for the craft to fit between waves. The result is greater buoyancy and a drier ride.

However, a canoe on a quartering tack is constantly on the edge of broaching to the wind. The stern person must be in total control. An error here and you'll swim for sure. That's why quartering is a tactic best reserved for experts. Beginners should wipe the technique from their memory banks and instead adopt the head-on approach.

Procedure: Both partners move closer amidships to lighten the ends of the craft so it will rise and fall more freely with the waves. Point the bow upwind and paddle! Simple as pie. There is no danger of broaching as you power upwind.

Motorboat Wakes

Experienced canoeists often seek out motorboat wakes for the thrill of riding them. Beginners, however, have somewhat cooler feelings toward the experience. Mix good current with a variable wind, add a speedboat wake, and you have a recipe for a broach, surf, swamping . . . or all three. Now introduce the wake from another powerful cruiser and you have the makings for a Class III rapid on your hometown river.

The solution for surviving this mess is to paddle head-on into the maelstrom—not so easy if you're being assaulted from both sides. And if the wave length is short, you may take on water unless you act fast. Pick the closest oncoming wave set and gently paddle straight into it. As the bow rises onto the first roller, angle off into the wave trough (quarter it) to shorten the canoe's waterline length. Keep this gentle quartering course (it gets easier with each passing wave) and you'll stay dry and in command. The opposite wave train you were worried about will be absorbed by the waves in which you are now safely nestled.

Tip: If you see a speedboat bearing full-bore your way, raise your hand high, execute a grimace, and give a forceful thumbs down. More often than not, the boat cuts power on your command.

Towing

You've finished your canoe trip in a quiet bay of the big lake. Ten miles of open-water travel stretch between you and your car. To save time, you hire a powerboat to tow you to the public landing. What are the safety concerns, if any?

Canoeing texts make towing sound like a lark. Just attach a harness around the canoe so the line pulls right from the keel, run a Y-trace off the powerboat transom (figure 7-2), and speed ahead, worry-free.

Don't you believe it!

On calm water a proper tow is safe enough. Cruise at moderate speed, make gradual turns—the canoe must not cross the wake path—and you'll have no trouble. However, when the wind comes up, it's a different story. Now, you must balance two variables—

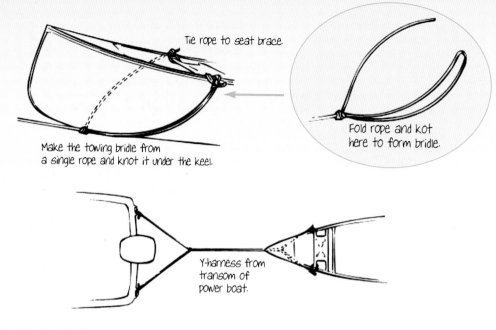

Tie rope to seat brace.

Make the towing bridle from a single rope and knot it under the keel.

Fold rope and kot here to form bridle.

Y-harness from transom of power boat.

Figure 7-2 Towing bridle.

waves and the speedboat's wake. Frequently, the two synergize (especially when making turns) and the canoe angles into the wake. The result may be a swamping or capsize and a severely damaged canoe.

The safest way to tow canoes is on an overhead rack built for the purpose. Failing this, you're best advised to wait for calm water—or paddle those 10 miles!

Two Is Company, Three Is a Load

Some canoeists take canoe capacity recommendations seriously. If the bulkhead sticker reads 850 POUNDS MAXIMUM, half that weight in human cargo should allow for ample freeboard. Or so they think!

First, be aware that manufacturers' load ratings are usually stated to a 6-inch freeboard capacity. Load any canoe that heavy and a few good riffles will sink it at the dock. As mentioned in chapter 1, a 9-inch minimum is more responsible. And movable weight (humans) juggles all the variables and synergizes everything. Place four 90-pound teenagers in an 800-pound-rated canoe and you'll understand. When one kid bounces, the other jounces. The result is an "upsetting" experience.

Obviously, it makes a difference if the human load is seated dead center and on the floor of the canoe. But even then, 800 pounds of flour is a more manageable load than half that weight of well-behaved kids. You can improve the odds by substituting grown-ups for children. But it's still safer to carry the equivalent weight of uncooked pasta!

I've traveled thousands of miles without incident with three in my canoe, and as long as weights are kept reasonable, it's safe enough. Nonetheless, a passenger is always a concern—one that prompts me to portage rapids I'd otherwise paddle with a similar dead-weight cargo aboard. Floatplane pilots frequently halve the useful load of their aircraft when carrying a canoe on the pontoons. I suggest you do likewise when you carry a passenger in your canoe.

CHAPTER 8

Canoe Rescue and Repair

Kettle River—a delightful blend of exquisite scenery and intriguing rapids, a federally protected wild and scenic river that deserves to be. And a favorite playground for midwestern kayakers and canoers.

Mike and I had made a deal: I'd help him teach the intermediate whitewater course, and he'd provide meals and lodging plus an opportunity to learn some new salvage and rescue techniques developed by the Nantahala Outdoor Center.

My mistake was bringing old Mantoy—a well-used, well-patched, wood-strip solo canoe that had seen tough service on some of the rockiest rivers in Minnesota and Canada. Mike watched enviously from shore as I ferried out, eddied in, and did a host of other playful maneuvers, all designed to solicit envy from the crowd.

For the better part of the day we practiced in easy Class I to II rapids. The crew gained skill, and by early afternoon they had learned their lessons well enough to begin the "canoe trip."

"Can I take her downriver?" asked Mike, pointing hopefully to the little wood canoe. Before I could answer, he climbed confidently aboard and slipped quietly into the water and out of sight around the next bend.

It was then I remembered that Mike had the pack with all the rescue gear—the climbing rope, carabiners, pulleys, slings, and the like. Suppose we wrapped a canoe around a midstream boulder? How on earth would we ever get it free?

Well, that wouldn't happen—I'd see to that!

It wasn't a big tree, but it was large enough to command concern. It jutted three-quarters of the way across the river on the inside of a tight hairpin turn.

But there was a clear 3-foot channel on the outside—plenty of space for a canoe to scoot through.

My partner and I slipped through the opening, then put ashore to wait for the students and signal them to the outside of the turn. They came through like veterans, first one canoe, then two, then . . . capsize! Suddenly, there were two paddlers in the grip of the icy water.

Seconds later I saw the comforting sight of two sunlight-yellow life vests skimming the surface. I thanked God that the tree had no submerged branches to entrap the swimmers. I quickly belayed the throwing line around a tree and tossed it out. The woman grabbed it, and together my partner and I towed her to shore. Downstream, in the shallows, I observed the man struggling ashore.

The water was a cold 47 degrees and the air temperature was only slightly warmer. But the flush of excitement had provided a surge of warmth and the pair had not yet begun to shiver. Nonetheless, an immediate change of clothes, hot tea, and affectionate hugs were in order.

And now to rescue the canoe. The Grumman had bellied up against the foot-thick log—open end exposed to the full force of the current. Reluctantly, I shuffled along the tree trunk to the pinned canoe. No way I could budge it. "Damn!" I said aloud. "If only we had the proper rescue gear!" But no sense whining; we would have to extract the boat with what we had—100 feet of ⅜-inch nylon rope and one carabiner (an aluminum link through which mountain climbers run their ropes).

The first step was to get a rope around the hull and attached so that it would pull the submerged gunwale up and away from the raging current—a feat of engineering that required the better part of twenty minutes. That accomplished, we rigged a makeshift block and tackle around an upstream tree with a power cinch (see chapter 10, Tying It All Together) and carabiner. Then everyone pulled . . . and pulled. No luck.

Next we tried prying the canoe free with a 6-foot length of log. Again, a blank. "Maybe if we pry and winch at the same time," suggested someone. That did it; the gleaming metal hull groaned and popped free like a cookie from a mold. All that remained now was to haul it ashore, dump out the water, and stomp it into a shape that could be paddled.

In this instance salvaging the canoe was no big deal. We could have simply returned with the rescue equipment. However, had this occurred on a wilderness river, miles from the nearest road, the picture would be much different. Then we could choose between our ingenuity and a long walk home!

Equipment

If you'll be leading groups down rivers where there's a real possibility that you might have to extract a pinned canoe, then you'd better carry some serious climbing gear—120 feet of climbing rope, about six carabiners, a couple of nylon pulleys, nylon webbing, and so forth. Otherwise, 100 feet of about ⅜-inch rope, two carabiners, and a rescue pulley should suffice. With these you can rig a 2:1 (or greater) mechanical advantage pulley over a short distance. If the canoe is hung up so badly that a solid harness, a pry bar, and your best efforts won't get it free, at least wait around for a few days before abandoning it. Rivers often fluctuate greatly from week to week, and an inch or two less water may provide just the edge you need.

If your canoe should ground firmly on a rock in a fast-flowing river and turn broadside to the current, the entire side of the craft will be exposed to the force of the rushing water. This force may equal several thousand pounds and may be enough to bend or break the canoe. However, as long as the craft is kept upright, the rushing water will usually pass harmlessly beneath the rounded hull. But if the upstream gunwale should dip below the water and expose the inside of the canoe to the power of the current, the craft may be broken in half or damaged beyond repair. Therefore, it is important that you never let

the open end of your canoe become exposed to the current. You should make every effort to keep the upstream gunwale up, even if it means leaving your canoe. Hold tightly to the gunwale and try to work the canoe loose. Usually the removal of your weight is all that's necessary to free the hull. Do not, however, enter the water downstream of the canoe under any circumstances. Should the craft slide off the rock while you are in the water, it could crush you against a downstream obstacle.

Repair

Modern canoeists use silver duct (furnace) tape almost exclusively for field repairs of canoes. Duct tape sticks to anything! In fact, canoe owners often neglect more permanent hull repairs simply because furnace tape works so well. A small roll of duct tape should be carried on all canoe trips—close to home or otherwise. In thirty-five years of canoeing I have yet to damage a canoe so badly that tape and ingenuity would not repair it.

In the case of aluminum canoes, there is little you can do in the way of field repairs other than apply tape. Where rivets have been pulled, they can be retightened by administering several blows with the backside of an ax. Small gaps and holes can be filled with liquid aluminum epoxy, and these items should be included in your repair kit. Since aluminum canoes usually bend rather than break, physical force will be required to straighten them. An aluminum canoe that has had its gunwales or sides caved in can be placed in shallow water, sand, or mud and stomped back into a semblance of shape. A wood block, the hammer face of an ax, and true grit will produce amazing results.

At home a break in the skin should be repaired by affixing a riveted patch. Complete patch kits available from Marathon Canoes include patching material, rivets, and instructions. Although a good-quality welding job appears to hold satisfactorily, the aluminum adjacent to the weld may become brittle and cause problems later on. I have seen some fine repair jobs by master aircraft aluminum welders, and these are probably adequate.

Fiberglass, Kevlar, and wood-strip canoes are easily repaired by applying epoxy resin and fiberglass cloth

Performing a canoe-over-canoe rescue, Pipestone River, Ontario.

directly to the break. (See my book *Canoeing Wild Rivers*—The Globe Pequot Press, 1989—for detailed methods of repairing structural damage.) You can substitute polyester resin for epoxy, but it isn't nearly as strong. (You can patch polyester canoes with epoxy but not vice versa.) Unfortunately, there are dozens of formulations for epoxy and not all are ideal for boat repair. I can heartily recommend these epoxies: West System, available from the Gougeon Brothers,* Ad-Tech, available from the Northwest Canoe Company,* and System Three.* (Addresses are in appendix 4.) These epoxies cure in temperatures as low as 45 degrees. Unique plastic pumps dispense the correct mix so there's no waste or mess.

It's unlikely that you'll ever have to repair major damage on a well-built fiberglass or Kevlar canoe. However, you may need to mend chipped gel coat on the nose of your canoe after every trip down a shallow rocky stream—easy enough if you don't follow the manufacturer's directions. The book procedure calls for filling the break with color-matched liquid gel coat, then sanding, buffing, and polishing to blend the repair.

Nothing could be more difficult—or frustrating! Catalyzed liquid gel coat is so runny that it's impossible to contain. The solution is to prop the boat at an awkward angle to level the flow, then build a well of masking tape around the resin. You then have to nurse the slowly hardening liquid with a flat stick to keep it from overflowing the well. If your patience holds out, the completed patch will hardly be noticeable.

There is an easier way. All you need is a can of white polyester putty (you can substitute gray auto-body putty), which is available at all marinas, and an aerosol can of acrylic enamel or auto lacquer to match the color of your boat:

1. Pick out the shards of damaged gel coat with the blade of your pocketknife.

2. Catalyze the putty (use extra methyl-ethyl-ketone-peroxide (MEKP) to produce a "hot" mix) and work it into the break to overflowing. The putty is thick and won't run, so there's no need to prop the canoe or build a tape well.

3. When the putty is firm (about five minutes), slice

off the excess with your pocketknife. Allow the remainder to cure completely (another ten minutes), then sand it level with progressive grits of sandpaper. Finish to silky smoothness with 400-grit wet sandpaper.

4. Spray-paint the patch. When the paint has dried, blend the paint to match the hull with a mixture of paste wax and pumice. Or polish with commercial fiberglass boat wax, which contains pumice.

The repair is hardly noticeable, and downtime on the boat is less than an hour.

ABS Royalex hulls are so tough that they are nearly puncture-proof. Repairs are usually made with fiberglass cloth and epoxy resin. Kits are available from nearly every company that manufactures these canoes.

If you own a fine wood-canvas canoe, you are probably well aware of how to maintain it. Old Town Canoe Company* offers everything you need to restore these craft. Wood-canvas canoes never die; they just accumulate new parts. For detailed instructions on how to repair wood-canvas canoes, consult the American Red Cross's canoeing manual, which provides a wealth of information on the subject.

C H A P T E R 9

The Art of Cartopping

Given enough rope—and time—anyone can tie down a canoe so it won't blow off a car. The fun comes when you have several boats to haul, or when the wind whips to impressive speeds. Then you'd better know what you're doing or you may have an airborne missile on your hands!

The safest arrangement is to get a cartop carrier that bolts directly to the automobile's drip eaves—an insurmountable problem now that nearly all vehicles come with airplane-style doors. Fortunately, several companies offer fitted brackets for gutterless cars, and these have proven reliable over the long haul.

Even if you never plan to buy a second canoe, you will often need to shuttle a friend's, so be sure to order double-length (78 to 82 inches) racks—the factory-standard 48-inch carrier is not long enough to carry two canoes.

As an added precaution, canoes carried in pairs should have a boat cushion or piece of carpeting placed between them and tied to one of the canoes. It is also essential to secure carpeting or heater hose to crossbars so the rails won't be damaged. Many canoeists (myself included) simply won't allow their canoes to be carried on nonpadded racks!

For Safety's Sake, Tie 'em Down

Most canoeists give only casual thought to securing their canoes to cartop carriers. A properly tied-down canoe should show little, if any, movement, even in high winds at speeds well in excess of those legally posted. As a rule of thumb, each canoe carried should be tied down separately. This will eliminate many embarrassing problems at highway speeds.

Attach a stout ¼-inch nylon rope to each car rack. Run the lines over the belly of the canoe and secure them to the other side of the rack. Tie each as close as

possible to the gunwales of the canoe to prevent wind shift. The power cinch (see chapter 10, Tying It All Together) is the most suitable knot and is the only one that should be used for tying down canoes. Additionally, tie two ropes to each end of the canoe and attach the free ends of these lines to their respective bumpers. Again, use a power cinch. Make up a special set of nylon ropes with S-hooks at each end, or install steel eye bolts in the bumpers. It is very difficult to attach naked ropes to today's plastic bumpers. *Caution:* Avoid the use of rubber truck tie-downs. They have too much stretch and can cause problems if the canoe is buffeted by wind. Lastly, if you cartop two canoes on one car, use a separate belly rope for each canoe. This is in keeping with the aforementioned rule of thumb, and it will also help keep paired canoes from rubbing.

Straps versus Ropes—The Big Debate

Many modern canoeists, and nearly all commercial haulers, prefer reinforced nylon cam-lock straps to ropes. Cam-lock straps are fast to operate and undeniably secure; you don't need to know special knots. But there are disadvantages:

- Straps are expensive and may be stolen if you leave them on the car when you're on the river.

- You must remember to put the straps on the crossbars *before* you rack the canoe. It's awkward if you do it the other way around.

- Each strap must be passed over the canoe to the far side of the rack. The straps are too short to carry around the vehicle, and if you toss them over the top of the car, the buckle may strike the vehicle and damage it. What you need is a helpful friend.

- If you carry two canoes side by side on the same

rack, you *must* remember to install all four belly straps on the crossbars *before* you load either of the canoes. Forget this and you may have to climb the hood of the vehicle to reach the crossbars!

Most experienced canoeists will admit that ropes are easier than straps. Leave them permanently tied to the racks when you're on the river and no one will take them. Load your canoe and throw them over the top of the car—you won't damage the finish. Will they loosen on a long trip? Not much. Polypropylene, polyester, and natural fibers stay drum-tight in any weather. Nylon ropes stretch slightly when they get wet. But cinching them takes seconds, if you use the right knots.

Canoe Cushions May Be Unreliable

This inexpensive rig (every marina has one) consists of two tie-down straps and four grooved foam blocks that snap onto the canoe's gunwales. Unlike conventional carriers, canoe cushions can be quickly installed and removed, and they're easily stored in the trunk of a small car. The downside is that you can only carry one canoe at a time, and the craft is questionably secure—more so if your car does not have rain gutters to which you can clamp the belly straps. A fairly safe solution is to crack the side windows and run the belly ropes or straps *through* the car. Even then, I question the safety of this rig!

How Do You Carry Three Canoes on a Car Rack Built for Two?

To carry a third canoe on a two-car rack, mount two boats on the carriers as described, then place 5-foot-long carpeted 1-by-2s across the belly of each canoe. Center the third craft on top of these wooden supports and tie it to the metal crossbars and car bumpers. On a long trip it's a good idea to tie the ends of the 1-by-2s to the steel carriers.

Canoe clubs frequently trek to the river with a half-dozen or more canoes and kayaks piled high on a vehicle. (I think the record—established at a national whitewater event—is ten boats!) Such displays of civil engineering are impressive, but not necessarily safe. Most canoeists would agree that you're tempting fate whenever you carry more than three boats at a time on the overhead racks of a car. If you need to haul more than three canoes, use a trailer—it's much safer.

Trailering

The best way to carry large numbers of canoes is aboard a trailer built especially for the purpose. Be sure the trailer has good-sized fenders so it won't throw dirt and gravel into the canoes and a high-enough "tree" so the ends of the bottom canoes won't bottom out on rutted roads. As always, use good nylon line, not rubber ropes, to secure the canoes to the trailer.

Caution: Well-tied-down canoes stiffen a trailer tree considerably. However, when the canoes are removed and the trailer is run empty over rough roads, substantial strain is placed on the unsupported tree. After a few years (or less) of bouncing around, the crossbars usually give way and require rewelding. A number of methods have been used to stiffen the crossbars, but the best is a vertical strut (see figure 9-1) that spans two bars. The strut bolts in place with wing nuts and swings aside to load and unload the canoes. This setup virtually eliminates stress . . . and trailer breakdown.

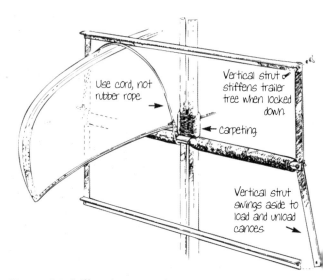

Use cord, not rubber rope.

Vertical strut stiffens trailer tree when locked down.

carpeting

Vertical strut swings aside to load and unload canoes

Figure 9-1 Stiffen the tree of your canoe trailer by adding removable vertical struts. This brace will take the strain off the crossbars when the empty trailer is shuttled.

Procedures for Carrying Fragile Canoes

Ultralight fiberglass, Kevlar, and wood-strip canoes should be handled with a loving touch. They should be carried on padded crossbars or foam gunwale pads only and tied with clean, large-diameter (¼- to ⅜-inch) ropes, which won't gall their delicate skin.

You can break the spine of a lightweight canoe if you snug its ends too tightly, so it's preferable to tie *only* the bow to the front bumper. If you cinch down the tail, you may bow the hull and damage it.

If you're hauling two canoes on a double rack, place the fragile canoe on the right side (passenger side) of the carriers. This will allow the sturdier (and more rigidly tied) craft on the driver's side to take the abuse of high winds generated by passing trucks. If you cartop three canoes, put the most fragile one on top.

Special Considerations When Traveling in Very High Winds

In very high winds you may want to rig a bridle around the bow (windshield end) of your cartopped

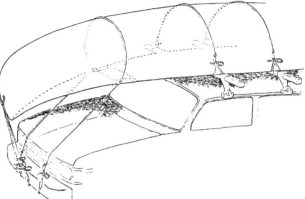

Figure 9-2 In very high winds you may want to rig a bridle around the bow of your canoe. All lines should go through eye bolts or S-hooks on the bumper.

canoe. To make the bridle, tie a length of rope tightly around the hull near the seat (loop it through the seat support) and secure it to the bumper (figure 9-2). The bridle will absorb wind stress and take the load off brass and plastic fittings, which may break or bend under stress.

Cartopping three canoes.

Part III

Applied Skills

C H A P T E R 10

Tying It All Together

You can get along very nicely with just the sheet bend knot and power cinch (tucker's hitch). Add the double half hitch and bowline, and you'll be set for every emergency.

The Double Half Hitch (Two Half Hitches)

The double half hitch is useful for tying a rope to a tree or to the towing link of a canoe. The knot is very secure and tends to tighten itself when a load is applied to the rope.

Figure 10-2 Sheet bend.

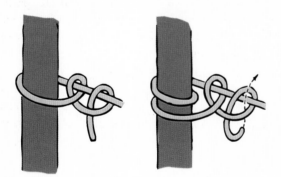

Figure 10-1 Double half hitch.

The Sheet Bend

Use the sheet bend for tying two ropes together. The knot works well even if the rope sizes differ greatly. The sheet bend is about the only knot that can be effectively used to join the ends of slippery polypropylene rope.

It is important that the free ends of the sheet bend be on the same side, as shown in figure 10-2. The knot will work if the ends are on opposite sides, but will be less reliable.

The Bowline

The bowline is a very secure knot that won't slip—regardless of the load applied. It is commonly used by mountain climbers to tie their climbing ropes around their waists. Use this knot whenever you want to put a nonslip loop on the end of a line.

Beginners are often told to make the bowline by forming a loop, or "rabbit hole." The rabbit (free end of the rope) comes up through the hole, around the tree (opposite or long end of the rope shown in figure 10-3), and back down the hole. The bowline will slip a few inches before it tightens, so allow an extra-long free end.

Use a bowline to secure your bow and stern lines to the canoe. Even a secure bowline can work

Figure 10-3
The bowline.

loose, so finish the knot by applying two tight half hitches around the main body of the rope.

The Power Cinch (Trucker's Hitch)

Perhaps the most ingenious hitch to come along in recent years is the power cinch (there seems to be no widely accepted name for this hitch, so I took the liberty of naming it the power cinch), which effectively replaces the tautline hitch and functions as a powerful pulley when used properly. Skilled canoeists use this pulley knot almost exclusively for tying canoes on cars. It is also widely used by truckers who tie heavy loads in place. The power cinch may be the canoeist's most useful hitch.

Begin the power cinch by forming the loop shown in figure 10-4, step 1. Pull the loop through as in step 2. It is important that the loop be formed *exactly* as shown. The loop will look okay if you make it backward, but it won't work.

If the loop is formed as in step 2, a simple tug on the rope will eliminate it. This is preferable to the common practice of tying a knot in the loop, which, after being exposed to a load, is almost impossible to get out.

If you are tying a canoe into place on top of a car, tie one end of the rope to the canoe's bow or stern and snap the steel hook on the other end of the rope to the car's bumper. Run the free end of the rope (a) through the loop in step 2. Now apply power to the free end. You have, in effect, created a pulley with a 2:1 mechanical advantage.

Complete the hitch by securing a double half hitch around the body of the rope or use a quick-release loop, as illustrated.

The Quick-Release Loop

There's nothing more frustrating than untying a bunch of tight knot when you're breaking camp in the morning. If you end your knots with a quick-release loop like that illustrated in figure 10-5, you'll be able to untie your ties with a single pull. Form the quick-release feature by running the free end of the rope back through the completed knot—the same as making a bow when you tie your shoes.

Use a simple overhand knot with a quick-release loop to seal the stuff sacks that contain your sleeping bag and personal gear. The plastic "cord locks" sold for this purpose are for people who don't know how to tie effective quick-release knots.

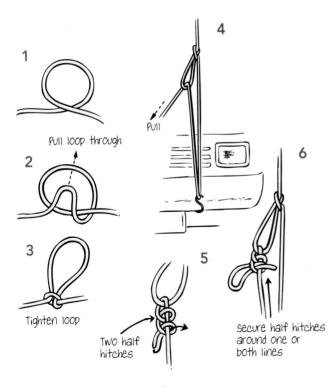

1

2 Pull loop through

3 Tighten loop

4 Pull

5 Two half hitches

6 Secure half hitches around one or both lines

Figure 10-4 **Power cinch.**

Figure 10-5 **Secure your stuff sacks with a quick-release loop.**

Securing a Line

On a wilderness trip some years ago, one canoe of our party swamped in a heavy rapid. There was a bouldery falls about 200 yards downstream, and it was imperative that we get a rope to the wet canoeists immediately in order to avoid disaster. Luckily, a 50-foot line was at hand and was properly coiled for throwing. The line was heaved to the two men, who were hanging on to the gunwales of the water-filled canoe. Fortunately, the men caught the rope, and both they and the canoe were pulled safely to shore, avoiding what might have been a serious mishap.

You should always keep your ropes coiled and ready for use. The best system I have found is an old navy method:

1. Coil the rope (taking care to lay each coil carefully into place), then grasp the main body of it with one hand and place your thumb through the eye of the coils to hold them in place, as shown in figure 10-6, step 1.

2. Remove the last two coils of rope, then take this long free end and wind it around the main body of the rope several times (figure 10-6, step 2). Wind the free end downward, toward the hand holding the rope body. Wind evenly and snugly. Don't make the coils too tight.

3. Form a loop with the free end of the rope, as shown in step 3, and push it through the eye of the rope body.

Step 2.

Step 3.

Step 1.

Step 4.

Figure 10-6 **Old navy method of coiling a rope.**

4. Grasp the wound coils with one hand and the rope body with the other, and slide the coils upward tightly against the loop. The rope is now coiled and secured (step 4). Pulling the front end of the rope will release the line, which can quickly be made ready for throwing.

I bind all my 50-foot utility ropes in this manner and store them under a pack flap so they'll be quickly available when I need them. When running whitewater, I often keep a throwing line tied around a thwart, as illustrated in figure 10-7. A single pull release the line from the thwart; a second tug makes it ready for use. Fast and convenient . . . and possibly a lifesaver!

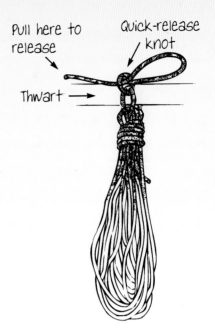

Figure 10-7 Bind your 50-foot line by the old navy method outline in figure 10-6, then tie it to a thwart as illustrated here. A quick pull of the free end releases the rope instantly.

CHAPTER 11

Solo Canoeing Is Different

Sunrise on Any River, U.S.A. A damp morning mist, warmed by the day's beginning, rises reluctantly above the cool, green water. Beneath the slowly burning fog, an ever-growing ribbon of gold expands confidently across the horizon.

In awesome silence you slip your trim, light solo canoe into the awaiting riffles, while nearby, friends in a tandem canoe follow suit. A gentle push of the paddle sets you free and in harmony with the determined current.

For a while you paddle powerfully, each stoke crisp and well timed. The quick canoe responds eagerly and glides whisper-quiet at what seems to be incredible speed. Around a bend a great blue heron curiously looks your way. In awkward slow motion he stretches his wings and with casual assuredness begins to fly. The muffled hiss of your wake has broken the spell!

The sun is in full posture now and the day is flooded with its warmth and light. Everywhere the sights and sounds of the river entice you to linger, so you rest your paddle, laze back, and wait for your friends to catch up. Above, puffy clouds of hushed white whisk quietly by, and for a time you are left alone with your dreams and the delights of the river.

Then you hear it—the hollow drone of rushing water. Falls? The shock of realization brings you bolt upright. Your eyes search knowingly for the danger signs—a broken tree line or crest of dancing white. Then you see it—a narrow band of discontinuous water that stretches entirely across your path.

Ledge! You call loudly to your friends behind. But don't panic; you're in control. A few well-placed back strokes bring the little canoe swiftly to shore.

The falls, a sheer 6-foot drop over sharp granite, is not negotiable. And neither are the rapids below.

You'll have to take the ½-mile portage that's indicated on your map. Single-handedly, you shoulder your 35-pound canoe, while a few yards away your friends struggle with their tandem craft of twice the weight. A smug smile flashes briefly as you jubilantly strike off down the trail. You're beginning to discover the joys of the solo canoe!

Partway through the portage you ascend a long, steep hill, at the top of which stands a well-worn canoe rest. But the little boat is no burden, so you unhesitatingly continue on. Seconds later you hear the hollow clunk of a canoe being set on the wooden brace you just passed—a reminder that your tandem friends don't share your unencumbered feeling. The smile returns!

Now the trail descends quickly and you move along at a furious pace. A glint of white suddenly appears among the blanketing foliage and you know the river is near.

You set the little canoe at the water's edge and stare unbelievingly at the river. You've canoed in low water before, but this is ridiculous! A shallow rock fan stretches well into the next bend, perhaps ¼ mile. There are 3, maybe 4, inches of water lying between the water's surface and its pebble bottom. And everywhere huge round rocks protrude like polished marbles on an earthen field. No way can the big canoe get through there without grinding, scraping, breaking.

But you can!

As you gingerly board your solo canoe for the slalom run, you watch amusedly as your friends put on their wading shoes. "It's gonna be a long walk," you tease. "Sure glad I can ride!"

Once under way, the little canoe comes alive. It leans when you lean, goes forward, backward, sideways on command. There's no argument from a part-

Soloing an easy rapid in the Boundary Waters Canoe Area.

ner, your spouse, or your mother-in-law. A screwup is a screwup, and you have no one to blame but yourself.

You discover that the tightest turns are possible if you brace far out on your paddle and lean the canoe until its gunwale barely touches the water. Ahead is a cluster of rocks with a 2-foot channel between. No problem; you tilt the canoe to one side and scoot cleanly through.

Now you're both bow and stern—sweeping, drawing, prying, bracing. Occasionally the muffled screech of fiberglass impacting rock rewards your indecision and carelessness. But no matter; these surface scratches do much more harm to your ego than your canoe.

Within minutes it's over, and you find yourself drifting aimlessly in the deep, still water below the rapid. A few lazy back strokes bring you to shore, where you get out and stretch . . . and wait for your friends to finish lining their canoe through the rock garden you just paddled.

These, then, are the joys of the solo canoe—joys that become more intense as the years creep by and you suddenly discover that you're not as athletic as you used to be. Small-framed men and women need no introduction to the pleasures of soloing, for they more than anyone else understand what it means to be always last on the portage trail and forever chained to the bow seat of a tandem canoe. Tough day at the office? Perhaps an hour's play on a park pond will provide the relaxation you need. Got a canoe trip planned and can't find a partner? Great; take your solo canoe. Extended wilderness tripping? You bet! A well-designed "little boat" can carry at least 300 pounds—nearly half the weight of an average tandem canoe. Unless you plan to bring along the kitchen sink, you'll have more space than you can possibly use.

"But I'm a family person," you say. "How can I take the kids along if I paddle alone?" Well, you can't, of course. But wouldn't it be nice if the children could paddle *their own* canoe rather than ride in yours? Easy enough if you outfit your solo canoe with seats fore and aft. Now your teenie-boppers can experience the joy of canoeing in a boat that's suited to their dimensions. Meanwhile, the grown-ups can tag along behind a big canoe. Two canoes—one tandem, one solo—per family is not an extravagance; it's common sense, and a delightfully good time!

Whitewater, flatwater, local streams, or the deep wilderness. The solo canoe will go anywhere a tandem canoe will go—a bit more slowly perhaps, but with a grace, style, and elegance that is unmatched by the most sophisticated large canoe.

But solo canoes *are* different, and many of the procedures and equipment used to paddle and portage them also are different.

Paddles

You need two paddles in case one breaks. As I mentioned in chapter 5, paddle length is determined by the reach of your arms and the type of boat you paddle. I alternate my solo time between a 13-foot Bell* Flashfire and 14-foot Wildfire. I use a 54-inch Zaveral* 12-degree bent paddle for cruising, then switch to a 56-inch Bell straight paddle for rapids. These two paddles cover all my solo needs.

Some canoeists prefer a double-blade paddle for everything. A well-designed solo canoe will dance across the water when powered by twin blades, but the standard kayak paddle is too short; you need a length of 8½ or 9 feet (not commonly available), which means you'll have to make your own.

Note: Twin blades are practical and powerful, but they can be awkward in tight places—such as threading your way down a narrow beaver stream. Be sure your double paddle breaks apart so you can store it in the canoe. Some soloists carry a snap-on T-grip so they can convert their break-apart double paddle into a single whitewater blade.

As I've noted, double paddles are considered gauche in fashionable canoeing circles. To many (myself included), soloing is an art form—one that necessarily demands efficient use of the single blade. Nonetheless, don't let me or anyone else spoil your pleasure. Double paddles are efficient. If you like 'em, use 'em! By the way, did you know that the Eskimos commonly used single paddles when hunting from their kayaks?

It's beyond the scope of this book to cover the techniques and equipment of whitewater solo canoeing. My book *Basic Essentials: Solo Canoeing* (Globe Pequot Press, 1999) provides a starting point. If you're serious about whitewater, join a canoe club and take lessons from an accomplished instructor. And do get Kent Ford's excellent workbook, *Solo Playboating.** Kent's superb video *Drill Time* will also get your blood pumping!

Portage Yoke

A solo-canoe yoke must be removable (unlike those on tandem canoes) so it won't interfere with paddling (you sit or kneel in the middle of the canoe, remember?). The best arrangement is to attach the yoke to the gunwales with hardwood clamps and wing nuts, or buy a pair of indestructible aluminum brackets from Old Town* or Mad River* Canoe Companies. Bell Canoe Works* has the neatest solo yoke I've seen.

Knee Pads

Solo canoes are more versatile than kayaks. You can sit or kneel (or even stand) if you wish. In rough water, kneeling is an option in big, steady tandem canoes; it's an *absolute must* in tender solo canoes! Glue knee pads into the bottom of your canoe for the ultimate in comfort.

Note: Some canoes, like the racy We-no-nah* models, are not designed for kneeling. These canoes have low-mounted bucket seats and foot braces that lock your body firmly into the hull. You *never* kneel in these canoes.

Packs

For day trips a small nylon pack is fine, as long as it's not too heavy. A solo canoe is sensitive to proper trim (the difference between the draft at each end). A few misplaced pounds, fore or aft of dead center, may unbalance it and adversely affect performance. Consequently, it's unwise to place all of your eggs in one basket, even if they all will fit. It's better to use two packs—a large, soft (no-frame) tripping pack of some sort and a medium-sized day pack.

Solo canoes set you free to follow your star in your own way at your own pace. Here, the author paddles his Bell Traveler in the Boundary Waters Canoe Area of Minnesota.

I place food, sleeping gear, tent, and cooking items into the large pack and set in front of my feet. The small pack, which contains extra clothes, rain gear, sweater, and other frequently used essentials, goes behind the seat (some canoeists reverse the position of these packs). By moving the packs forward or back, I can balance the canoe perfectly.

An annoying characteristic of all open solo canoes is that they are always wet inside. Every time you change sides with your paddle ("HUT"), which you do often to steer and rest muscles, water drips off the blade and into the canoe. Keep a large sponge secured beneath a loop of shock cord tied around the side of your seat frame. Sponging our accumulated water is a never-ending process!

For a weeklong trip your solo canoe will easily carry more cargo than you'll ever want to bring along. Nevertheless, that's no excuse to bring too much. The price of gluttony is a sluggish canoe, or at best an unspirited one. If you choose items carefully, your heaviest pack should weigh less than 50 pounds, and your light pack around 15 pounds. (See chapter 3 for a discussion of the things you really need.) Carry the heavy pack, paddles, life vest, and camera over the portage first. On the second trip take the canoe and small day pack. This works out to about 55 pounds per trip.

Touring the wilds in a solo canoe is easier if you travel in the company of other canoes, since you can share the weight of community essentials—tent, cook set, ax, saw, and so forth. I recently completed a ten-day canoe trip on an Ontario river along with three other solo friends. My share of the outfit (including food and personal gear) was 60 pounds—less than I commonly carry on tandem canoe trips of the same length.

It's important to fit all your camping gear into two packs so you can complete the portages in three trips (one round trip plus the return leg). A third pack means *two* additional portage crossings, so plan wisely and go light.

Map and Compass

You are your own partner in a solo canoe; there's no time to fumble for navigational aids when you're fighting waves on a wind-tossed lake. A few moments of distraction and you may find yourself lost . . . or upside down!

For these reasons, it's essential to secure your map under a loop of shock cord strung through holes drilled in the front thwart, as suggested in chapter 2. Also, I carry two compasses—a small but highly accurate Silva Huntsman (for plotting the course from the map) and a Silva wrist model (for easy reference while paddling). The Huntsman rests in my shirt pocket, protected against loss by a lanyard attached to a buttonhole. I keep the wrist compass strapped to the forward thwart. With this setup my map and compass are always visible, regardless of how actively I paddle.

Note: Silva design compasses are now sold under the Bruton Company, Nexus name.

Paddle Strokes

As you gain solo experience, you'll develop a repertoire of special strokes—the C, draw, low brace, and so forth. But you don't need all these to use and enjoy your solo canoe. In fact, the most efficient way to paddle alone is to simply switch sides whenever the boat begins to waver off course. Though some people consider the practice boring, it is very powerful and state of the art for racing.

Some paddlers prefer a hybrid style of paddling. They use a double paddle on open water and change to a short single blade and racing switch stroke on the river. In rapids they select a long single paddle and twist their way between obstacles with a variety of hard-to-define sophisticated strokes. That's the beauty of soloing: You're free to chase your star in your own way at your own pace.

You'll find a wealth of solo procedures and paddling techniques in the revised edition of my book, *Basic Essentials: Solo Canoeing* (Globe Pequot Press, 1999).

Evening on a quiet lake in the Boundary Waters Canoe Area.

CHAPTER 12

Day-Tripping

Day-tripping—where all the hours of planning, packing, and fear of rain come together. You're at the river at last, sun rising warmly to the newborn day, and there's not a cloud in the sky anywhere.

You rest momentarily against the car fender and watch your friends repeat the age-old procedures for putting in. Down the way an older man and woman struggle to remove an aluminum canoe from the high roof of their van. You leap to their assistance.

It's a bit of a hike from the roadway to the mud bank of the river, so you offer to portage the canoe the entire way. On your return you're greeted by gentle smiles and gracious thanks. What a way to begin the day!

With the help of your spouse, you unload your canoe and carry it down the bank to the waiting river. There's no "landing" per se, just a small, sandy flat that is already occupied by a half-dozen canoes. "Dang!" You mutter. "No place for me." Unwillingly, you set down the canoe on the steep incline—bow in the river, stern on land. For safety's sake you tie the stern painter to a nearby tree. A smug smile flashes briefly when you discover that no one but you remembered to attach ropes to the ends of his or her canoe. Ah . . . expertise!

Your eyes knowingly inventory each item. In the big packsack is a change of clothes, light jacket, and rain gear for everyone, along with two pairs of socks (just in case!) for six-year-old Peggy Anne. And it's all safely protected from rain and the river by two nested plastic sacks.

Your inventory continues: two adult-sized life jackets and a "pee-wee" vest for little Peggy, a small ice chest, a closed-cell foam pad for your daughter to sleep on, an aluminumized space blanket for the picnic shore lunch, and a nylon pack filled with fried

chicken and chips, candy bars, paper plates and cups, silverware, and paper towels for cleanup. And oh yes, toilet paper in a Ziploc bag.

Tied to the pack strap is a sturdy nylon bag for hauling out trash—yours and that of others who are less thoughtful!

It's quite a heap, but you may need it all. At any rate, it pays to be prepared.

Two trips down the bank and everything is safely stowed inside the waiting canoe. This will be a simple float trip—no real rapids—so there's no reason to tie anything in. Now all that's left is to wait until the cars return from the takeout point. Within the hour you'll be on your way.

The shuttle is completed and the apparent disorder of earlier comes to an abrupt halt. Suddenly everyone knows exactly what they're doing. In a flash canoes are loaded and launched. The day begins!

The first few minutes you paddle hard. It feels good to stretch your muscles, to work out the city kinks. Then as the uniqueness of the day begins to fade, your strokes slow to an easy all-day pace.

Around the bend you spot a dappled fawn standing ankle-deep in water near the shore. A hush falls on the group and someone points. In unison everyone rests their paddle and simply watches the deer.

Downstream the river changes from stagnant backwater to joyful riffles. Peggy tries her miniature paddle and drops it instantly. No matter; it trails safely behind, tethered to a length of cord you attached for just such an occasion.

A dozen bends later you come upon the quiet pool that marks trip's end. Already there's a jam-up at the landing, so you rest your paddle and just wait around. Another canoe pulls alongside and you strike up a

Sue Harings, the author's wife, models some essential items.

Checklist for Daytripping

Besides the obvious—life jackets and paddles—you'll need:

- Complete change of clothes for everyone (in a waterproof pack)
- Light jacket or sweater
- Brimmed hat and sunglasses
- Rain gear
- First-aid kit
- Pocketknife
- Matches
- Ropes (lines) for the ends of your canoe
- Water bottle, soft drinks, snacks, and so forth
- Flashlight: It's amazing how many trips begin in daylight and end in darkness
- Map of route and compass

friendly conversation. You've never met these folks before, but immediately there's a bond. As you bid farewell, you both agree to meet again on next week's day trip.

These, then, are the joys of the river. Joys born of love and friendship, of artistry and motion. The river passes as a fleeting moment: but it is always there, waiting for you to return.

CHAPTER 13

Canoeing in Winter

At the outset I should make it perfectly clear that when winter comes to my home in River Falls, Wisconsin (a stone's throw from St. Paul, Minnesota), I don't go canoeing! Not that I haven't tried, mind you. It was February when I finished building the wood-strip prototype of Mad River's* popular Slipper, and I couldn't wait till spring to try it. A patch of blue in a nearby pond suggested there might be space enough to pirouette a new boat.

A balmy 15-degree temperature suggested perfect paddling conditions. Dressed in warm woolens, I felt snugly comfortable. No matter that my paddling hole—kept open by an air bubbler—was barely large enough for a canoe, or that water droplets froze on the gunwales whenever I switched paddle sides. I was canoeing. In winter. In Viking land!

Then I saw the ice chunk that a gentle breeze was pushing my way. To my left was the jagged icy shore; to my right, a bathtub-sized block of ice. Seconds later I was neck-deep and hyperventilating in icy water. Fifty feet to shore seemed an impossible distance to swim, even with a life jacket on. Right then I learned that the most important lesson in winter canoeing is: *Don't tip over!* To this add good judgment, the right equipment, and a friend to bail you out if you screw up, and you'll be okay.

The Right Equipment

Ask an expert paddler what to wear for winter paddling and you'll hear a dissertation on wet suits (farmer john or standard two-piece?), dry suits (side zipper, back zipper, or no zipper?), and watertight nylon paddling shells (fitted neoprene collar and cuff, or leaky Velcro closure?). When the smoke clears you'll discover that these solutions are all hot, uncomfortable, and expensive. If like me, you love cruising gentle waters before ice-in, you'll forget waterproof attire and choose more versatile clothes.

Fabrics

Fleece, polypropylene, wool, or polyester—they all work, and differences are less pronounced than users will admit. Winter cruising is not whitewater canoeing, so you won't be going swimming! Instead of protection from the icy wet, you need warmth, resistance to spray, and protection from the howling wind.

Consider the bulk of your garments. Fleece sweaters, for example, are luxuriously warm and comfortable. But they don't layer well under other garments. If you choose fleece—and most serious paddlers do—select a roomy wind shell that will fit over it.

My preference? I wear Thermax, wool, or polypropylene underwear beneath an all-wool shirt and trousers. A short-sleeved fleece paddling shirt goes on top, followed by a fleece neck warmer and nylon wind shell. In bitter weather I add a two-ply rainwear-without-compromise Gore-Tex parka or a foul-weather (sailing) rain suit. A genuine sou'wester hat worn over a wool stocking cap tops my outfit. Gloves are neoprene, 3-M Thinsulate/Gore-Tex, leather-faced wool, or rubber-dot acrylic.

Footwear

For cold-weather trips that include portaging and wading, I usually wear soft Steger Mukluks* inside Tingley rubber overshoes. Sixteen-inch high rubber boots (barn boots) also work well, but they're not as flexible. Some paddlers wear neoprene wet-suit socks inside sneakers or serious river shoes, but this combination can be mighty cold. In today's high-tech world, options abound. There is no right way to dress for winter paddling.

The closest I get to winter canoeing in Minnesota is a late-October solo trip in the Boundary Waters

Canoe Area. Here the daily high can be just above freezing, while nighttime temps often plunge into the teens. The rocky portaging/camping nature of this area suggests a traditional (wool, fleece, and polypro) approach. Scuba gear would be too uncomfortable, especially where frequent portages are the rule. And neoprene clothes would freeze solid when the mercury dips below freezing at night.

Boats

If you paddle a tender slalom beast, you'll want to follow the lead of the whitewater crowd and clothe yourself in sweaty neoprene. Otherwise, it's best to wear more traditional (comfortable) clothing and adapt your canoe for cold-weather travel:

If you paddle solo, you'll want a *two-piece* fabric splash cover (see photos on pages 95 and 97) for your canoe. The revised edition of my book *Basic Essentials: Solo Canoeing* shows how to make one. Without a cover, icy water will drip into the boat (and freeze there) every time you change paddle sides. A cover will also cut wind resistance and keep you warm in blowing rain and snow. I can't say enough good things about my canoe cover!

For tandem canoes, you'll want a three-piece splash cover with removable belly, like the one I described in chapter 2.

Other Equipment Concerns

For day trips, *two* changes of clothes—from nose to toes—generally provide enough protection against hypothermia or a capsize. Overnighters require the ability to dry wet things, which isn't easy in frigid weather.

For this reason I always carry full-bore fire-making equipment, which includes a strong knife, folding saw, hand ax, chemical fire-starters, and candle.

A nylon rain tarp, customized with extra ties on the face and edges as described in chapter 17, allows you to cook and work in sleety weather. And in the event your woodsmanship fails, don't forget a stove!

Canoeing in winter—in Viking land!

Good Judgment

Capsize on a farm pond when air and water temperatures are both below 40 degrees and you'll understand the need for caution. So unless you're wearing full scuba gear or a nylon paddling suit over polypropylene and fleece, you'd best confine your winter travels to easy waters in the company of friends.

It takes time to develop the proper respect for a waterway on which help is not available—and in winter, almost every lake and river qualifies. Don't rush the learning curve. Fear is nature's way of telling you to slow down and think before you act. Icy undercut banks, floating ice chunks, a combined air/water temperature of less than 100—all spell trouble even when you're well prepared. Start out easy, equip right, surround yourself with caring friends, and you'll be well prepared for winter paddling.

Don't Forget

1. A detachable seat pad makes a convenient duff warmer in the canoe and in camp. Commercial models are available, or you can make your own.

2. The inside of your canoe won't dry in chilly winter weather, so bring along a sponge to clean up icy paddle drips and accumulated water.

3. Nights are much longer in winter than in summer, so campouts will require long-lasting batteries (extras, too!) for your flashlight. A full-sized headlamp is a welcome companion this time of year.

4. A glass or stainless-steel vacuum bottle brings you hot coffee, tea, or soup any time of day.

5. A telescoping candle lantern raises tent temperatures 10 to 20 degrees.

6. A large brimmed hat keeps blowing crud off your glasses. I prefer a traditional sou'wester worn over a wool stocking cap.

C H A P T E R   14

Canoeing with Children and Pets

The Indians call it *chautauqua*, which means "traveling show," and it aptly describes a family of canoeists on a pleasant float downstream. Put these together in the same canoe: Mom and Dad, a wiggling two-year-old and inquisitive five-year-old, a floppy-eared dog, waterproof packsacks filled with dry clothes, an ice chest stocked with pop, a thermos of milk, bags of disposable diapers, sunscreen and bug dope, toilet paper, facial tissues and Handi-Wipes, jackets, hats, paddles, a camera and pair of stuffed teddy bears, potato chips, pretzels, and candy . . . and the view from dockside is, in every sense, a chautauqua!

At these times you're sure to wonder if all the pre-trip planning and packing, the stern instructions to the kids, and the hopeful prayers for a brilliant rain-free day are really worth the joys of a family canoe outing. Is canoeing with children all that it's cracked up to be? Or is it really more trouble than it's worth?

The first time you see the bright eyes of your child come alive with wonder at the sight of a big blue heron standing knee-deep in sea-green duckweed a dozen feet away or soothe the frightened cry that results when a foot-long fish jumps brashly across your bow or thrill to the bubbly laughter of a breezy glide down gently rapids, you'll know. Then no amount of pre- or post-trip drudgery will ever again chain you to the dull confines of house- or garden-work when on the river there awaits the sunlit morning of a new day.

Children are magic. And canoes are the perfect vehicle to transport them into the ever-changing, always entertaining world of nature. There's no better way to keep a youthful heart than to paddle with young people. Canoes provide all the entertainment kids need to provide all the laughs you need!

So much for philosophy. Now let's be deadly honest: Canoeing with children can be a trying experience,

even when you do everything right. Your role as parent and leader requires canoe-handling knowledge, a perceptive eye, and patience, patience, patience! Even then, don't expect miracles. Kids *will* behave like kids.

The Right Attitude

Uppermost in your mind should be the realization that you're canoeing for the *sake of the children*, not the adults. Everything should be structured around their safety, well-being, and concerns. I've seen parents set toddlers on the cold, damp floor of a metal canoe without so much as a square of plastic for insulation. Without a dry place to sit, a comfortable backrest, and a soft pad to sleep on, they'll respond by crying, screaming, and kicking—exactly what you can't tolerate in the tippy confines of a canoe. The right equipment and a detailed battle plan will eliminate most problems.

Dangers

I am always surprised when I hear people talk about the dangers of canoeing with children. Fact is, most of the rivers in North America were once routinely traveled by Native American families that hunted and fished from canoes, harvested wild rice from canoes, and traveled (often for days) by canoe to visit relatives. Indian families didn't take chances with the lives of their kids—they had the good sense to portage rapids that modern recreational paddlers prefer to run, and they stayed ashore when the wind was up and the weather was bad. Occasionally, there was a capsize and someone got hurt. But overall, the experience was probably a lot safer than commuting by car.

The best modern canoes are superior to anything the Native Americans ever built, and today's best paddlers are far more skilled than their predecessors. Canoeing—especially lazy-water family canoeing—is among the safest of all sports. Indeed, you are far more likely to be killed driving to and from a river than paddling it.

Skills Are More Important Than Things

The best way to keep kids safe is to be an accomplished canoeist. Swimming and water-rescue skills are important, too, but canoeing skills are more important. After all, you won't have to deal with an accident if you don't have one.

Begin by reading all the canoeing books you can find. Check out some paddling videos—Bill Mason's *Path of the Paddle* series is timeless. Most canoe stores have them. If there's a canoe club nearby, join it. You'll paddle with other families that love canoeing and share your concerns. Besides, it's nice to know that if a problem develops, knowledgeable folks are there to help. Between club trips, get out and practice—without the kids. As your skills improve, your fears will disappear.

Where to Begin

It's simple, really. Start with a friendly river that you've paddled many times before. Try to act excited even though you know what's around every bend. Remember, it's all new to your child—every floating leaf and riffle.

Remember, canoeing with children can be trying even when you do things right. Children will complain when they're cold or hungry or uncomfortable. The good news is that sun, water, and the wonder of wild things will provide all the entertainment and diversion they need. And the rocking motion of a canoe will encourage frequent naps and long periods of quiet time for adults.

I might add that well-trained dogs are always welcome on my canoe trips. Topsy, my little Sheltie, loved canoeing. She'd prick up her ears and bark as soon as I started loading the canoe. If I paddled out without her, she'd bark angrily then swim out to the canoe—and then, of course, I'd have to haul her in. If she saw something interesting on the river, she'd jump out and swim after it. Minutes later, she'd swim back to the canoe and we'd pull her in. I was surprised that she knew how to ferry across strong currents.

Anyone can safely paddle a pond on a bright sunny day with a child and dog aboard. But you'd better know what you're doing when the wind comes up and currents flow quick. And if you capsize or the weather turns sour, you'll be glad everyone is outfitted right.

Personal Paddling Gear

Everyone needs a *correctly sized* life jacket. Coast Guard approval tags will tell you what fits whom. A vest that's too small may not support the child; one that's too large may turn the child head-down in the water! Adults have a centrally located body mass, but children are head-heavy; they need a life vest that has a more positive righting moment. Junior-sized PFDs are designed with these important differences in mind.

You can even get special life jackets for dogs. The dogs don't seem to mind them at all.

Special downsized life jackets for preschoolers are expensive, and worth it, even though it means they will be outgrown in a year or two. Children should *never* be outfitted with inexpensive (not Coast Guard approved) swim aids, which will not keep the head of a nonswimmer afloat!

Every child should try his or her PFD in a swimming pool. Does it chafe under the armpits? Are there thigh straps to prevent ride-up? Does it float the child *head-*

Figure 14-1 Downsized life jackets for preschoolers are expensive—and worth it.

up? One popular vest has a large collar that provides a positive righting moment. Some youngsters find this intolerable, because the collar prevents them from seeing their feet.

The important thing is to provide a vest that your children will wear for long periods of time without complaining! Some psychology helps, and this means that both Mom and Dad should set an example. The rocking motion of a canoe encourages naps, so the PFDs must not interfere with sleeping.

Clothing

What you need, they need. Period! This does not mean you need to buy expensive Gore-Tex parkas and neoprene wading shoes. You can cut corners and be safe.

Start with a complete change of clothes from nose to toes. No blue jeans! Cotton T-shirts and trousers are fine for July heat, but be prepared with polypropylene, polyester, wool, or acrylics if the weather turns bad. You'll treat serious sunburn unless you rule that shorts are for swimming, not for canoeing.

Bring a fleece or acrylic sweater instead of a cotton sweatshirt. A long-sleeved windbreaker (not waterproof) substitutes for a long-sleeved shirt, and it dries fast if it gets wet.

Don't forget a brimmed cap, sunscreen, and a bandanna. You can tie the bandanna around the child's neck to prevent sunburn. Kids think it looks cool.

Footwear

Light nylon sneakers and thin rubber overshoes are ideal. Children wear the rubber boots over their sneakers when they slosh through shallows. They kick them off when they're settled in the canoe.

Avoid cotton socks unless you want to deal with cold, damp feet. Alternatives are acrylic, polypropylene, polyester, and wool. Bring two extra pairs of medium-weight socks plus one super-heavy pair. A pair of closed-cell foam insoles for the rubber boots is always a good idea.

Scenario: The day turns sour and Judy gets her rubber boots and tennies wet. You wipe out the rubber boots with a handkerchief and install the thick foam insoles. Judy puts on two pairs of socks—one light, one super-heavy. Voilà! Her feet are dry and warm again.

Rainwear

No one wants a wet, whiny kid on a canoe trip—and you'll have one for sure if your child gets wet and cold. A light plastic poncho worn over a rain suit will deter a deluge. And the long, flowing poncho will cover the entire body—legs and all—when the child sits in the canoe. Trim the poncho to child size so it won't become a sail in wind.

Tip: Bring a 3-foot square of plastic for your dog. If you get caught in a severe rain, lay the plastic over your curled-up pet. Dogs get hypothermia, too!

Toys and Treats

Each child should have his or her favorite blanket and toy. A "raincoat" (plastic bag) for teddy bears and blankets is a must. And do bring downsized canoe paddles so the kids can join in the fun. Leash the paddles to a canoe thwart so you won't have to chase them downriver every time the kids drop them overboard.

Besides food and drink for the day, you'll want a thermos of milk and some cookies or penny candy. Don't forget diapers (and disposable bags for hauling them out). Plan to stop for a few minutes each hour and allow the kids to explore. Four hours afloat is about right with preschoolers.

The rocking motion of a canoe encourages naps.

Insects

Mosquitoes and canoe trips go together, but there are some slick solutions to keeping your sanity.

- *Bugs love blue:* Mosquitoes home in on anything that is navy blue in color. They also like black, purple, and other heat-absorbing colors. Really! Remember this when you buy clothing and rain gear.

- *There's hope in bug dope:* The most effective repellents contain deet—a chemical that contains N,N-diethyl-m-toluamide. Generally, the more deet a repellent has, the longer it works. However, too much deet may burn sensitive skin. Children should use a mild, cream-based repellent that contains very little deet. Natural (citronella-based) repellents are a better plan, though most don't work very well for very long.

Better yet, nix the bug dope on the skin and have the child wear long-sleeved shirts and trousers. A light repellent spray on the outer clothes will keep bugs away.

Kurt Avery, president of Sawyer Products, Inc., suggests you rub sunblock deep into your skin, wait ten minutes, then apply the repellent. The sunblock keeps your body from absorbing too much of the repellent. If possible, select one of the new bonding-base sunblocks that penetrate deep into your skin. Film-based sunblocks cover just the surface of your skin.

Children have less tolerance to bugs than adults. Even a few mosquitoes can drive them batty. A head net that rolls to fist size and fits in your pocket can spell the difference between delight and insanity. Most camping stores and military surplus stores have insect head nets.

Outfitting the Canoe

Place a closed-cell foam sleeping pad into the bottom of the canoe. The pad provides a warm, dry place for children and pets to nap.

For an overnighter, you'll need two large, *waterproof* packs; two small, nylon day packs; and a small ice cooler for drinks. You can substitute a large plastic ice chest or Tupperware container and a duffel bag for packs. Clothing and sleeping gear go in one pack;

food and cooking gear go in the other. Keep frequently used essentials (rain gear, sweater, spare socks, and the like) in the day packs.

Seal the liners of the packs so everything is watertight. Duct-tape the lids of ice chests and plastic containers.

Place one large pack against the stern thwart and the other in front of and against the center thwart (yoke). Set a boat cushion (technically, a throwable lifesaving device) on the floor for each child to sit upon. Now the kids have an elevated seat (out of contact with bilgewater) and a comfy backrest. The closed-cell foam pad keeps legs and feet warm.

Note that the two children are isolated from one another—which means they can't fight! Naturally, you can place them side by side if they behave.

The children will need more insulation when they fall asleep, so bring a spare blanket or an old sleeping bag. A small nylon tarp may be useful in a light rain, both in the canoe and at lunch stops.

When Dogs Are Along

The best place for a well-trained dog is seated between the legs of its master. The dog must obey your commands to sit, stay, and come.

Bring along some snacks for your pet, and a large towel to wipe wet, dirty paws that track mud into the canoe.

And What If You Do Capsize?

A capsize in warm, calm water isn't serious. But it is a mess. The kids may even think it's funny, and it won't bother the dog at all. But you will have to rescue everyone and everything, and all of it will be soaking wet.

It should go without saying that you shouldn't paddle rapids, even if you are highly skilled. Mild, bouncing water is okay, and children will respond with excited giggles.

You should have a battle plan if you do tip over. Generally, one parent goes after one designated child. *Do not* take three children canoeing unless there are three adults to watch them. Should you overturn,

Canoeing with children encourages smiles.

your children are your first concern. If everyone is wearing life vests and the water is easy, rescue will be, too—especially, if another canoe is nearby.

When Kids Get Older

A lot of families give up canoeing when their children get so big that they overload the family canoe. Other families just buy a bigger canoe and keep paddling. However, even a large-volume 17-foot expedition canoe is overburdened with four people, a dog, and overnight camping gear. When children reach six or seven, they are old enough and big enough to paddle their own canoe—and if you want to keep your sanity, you'll encourage it. Some parents split up—Mom captains one canoe, Dad the other, while a child paddles in each bow. However, if you want your kids to learn canoeing, they need to paddle by themselves while Mom and Dad gently coach from the sidelines.

When my girls were small, I outfitted my narrow solo canoe with a low slung seat at each end. I set a heavy pack in the middle of the canoe for ballast and let the kids go at it. The solo boat made a perfect tandem canoe for the little girls, who easily outpaced us.

They had a great time chasing frogs and fish while we watched protectively from our canoe. They tipped over only once. My wife, Sharon, and I had the food, equipment, and dog in our canoe, so there was no cause for alarm. Rescue was easy: We just towed the canoe ashore while the girls dog-paddled in. Ten minutes later we were canoeing again.

Teach Your Children Well

I've taught environmental science to eighth-graders for more than thirty years. I've learned that once children develop a love for wild places and wild things, they become serious about preserving those places and things. A delightful television commercial for a popular summer camp sums it up:

A boy and girl are punching keys on their computer in a dimly lit room—each is trying to win a video game.

Now flash to the same pair floating through a bubbly riffle in a canoe on a sunlit day—paddles flying, smiles flashing. The caption reads: GIVE YOUR CHILDREN AN EDUCATION FOR LIFE. SEND THEM TO CAMP THIS SUMMER.

It's a warm summer day and a friendly waterway is minutes away. The dog is wagging to go. Nix the sports and video games: Go paddle the river of life with the ones you love most.

Tripping with Teens

Scenario: The youth director of your church just phoned to ask if you—the local canoeing and camping expert—would help him lead some teenagers on a weeklong canoe trip to Any Park, U.S.A.

Flattered by his confidence in your ability, you dutifully answer, "Sure." After all, you'd planned to canoe the park this summer anyway. Why not share the experience with a group of appreciative kids and, in the process, teach this inexperienced youth leader the ropes?

"Uh, how many kids are we talking about?" you ask.

"I dunno, maybe eighteen if all the older kids go," he answers.

"Eighteen fourteen-year-olds, and just you and me? You've got to be kidding!"

"Hey, I took twelve of 'em to Mexico alone last year. No problem. This time there'll be two of us. You handle the canoeing and camping stuff; I'll take care of the rest. Okay?"

Numbly, you mumble acceptance, keenly aware that the "canoeing and camping stuff" says it all. Your spouse lovingly pats your shoulder and offers help. "Congratulations, honey, you're the leader!"

Getting Started

Make no mistake, *you*, not the tenderfoot youth director, are the leader, and you'd best make this fact abundantly clear at the start. *You* must have the final say in matters of organization, safety, equipment, training, routes, and rules of the road. Even the menu must reflect your knowledge of backcountry needs and what kids will eat. The counselor may make recommendations, of course, but it is *your* responsibility to bring these kids back with a smile on their face and a song in their heart. Call this guy back right now and set the record straight. You should take the job only after agreement is reached here.

Meeting the Kids

The first order of business is to meet the kids and parents, show some slides and canoeing gear to gather interest, explain expectations, and go over the necessary forms. Each participant must have a copy of the following documents:

- *Parent medical release:* If a youngster is injured and must be evacuated to a hospital, the medical release gives the attending physician authority to administer drugs or perform surgery without the okay of a parent. A simple statement that gives you the authority to act in lieu of a parent in the event of emergency is all you need. Include the phone number of parent(s) or guardian(s), family physician, and a relative or friend who can be reached in an emergency. You *must* carry this document on the canoe trip.

- *Parent permission form:* You cannot take kids across a state or international border without permission of a parent. This fact was made abundantly clear to

Tripping with teens is a rewarding experience *if* you plan ahead.

me some years ago when I attempted to cross into Canada with nine teenagers in tow. When the young customs officer refused to admit us, the kids began to act like normal teenagers. They whined and cried and claimed that I was their dad. Then they began to yell and throw things. Finally, the poor woman could take no more and we were reluctantly waved on through. When we arrived in Thunder Bay, I bought them all pizza for their cunning bravery in the face of adversity.

- *Swim form:* Most summer camps have a 100-yard swim requirement. Frankly, I think that's overkill for a gentle river or lake-country canoe trip. If a youngster can swim 50 feet unaided and is comfortable in deep water while wearing a life jacket, that's enough. Conversely, it's unwise to take along nonswimmers, no matter how loudly they or their parents complain.

- *Behavioral contract:* Cigarettes, alcohol, or hard drugs can ruin a trip in short order. Teenagers *must* understand that they will be immediately dropped from the trip if they're caught with an illegal substance. Don't minimize the importance of the behavioral contract. It is your ticket to a sane, well-mannered good time!

- *Equipment list:* I require that teenagers religiously follow the equipment list detailed in appendix 2. I go over each item, carefully explaining the rationale for every choice. Kids and parents will want to save money by substituting plastic ponchos for reliable two-piece nylon suits, tennis shoes for sturdy boots, hooded cotton sweatshirts for wool or fleece sweaters, cheap slumber bags for genuine sleeping bags, and blue jeans for quick-drying pants.

Allow no substitutes! You are the responsible adult on this trip. Everyone in your charge must be prepared to endure a week of cold, penetrating rain and muddy portages without complaint. That means wool, fleece, polypropylene, or acrylic clothing, sturdy boots, and rain gear that won't destruct on the first portage.

Youngsters can find what they need at surplus stores and garage sales. In their search for the right stuff, it pays to remind them that a canoe trip is not a fashion show. What looks good and what works are often two different matters!

Group Size

Five teenagers per adult leader is about right. Nine is the absolute maximum! Split up groups larger than ten (including the leader). Large groups are noisy and wreak havoc on the environment—the reason why most U.S. and Canadian wilderness areas impose a maximum limit on party size. Remember this if you have to split the group: Strive for a fifty-fifty gender split, and pair everyone with at least one good friend.

Question: John, Tom, and Bill are close friends. Alone, they are well-mannered, good kids. But put them together and all hell breaks loose. Since there are only two groups on this canoe trip, you can remove only one of them from the trio. You should (a) give all three their money back and tell them they can't go, (b) put all three together and take your chances, or (c) put one of the three in a separate group.

Answer: B and C are both reasonable choices. I've found that kids who cause trouble back home are often wonderful in the outdoors. In fact, some of my best teenage crews have been composed of "at risk" kids who go the extra mile to impress their friends and me. The wilderness is foreign turf to most teenagers, and respect is earned by doing more than your fair share in camp and on the portages. Keep an open mind—you might be pleasantly surprised!

Group Gear

If you want to really evaluate a piece of equipment, give it to a teenager for a week. Kids have an uncanny way of damaging or losing whatever they touch. On one of my trips, a boy burned up a new boot and part of his sleeping bag. He also lost a wool shirt and life jacket. While fishing he cast out his lure with such force that the reel and rod tip flew into the lake. Some time during the trip he broke an "unbreakable" synthetic paddle!

For this reason *do not* borrow canoes and gear from anyone whose friendship you want to retain. Renting is safer, especially if the kids know they will have to pay for the damages. A twenty-dollar damage deposit, to be reimbursed at trip's end, will make the point abundantly clear.

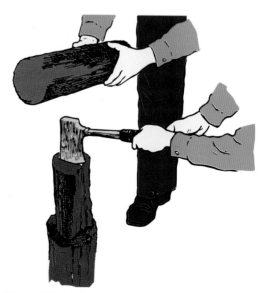

Figure 14-2 Splitting wood is easy if you use the ax as a splitting wedge rather than a chopping tool. Thick logs can easily be split by this method.

Figure 14-3 Kindling splits easier from the end grain—a process that is made easier (and safer!) if you use a stick of wood to hold the upright piece in place.

Remember these equipment tips: Fourteen-year-old boys and girls are perfectly capable of carrying 75-pound canoes—that is, if they have a properly fitted yoke. The pads on standard canoe yokes are spaced too wide for narrow teen shoulders. Yoke pads should be set 6½ to 7 inches apart (inside measurement) rather than the customary 7½ to 8 inches.

Make downsized wood yokes for all your rental canoes and secure them to the gunwales with quickly removable wood or metal clamps. Most outfitters will allow you to remove their yokes and install your own if you supply the labor. When traveling with three to a canoe, remove the yoke to provide more room for your passenger.

Other Essentials

Scenario: The trip begins in light rain, which intensifies throughout the day. By the time you camp, it's coming down in cold, determined sheets. You have polypropylene and fleece, a sophisticated watertight pack, and a class-act tent; the kids have cotton and acrylics, aging Duluth packs with patched plastic liners, well-abused rental tents, and no knowledge whatsoever as to how to keep things dry.

As the leader it's your job to keep hot meals coming and a dry roof over your crew. As a wilderness canoeist you know what gear is necessary; you just

need more of it. Be sure you carry these important items:

- One 4-mil-thick plastic ground cloth for the inside of every tent. Make each ground cloth oversized so it flows up the sidewalls of the tent. Water that wicks through worn fabric and floor seams will be trapped under the plastic, and the tent will stay dry in heavy rain.

- One 10- by 12-foot nylon rain tarp for every five people. Build a fire out front and string a clothes-line under the fly so the kids can dry wet gear.

- Two one-burner or one two-burner stoves per each group of ten.

- A sharp folding saw and hand ax. All wood is cut with the folding saw. The ax is used only as a splitting wedge; it is never used for chopping! I permit only one method of splitting (figures 14-2 and 14-3). The hand ax is set lightly into the upright log with just enough force to hold it in place. Then the splitter pounds the ax on through with a chunk of log. There are no "axidents" because the tool is never swung through the air!

- A 20- to 30-cup tea or coffeepot to satisfy the demand for soup and hot chocolate.

- Sitting pad: Most teen groups travel with three to a canoe, which means that one person rides "dead weight" in the cold, wet bottom of the hull. A sitting pad—boat cushion or square of waterproof foam—for each passenger is essential.

Accidents invariably fall into the following categories:

- Cuts due to whittling. Prevention? *Do not* allow kids to whittle!

- Blisters. Bring plenty of Spenco Second Skin.

- Sprained ankles (often results from horsing around). The worst sprain I ever saw resulted when a girl fell off the log on which she was dancing. It was midnight and she was showing her friends a new routine! Fortunately, I had an air splint and plenty of aspirin.

- Foreign object in the eye (scratched cornea). I carry Polysporin ophthalmic ointment. You'll need a prescription from your doctor to obtain it.

- Fishhook in the skin. I carry injectable Xylocaine but have never need it. Learn the painless string pull method of removing a fishhook if you plan to fish (see page 76).

Add the usual complement of gauze and tape, Tylenol, aspirin, Band-Aids, and antacid. A fire-making kit consisting of a flattened milk carton, some cedar shavings, fine kindling, a candle, and chemical fire-starter will help combat the cold.

Basic Training

Training is fun for everyone and especially rewarding for the leader. I start by showing all the old Bill Mason *Path of the Paddle* films, which are available from most public libraries in 16 mm or videocassette. Sometimes I photocopy selections from the canoeing literature and assign them for homework. The kids enjoy learning about hypothermia, first aid, and camping procedures. As the trip nears, plan an overnight shakedown cruise, or at least several practice sessions.

Ethics

Explain backcountry ethics *before* you take to the woods so every youngster understands the ecological concerns behind them. Leaders must model every rule and adopt an uncompromising attitude toward any practice that might harm the environment. School them in the ways of how to make camp, cook, wash, and go to the bathroom in the woods. Kids want to be part of the solution to pollution, and they will willingly follow your lead.

Kids also will be curious about their wilderness hosts—the fish, frogs, chipmunks, deer, and, yes, bears! Teaching kids to respect wildlife is integral to instilling a general respect for nature.

Unfortunately, most educational material on wilderness ethics is geared to adults. You'll have to simplify. I introduce the subject by giving the ethics quiz in appendix 3. We discuss the quiz, then see a short slide show that details various backcountry abuses.

How to Plan Your Route

Kids may plead for a week of layover days so they can swim and socialize, but inwardly they want the physical challenge of a real canoe trip. A 15-mile day, or six hours on the water, is a good daily goal. One "gut-buster" day followed by a layover day should be included to meld the group. Begin at dawn; finish near sundown. Paddle hard and choose tough portages that will wear everyone out. That night rekindle the day's events over a crackling fire and bottomless pots of soup and hot chocolate. Laze back, watch shooting stars, and tell stories until exhaustion overwhelms. Then snooze until 10 A.M., serve a lazy pancake breakfast, and dedicate the rest of the day to swimming, fishing, and exploring. Or place each kid on a barren rock for a three-hour isolation experience. At first they'll react negatively to the idea, but afterward they'll pressure you for more. Most teenagers have never been alone (or quiet!) for that long in a wilderness environment. This will be one of their most meaningful experiences.

When It Rains

Scenario: The last two days of your trip have been hot and sunny; you've been making good time and are, in fact, ahead of schedule. This morning, you awake to a cold, persistent rain. You should (a) sleep in and take your layover day here, or (b) rouse 'em up now and get paddling!

The correct answer is b. The worst thing imaginable is a bunch of grumbling kids massed under the rain tarp with nothing to do.

If you think you have problems now, try ten hours of confined, unplanned activity! Feed 'em well, dress 'em warm, and work 'em hard. They'll respond enthusiastically and with the understanding that you have their best interests at heart. Later, when the sun returns, you can stop and spend the day. Kids find plenty of ways to entertain themselves when the weather is cooperative.

Delicate Concerns

Seemingly insignificant things like how and where to go to the bathroom really frustrate teenagers. So develop rules that everyone understands. For riverside rest stops I simply point and say, "Girls upriver, boys go thataway." Coed overnights, however, require more finesse. If there's a unisex latrine, you'll need a policy that provides for privacy. For example:

I simply hang the nylon bag that contains the toilet paper in a conspicuous place at the edge of camp. When someone needs to use the facility, he or she takes the bag and goes. No one is to use the latrine until the TP bag returns. If the latrine is visible from camp, you should rig a privacy screen. I often carry an old nylon tarp for this purpose.

Before the trip the girls should be taken aside and told how to dispose of sanitary napkins. The excitement and intense physical activity may cause some girls to menstruate early or to have painful cramps. A wise leader is sympathetic and understanding, and carries appropriate medication.

The Inexperienced Leader

In case you've forgotten, there are eighteen kids going on this canoe trip. That's nine for you, nine for the inexperienced youth director. Granted, your colleague means well, and he's willing to learn, but he is not proficient in the bush. Nonetheless, he is responsible for nine kids. How can you smooth the way for him without affecting the social structure of his group?

At camp: Camp far enough apart so the groups can't see or hear one another, but close enough so you can help should an emergency arise. To retain individuality, each crew must operate on their own. So except on planned occasions, *do not* let kids from one camp socialize with those from another. I cannot stress this point enough! Remove kids from the rules and social order of their own group and they'll create endless problems.

On the water: Locating portages often calls for resourcefulness, patience, and good map-reading skills—attributes that your inexperienced colleague is just beginning to develop. To allay your friend's fears, suggest a time to start the next day's paddling. Then, at the appropriate hour, cruise by his campsite and casually signal him to follow. Stay close enough to instill confidence but distant enough to prevent socializing. Continue visual contact throughout the day, breaking off for lunch and to camp. After a day or two of this your friend will have his sea legs and you can go your separate ways.

Safety

Continually stress safety. Admonish kids to slow down and look where they're going when carrying a canoe or pack. Nearly all accidents are the result of hurrying a task or packing an oversized load. A particularly dangerous practice is "double packing" (carrying two packs, one on the back, the other on the chest), which obscures your view of the trail and your feet.

Rules

Kids are apt to forget items of equipment when they portage or break camp. So establish a foolproof system that makes every group member accountable. Everyone should commit the following rules to memory:

1. Everyone, regardless of swimming ability, must wear a life jacket when canoeing or lining canoes.

2. Take life jackets inside your tent when you retire. Do not sit on them or throw them around! No one wants to wear a PFD that has been left in the mud or rain.

3. Before retiring, canoes are turned over and tied to a tree so a high wind won't turn them into kites. The first time you chase an empty canoe down a bleak river in the black of night you'll understand the importance of this rule.

As you can see, canoeing with teens is an exercise in commitment. At times you'll be mother, father, doctor, and teacher. You'll have to find ways to include unpopular kids in group activities and to get the rest of the crew to accept them. Occasionally, you may even have to give up the shirt on your own back to warm that of a child.

Rewards? You bet! I've paddled dangerous whitewater and remote rivers north of the Arctic Circle. I've stood among thousands of caribou and have even been charged by grizzlies. But nothing warms my heart more than the tearful hugs and "Thanks, Cliff," that I receive at the end of a canoe trip.

Canoeing with teens helps me to rediscover the forgotten innocence of being young.

CHAPTER 15

Wilderness Navigation

The Fond du Lac River begins in the northwest corner of Saskatchewan at the far end of Wollaston Lake. It is described by Eric Morse (author of *Canoe Canada*) as a "remote challenging river for expert whitewater canoeists." The Fond du Lac is all of that and more, though getting to the river is the hardest part of all.

First, there's the bone-jangling ride over the Missinippi Tote Road—200 miles of fist-sized gravel that is guaranteed to fully depreciate the toughest vehicle. Then there's the 30-mile crossing of Wollaston Lake—a sprawling piece of water with hundreds of islands and bays to confuse you. The Fond du Lac begins innocently in an obscure bay at the northwest corner of the lake. All you have to do is find it!

The trip sprang from an assignment for *Canoe* magazine—one whose article deadline came just five days after our scheduled return. No way could I knock out a story that fast. I'd have to do some writing en route and find a way to shorten our time on the river.

The solution was to hire a tow from Wollaston Lake Lodge to the mouth of the Fond du Lac. That alone would save two days of paddling. The tow would cost us seventy Canadian dollars; but no matter, we'd come to run the river, not fight wind and waves.

We unloaded our gear at the Wollaston dock, packed the canoes, and tied them to the waiting motorboat. The sandy-haired man who was to guide us to the river seemed amiable enough. He was a college student from Toronto—a crackerjack fishing guide who purportedly knew the lake blindfolded.

Within minutes we were waterborne, skimming northward at full throttle. Casually, I looked at my map, then nudged my friend beside me. "Look here,

Darrell . . . this guy's going the wrong way, too far east. Whatcha think?"

"Aw c'mon, Cliff; he's the guide! Keep the faith, friend!"

"Yeah . . . okay."

With that I folded my map contentedly and simply watched the scenery pass. Ultimately I heard a coughing sound that suggested we were out of gas. No problem; our guide shut down the twin Mercs and plugged in the auxiliary tank. Then he quietly drew forth a tiny Xeroxed copy of a 1:500,000-scale map of the area and squinted boldly at it.

"Hey, this guy's really a pro," I muttered to my friend. "Look at that map. Man, I'd need bifocals just to tell the water from the land!"

There was a long silence. Then came a sheepish grin and the words, "Any of you guys know where we are?"

I looked at Darrell and together we burst out laughing. Our guide was *lost*!

Reluctantly, I pulled out my detailed 1:50,000-scale map and stared intently at it. "I dunno," I replied, "but one thing's certain; we're too far east!"

After that, it was merely a matter of intensive map study and fancy compass work to determine our location. Within the hour we chugged confidently to the hidden bay that marked the Fond du Lac—no thanks to our "expert" guide.

As this case illustrates, anyone can get confused on a complex waterway, even when it is familiar turf. The wilderness has a delightful way of humbling the most confident of egos. The remedy is to carry a good map and compass and to become expert in their use.

Maps

Topographic maps can be purchased by mail from the sources below.

For U.S. topographic maps, call (888) ASK–USGS or write:

United States Geological Survey
Box 25286, Federal Center
Denver, Colorado 80225

Canadian maps must be ordered through U.S. or Canadian map distributors. Write or call the Canada Map Office for a list of distributors:

The Canada Map Office
Department of Energy, Mines and Resources
615 Booth Street, Ottawa, Ontario
Canada K1A 0E9
(800) 465–6277

For charts and tide tables of U.S. coasts, the Great Lakes, and sections of major rivers, write:

National Ocean Survey
Division C44, 6501 Lafayette Avenue
Riverdale, Maryland 20840
(301) 436–6990

Canadian charts and tide tables are available from:

Hydrographic Chart Distribution Office
Department of Fisheries and Oceans
1675 Russel Road, P.O. Box 8030
Ottawa, Ontario
Canada K1G 3H6
(613) 998–4931
Fax (613) 998–1217

Request a free *Index to Topographic Maps.* This index will tell you what maps are in print, in what scale, and the cost. If much of your travel will be on large, complex lakes, request the largest scale available. Maps in 1:24,000 scale are best for picking your way across mazelike lakes, although at this large scale you'll need several of them. Smaller 1:50,000-scale maps are ideal for most wilderness canoe travel (the larger the denominator of the scale, the smaller the actual map scale). Usually, however, you can't afford to be so choosy. Large-scale maps are readily available for heavily traveled or civilized areas, while more remote sections of the continent may be available only in small scale. Avoid maps with scales smaller than 1:250,000 (1 inch = 4 miles). Such small-scale maps are useful to experts, but they don't inspire confidence in beginners.

When you have secured your maps, mark the route with a colored highlighter and number each map sheet in the order you will use it. To save weight and bulk, trim off and discard all unprinted margins. I prefer to coat nonwaterproof topographic maps with Thompson's Water Seal—an industrial-strength compound used for sealing wood and concrete blocks. Every hardware store has it. A single light coat of TWS, applied with a foam varnish brush, makes maps reasonably waterproof and allows you to write on them. Or for a waterproof seal, cover maps with clear contact paper. If you like more stiffness to your map, purchase some Chartex dry-mounting cloth for the backing from Forestry Suppliers, Inc.* This company has a number of navigational aids that you might find useful. Its catalog is free.

Map Case

A map case is essential, whether maps are waterproof or not. Plastic map cases take a lot of abuse on canoe trips, so get something sturdier than a Ziploc bag. If your canoe is properly outfitted with shock cords, as explained in chapter 2, your map case can be secured by sliding it under a shock-corded thwart. When you encounter rapids, stuff the map into your nylon thwart bag for the ultimate in security. Cook Custom Sewing* and Grade VI* make excellent map cases.

Compass

The most versatile and suitable compass style for the canoeist is the orienteering model. Orienteering compasses have built-in protractors that allow you to quickly and accurately compute direction and scale distance from a map without first orienting the map to north. This means you can define a precise direction—to the nearest degree—while sitting in your bobbing canoe. The direction is physically set on the compass by turning a dial, so there's nothing to remember or write down.

To determine the bearing of an object with an orienteering compass, point the compass at the object and, while holding the base steady, rotate the graduated

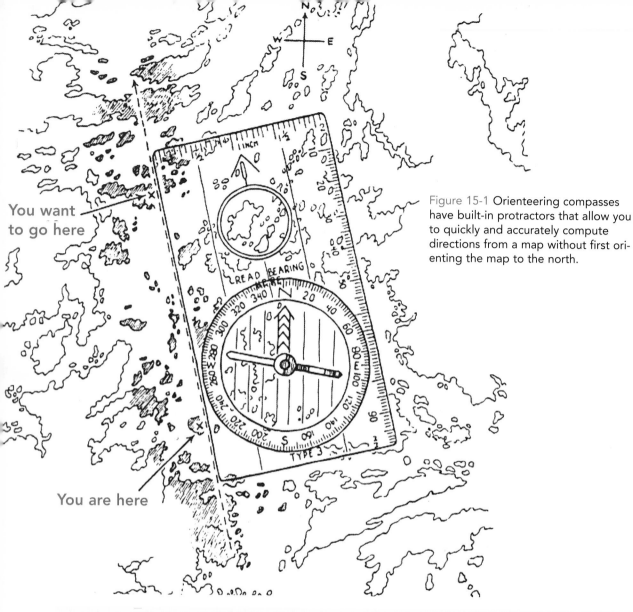

You want to go here

You are here

Figure 15-1 Orienteering compasses have built-in protractors that allow you to quickly and accurately compute directions from a map without first orienting the map to the north.

To Determine the Bearing of a Point on Your Compass

1. Place the left or right edge of the compass over your position in line with your destination.

2. Hold the compass base steady and turn the needle housing until the north on the dial points to north on the map (top of the map).

3. Read your bearing at the index (350 degrees in the illustration). Note that the magnetic needle is not used for this computation!

4. Now, remove the compass from the map and turn it (turn your body with the instrument) until the north end of the magnetic needle points to the north on the dial. You are now facing in a direction of 350 degrees. Simple, isn't it?

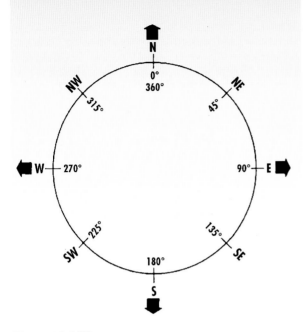

Figure 15-2 The compass rose.

housing until the north end of the magnetic needle points to N (north) on the dial. The direction you are facing, in degrees, is locked onto the compass dial and can be read at an index inscribed on the base. The compass can then be slipped back into your pocket for reference later. And you don't have to remember the direction that was set on the compass, because it will remain positioned on the dial until you turn the housing. To verify your direction with this style of compass, merely point the instrument away from your body and rotate your body and the compass until the north end of the magnetic needle points to N on the dial.

Since you don't have to read the numbers set on the dial, orienteering compasses are ideal for use at night or under conditions of rain or poor visibility.

Hint: Strap a small wrist compass around a thwart or seat frame and you'll be able to check directions without fumbling for your pocket compass.

Although all good compasses come with adequate instructions for average use, you should have an in-depth understanding of basic navigational principles if you intend to engage in serious route finding. For a thorough treatment of navigational procedures, see my book *Basic Essentials: Map and Compass* (Globe Pequot Press, 1999).

At the end of this chapter is a practice map that you can use to test your route-finding ability. If you can successfully complete the map exercise, you are ready to set out on a wilderness trip on a reasonably complex waterway.

First, the Basics

The compass is graduated in degrees. There are 360 degrees in the compass rose. The cardinal directions (north, south, east, and west) are each 90 degrees apart. The northeast (NE) quadrant encompasses the direction from 0 to 90 degrees, the southeast (SE) quadrant from 90 to 180 degrees, and so on. Learn to think in quadrants. Before determining the precise direction you wish to travel, ask yourself, "In which quadrant am I traveling?" This will help eliminate the most common of compass errors—the 180-degree error. For example, if your map tells you to go southwest and your compass points to 45 degrees (NE quadrant), you know something is wrong; you are facing 180 degrees in the wrong direction. It is not uncommon to transfer data from map to compass and make serious directional mistakes. Your approximate direction of travel should be known *before* you get down to the specifics.

Using the map of Lost Lake on page 121 (figure 15-6), assume you are at point A. You want to go just north of point H and take the portage trail to the South Arm of Maze Lake. A glance at the map tells you to begin heading northwest until you hit the shoreline, follow it around until you pass Bays 1 and 2, then paddle on into Bay 3 and straight to the portage. Very simple, right? Wrong! Look at the map scale. You won't be able to decipher island from mainland or one bay from another. When you look out across a lake of this size and complexity, you will see green as far as the eye can see. Physical features will blend with one another until the entire landscape is one of sameness. Because of wind and waves, you will lose all sense of distance traveled. You can rely on your watch for a rough estimate, but it will be difficult for you to judge whether you have completed 2 miles or 3. You can easily bypass Bay 3, or you can get completely turned around and become convinced that a channel between islands is a large bay, or vice versa.

One of the greatest tragedies of twentieth-century

canoeing occurred because of a map misinterpretation. In 1904 Leonidas Hubbard, Dillon Wallace, and George Elson attempted to penetrate the interior of an unexplored part of Labrador. "How vividly I saw it all again," said Wallace later. "Hubbard resting on his paddle and then rising up for a better view, as he said, 'Oh, that's just a bay and it isn't worthwhile to take the time to explore it. The river comes in here at the end of the lake. They all said it was at the end of the lake.' And we said, 'Yes, it is at the end of the lake; they all said so,' and went on." The Susan River they wrongly ascended was a dead end. With provisions gone and winter setting in, the expedition ended at Lake Michikamau, many miles from their destination.

Hubbard, weakened by hunger and exhaustion, could not continue. He died on Sunday, October 18, 1904. His two companions, Elson and Wallace, retraced their fateful steps down the Susan Valley to civilization. We will never know why Hubbard, a man of experience, did not take the time to check his map and compass at such a critical point in his journey.

Using Compass and Map for Precision Direction Finding

In order to keep track of where you are on a body of water of any size, you must know, within reason, your position at all times. This means you must proceed along an established direction—or bearing, as it is called.

Assume you have begun a canoe trip at point A on Lost Lake (again, see the map of Lost Lake on page 121). You plan to paddle the full width of the lake and portage into the South Arm of Maze Lake, which lies just to the west. Horseshoe Island, you've heard, has an excellent campsite on its south end (point B), so you decide to make your first camp there. You choose to paddle straight to the campsite rather than take the longer, more confusing route around the shoreline to your west. To accomplish this, you will need to determine the *exact* direction (bearing) in degrees from point A (your location) to point B (your destination).

You can use your orienteering compass or a simple protractor for this computation. To use an orienteer-

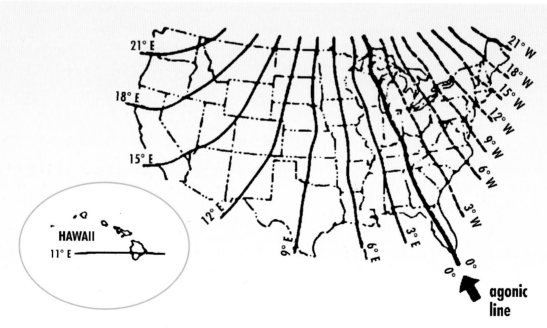

Figure 15-3 Standard declination chart.

ing compass, place either the left or right edge of the compass base plate on point A. Place the forward edge of the same side of the base plate on point B. Your compass is now pointing in the direction you want to go—from A to B (not from B to A). While holding the base plate tightly in position, turn the compass housing until north on the dial points to the top (north) of the map. *Caution:* Don't use the magnetic needle! Your direction of travel—292 degrees—is now locked onto the dial and can be read at the index inscribed on the compass base. Now while holding the compass in front of you with the direction-of-travel arrow inscribed on the base pointing *away* from your body, rotate your body and compass (you may have to turn the canoe to do this) until the magnetic needle points north on the dial. You are now facing in the proper direction. Locate a notch or visible incongruity on the horizon that you can identify as being on this course of travel. Put your compass away and paddle toward your objective. Do *not* attempt to watch the compass needle and paddle at the same time! In time your objective (point B) will pop into view and you will have found your campsite.

Once you have reestablished your position at point B, you can continue your voyage to C, then to D, and so on. In this manner you can cross a large, complex waterway without fear of becoming lost, for you will know where you are all the time.

Aiming Off

Assume you are at point G and you want to locate the portage to South Arm just north of H. There are three portages leading out of Bay 3, but only one goes to South Arm. Since 1 degree of compass error equals 92.2 feet per mile (tan. 1° x 5,280 feet), even a slight error can be disastrous.

From G to the south Arm portage is about 3 miles. A 4-degree error over this distance would cause you to miss the portage by at least 1,100 feet, or nearly ¼ mile. You would, in effect, be lost, since you'd have no idea which direction to go to find the portage. Instead, "aim off." Determine the bearing from G to a point just south of the portage—in this case, point H. Locate a notch on the horizon that corresponds to the bearing you have computed and start paddling. When you reach the shoreline, you will be somewhere near H, although you may be a few hundred feet north or south. But one thing is certain—you are south of the portage to South Arm. You merely have to paddle up the shoreline (north) until you come to the portage. This principle of aiming off is equally useful on land or for locating the mouth of a river. By aiming off you minimize the possibility of error.

Declination

A compass points (actually, it doesn't point—it lines up with the earth's magnetic field) to *magnetic* north, not *true* north. This angular difference, called declination, must be considered whenever you use your compass (see figures 15-3 and 15-4). In the eastern United States the declination is westerly, and in the western United States the declination is easterly. If you live right on the imaginary line that goes directly through both the true and magnetic north poles (called the agonic line), your declination will be zero.

If you live east or west of the agonic line, your compass will be in error, since the true North Pole is not in the same place as the magnetic north pole. As you can see from the declination chart, the farther away

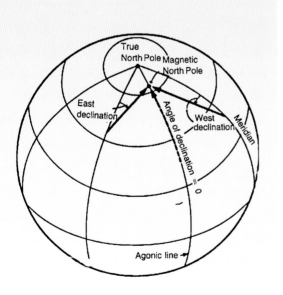

Figure 15-4 **Compass declination: The angular differ-ence between true north and magnetic north (the direction the compass points).**

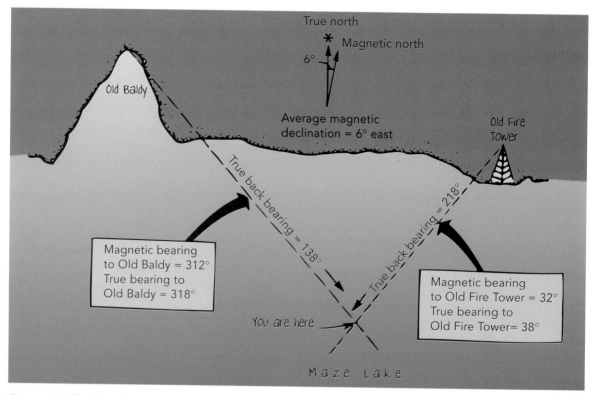

True north

Magnetic north

6°

Average magnetic
declination = 6° east

Old Baldy

Old Fire
Tower

True back bearing = 138°

True back bearing = 218°

Magnetic bearing
to Old Baldy = 312°
True bearing to
Old Baldy = 318°

Magnetic bearing
to Old Fire Tower = 32°
True bearing to
Old Fire Tower= 38°

You are here

M a z e   L a k e

Figure 15-5 **Position of triangulation.**

you are from the agonic line, the greater the declination. Moreover, the magnetic north pole is constantly moving, so declination varies from year to year as well as from place to place. To find the exact declination for your area, consult a topographic map or call a surveyor. In the continental United States, declination can range from 0 degrees at the agonic line to more than 20 degrees in New England and the Far West. Unless your canoeing will be limited to those states very close to the agonic line, you will have to consider declination.

The easiest solution to the declination problem is to purchase a compass that can be adjusted for declination. Many orienteering models have this feature. Or you can compute magnetic variation mathematically, according to the following rhyme: *Declination east—compass least* (subtract east declination from your map direction); *declination west—compass best* (add west declination to your map direction).

Maps are almost always drawn in their true perspective (any variation is so small that it can be ignored). So when you determine a direction of travel or bearing from a map, it is a *true bearing*. The true bearing taken from your map will have to be converted to a *magnetic bearing* to be set on your compass.

Assume a declination of 10 degrees east. Apply the rhyme "declination east, compass least," and subtract 10 degrees from the true bearing computed from your map. In the Lost Lake map exercise, a true bearing of 292 degrees from A to B would equal 292 degrees minus 10, or 282 degrees, using the declination given above. Conversely, if declination were 10 degrees west, it would be added (292° + 10° = 302°), and this value would be set on your compass. If this is confusing and you plan to travel in areas where the declination is large, you would be well advised to spend the extra money for a compass that can be manually adjusted for declination.

Position by Triangulation

Suppose you find yourself on a large, mazelike lake where you can identify two or more topographical features but you don't know exactly where you are. Finding your position by triangulation is simple with an orienteering compass (or you can use a protractor with a more conventional compass). Pick out one point on the horizon that you can identify—Old Baldy in this case (see figure 15-5). With your compass shoot a magnetic bearing to the point (bearing = 312 degrees). Change this magnetic bearing to a true bearing by reverse application of the rhyme (312° + 6° =

318°). Draw the *back* (reciprocal) bearing (318° − 180° = 138°) through Old Baldy, using your compass base plate and a sharp pencil. (When using an orienteering compass, you don't have to compute the back bearing at all.) Set 318 degrees on the compass dial, place your pencil point on Old Baldy, and put the forward edge of one side of your compass base plate against the pencil point. Rotate the entire compass in an arc around the pencil until north on the dial (not the needle) points to the top (north) of the map. (*Caution:* Do not turn the compass housing during this operation, since the true bearing that you just computed to Old Baldy (318 degrees) is set on the dial. This procedure will *not*

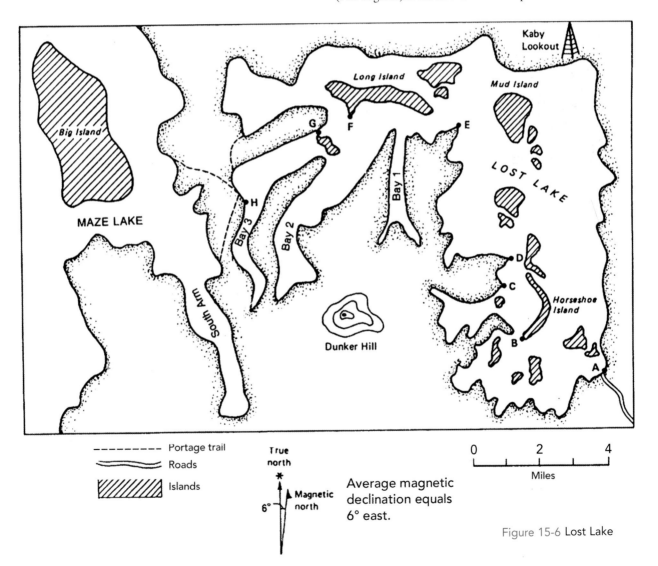

Portage trail
Roads
Islands

True north

Magnetic north

6°

Average magnetic declination equals 6° east.

0   2   4
Miles

Figure 15-6 **Lost Lake**

Point	True Bearing	Distance (miles)	Approximate Travel Time	Magnetic Bearing (to be set on your compass)
A to B	290°	2¾	1½ hours	284°
B to C	341°	1½	¾ hour	335°
C to D	15°	⅔	20 minutes	9°
D to E	338°	4	2 hours	332°
E to F	274°	3¼	1½ hours	268°
F to G	244°	1⅛	½ hour	238°
G to H	227°	2½	1¼ to 1½ hours	221°

H to portage (paddle north up the shoreline to portage): Time—about 15 minutes.

work if you change the dial setting! Using the base plate as a straightedge, draw your line. Repeat the exercise using another point on the horizon that you can identify (Old Fire Tower). You are located where the two lines cross. For greatest precision you may wish to take three sightings.

Navigation at Night

Canoeing by moonlight on a slow-moving river or calm lake is an enjoyable experience. However, no canoeist's repertoire is complete until he or she has done some black-night travel by compass. Some years ago while canoeing in Minnesota's Boundary Waters Canoe Area, I was awakened to find three bears in camp—Mama and two babies. In spite of previous stern warnings, the youth group that I was guiding had left food scattered around the camp. The dehydrated fruit that was on the lunch menu evidently had featured a super-abundance of prunes, and the youngsters had elected to have a prune fight. Even after a thorough policing of the grounds, enough prunes remained to attract the bears. We blew whistles, banged on canoes, clanked pots and pans, and made a variety of other noises in the hope of frightening away the hungry bruins, but to no avail. Our bears were used to people. After they knocked down one tent, we became convinced it was time to leave, and within a few minutes we put to sea. The night was black as pitch, but locating a new campsite without a moon to guide us was not difficult. We set course by compass and located a new site within an hour. My compass, a Silva Ranger, had a good luminous night-sighting device.

Lost Lake Exercises

Referring to the map of Lost Lake (figure 15-6), assume you are at point A. Using your compass or a protractor, determine the bearing and approximate time of travel from point to point. Proceed alphabetically, ending your trip at the portage into South Arm. Assume a travel speed of 2 miles per hour. When you have finished and your answers check, work the triangulation problem below.

Triangulation Problem

You can identify Dunker Hill at a magnetic bearing of 256 degrees and Kaby Lookout at a magnetic bearing of 4 degrees. Where are you located? *Clue:* Don't forget the apply the declination.

Answer to Lost Lake Exercises

You are located at the north end of Horseshoe Island.

River Navigation and Trip Guides

No discussion of canoe route finding would be complete without mentioning trip guides and river navigation. With the impact of humans on river systems, it is becoming more and more important for the prospective river paddler to know what the water conditions are like before setting the canoe in the water. Many local and even far northern rivers are now dam-controlled and are very dangerous at high water or impossible at low water. Barbed-wire fences strung across rivers maim and kill canoeists each year, and the people who string the fences generally have the law on their side. Each year we read about canoeists who inadvertently paddled over a dam because they didn't know it was there. If you paddle rivers, you must be able to accurately locate and identify dams, rapids, fences, and other obstacles in the water that can endanger your trip.

Unlike lake navigation, it is very difficult to fix your position on a river. A compass will be useful for rough directions only. You can reaffirm your location at major river bends, identifiable rapids, or incoming streams. On wilderness canoe trips where it is necessary to ascend an incoming stream and thereby change watersheds, a high degree of resourcefulness and competence in map reading may be required, especially if there are many streams to confuse you.

Lastly, some of the best maps of river conditions are the local people who live in the area. Always check with them before embarking on a river, even if you have run it many times. Many things may have changed since your map was drawn. Although you should heed the advice of locals, bear in mind that most don't understand canoes, and they have a tendency to exaggerate the dangers of their rivers. Nevertheless, they will provide you with much good information. Especially seek out foresters or professional people who work in the area. Outdoorspeople will generally tell it like it is, or at least they will exaggerate less.

Global Positioning System

It would be unfair to leave the subject of navigation without mentioning the wonderful new GPS (Global Positioning System) units that receive signals from orbiting satellites. With a GPS, you can locate your position (within 100 meters) anywhere on earth in a matter of minutes. Or you can enter the set of coordinates of a place you want to go; the GPS receiver will provide a (true or magnetic) compass bearing and distance, which will be updated by satellite information as you progress. Press a button and you get a speed readout (it's inaccurate if you're going slower than about 11 miles an hour) and an estimated time of arrival (ETA).

Outdoorspeople are buying GPS units like mad, though precious few know how to use them. To use a GPS effectively, you must know how to read a map and compass. And your maps must have a coordinate system that the GPS unit can understand. Maps that do include all U.S. and Canadian topographic maps marked with degrees of latitude and longitude. Some topographic maps also provide decimal-based Universal Trans Mercator (UTM) coordinates (grid lines), which are much easier to use than latitude and longitude. Any GPS can be set to read latitude and longitude or UTM coordinates, as you prefer.

Maps that don't have a coordinate system to which the GPS can relate include nearly all public road maps, most state and national park hiking and boating maps, and special-purpose recreational maps, like those drawn for the Boundary Waters Canoe Area of Minnesota and Canada's Quetico Provincial Park. If you use one of these special-purpose maps, you'll need to draw your own grid lines on the map face or carry a GPS-compatible topographic map. However, things are changing fast in GPS land—several companies now offer detailed maps on CD-ROM computer disks that provide precise coordinates with a click of the mouse.

The bottom line is that your map must have integral GPS coordinates or you won't be able to plot the fix your GPS calculates!

Finally, be aware that all handheld GPS units operate on small batteries—which could fail when you need them most. And few civilian GPS models are truly waterproof, which is important for canoeing.

How much should you pay for a GPS? Even the least-expensive (under $200) receivers will provide accurate coordinates, times, and routing information. Unless you're a GPS guru, you won't miss the frills they lack.

Sadly, I use my compass far less frequently now that I carry a GPS on my canoe trips. Deep down, I hope my reliance on this new technology won't cause my compass skills to atrophy.

If you're serious about learning the GPS system, first master the basics in this chapter, then study Michael Ferguson's excellent *GPS, Land Navigation* (Glassford Publishing, 1997). It's by far the best GPS text available.

Part IV

Camping Skills

CHAPTER 16

Quick Fixin's

A compendium of luscious fast-food ideas for those who'd rather canoe than cook

Breakfast

Seven A.M. and breakfast in the backcountry. Yesterday you served scrambled eggs and diced/fried Canadian bacon. Today there is instant oatmeal, dehydrated fruit, and leftovers from the day before. On hand is one egg and a cinnamon bagel apiece, ¼ pound of "still okay" bacon, and a fist-sized chunk of cheddar from Monday's lunch. Hmmm. Why not forget the gruel and wow 'em with Egg McBagel?

You pump some air into the cold steel tank of the Peak 1, then adjust the valve to a gentle simmer. Your culinary talents are about to be unveiled. But the first order of business is to make some gourmet coffee.

How to Make Gourmet Camp Coffee

Use the very best fine-ground coffee. Add a scant pinch of salt to your coffeepot and bring the water to a rolling boil. Remove the pot from the heat source and add 1 heaping tablespoon of coffee per cup. If you want cinnamon-flavored java, toss in about ¼ teaspoon of cinnamon for every 8 cups of brewed coffee. For almond- or mint-flavored coffee, add an equivalent amount of liquid extract to the brew. Stir once to mix everything, snap on the lid, and set the pot near the fire. Do not allow the coffee to boil! Doing so will kill and bury a fine brew. Allow the grounds to settle for three minutes, then pour off the sludge at the spout. Now lie back and contemplate what you've been missing at home.

To make North Woods Egg coffee, mix the grounds with beaten egg (use just enough egg to thoroughly moisten all grounds). Bring the water to a rolling boil, then drop in the egg-saturated grounds. Immediately turn the heat to simmer. Simmer very gently (do not boil!) about five minutes. Then remove from the heat and add a dash of cold water to settle the grounds. The result is a clear, rich coffee everyone will rave about.

For an added treat, fill your coffee cup with pre-mixed cocoa powder and top off with fresh-made camp coffee. The result is class-act cinnamon, mint, or almond mocha served steaming hot in the heart of the backcountry.

Egg McBagel

Each Egg McBagel requires about two minutes to make. First, fry some Canadian bacon—thirty seconds per side in a good hot pan will do the trick. (*Note:* Vacuum-sealed Canadian bacon will keep at least a week in the heat of summer. American slab bacon will last almost as long.) Drain the bacon on a few sheets of paper toweling and set it aside. Lubricate your skillet with a squirt of vegetable oil and fry an egg (break the yoke). Opposite the egg, place the two bagel halves facedown. Cover the pan immediately and use low heat. After thirty seconds, flip the egg.

While the egg is cooking, place a slice of Canadian bacon on the face of one of the bagel halves and flake some cheese on top. Top with the well-done egg. Add the other bagel half to complete the sandwich, then cover the meal for thirty seconds or until the cheese melts. Ferry your Egg McBagel onto an awaiting plate and chow down.

Important tip: If you add a dash of cold water to the hot skillet partway through cooking, then cover immediately, the water will turn to steam and quickly cook your food to moist perfection. This is a great way to revitalize week old bagels and to make grilled cheese sandwiches.

Cinnamon Burritos, Brown Sugar-stewed Apples, and Smoked Pork Sausage

These big-time favorites taste like cinnamon rolls!

Ingredients: You'll need (per person): 1 giant tortilla, 3 tablespoons brown sugar, ¼ teaspoon cinnamon, dehydrated apples, liquid margarine, smoked pork sausage.

Preparation: Evenly distribute a generous amount of liquid margarine, brown sugar and cinnamon on the face of each tortilla. Roll to form burritos, and place them seam-down on a warm pan that you've lightly oiled with liquid margarine. Cover and fry over low heat for twenty seconds, then turn the burritos (use bamboo tongs) and add a dash of water to steam. Cook thirty seconds more, then serve.

Start the stewed fruit and smoked porkies before you begin the burritos. You'll need one pot to boil the sausage, and another to boil the fruit. To the fruit, add brown sugar and cinnamon to taste. The fruit will absorb only so much sugar, so there's no need to measure. When the water boils, give the fruit a stir, then remove the pot from the heat and set it on an insulated pad. Add a cozy cover (as suggested on page 130) and allow the fruit to stew for ten minutes before serving.

Bacon, eggs with salsa, and toasted bagel with honey. A hearty breakfast.

Lunch Ideas

The ideal canoe lunch is tasty, nourishing, compact, lightweight, crushproof, immune to spoilage, and can be consumed on the run. If you can't unwrap it, slice it, spread it, or spoon it from a can, forget it. When the weather howls bloody murder, you may consciously cheat and prepare instant soup or hot, sweet tea on your gasoline stove. But the traditional fire-brewed shore lunch of fishing guides is out of place on the typical canoe trip—that is, if you'd rather canoe than cook.

On my early canoe trips, I relied exclusively on high-tech crackers like Rye-Crisp and Wasa Brot, on which I heaped oily synthetic cheeses that came in cardboard boxes and squeeze tubes. A poly bottle of peanut butter, another of jam, and a stick or three of beef jerky constituted lip-smacking traveling fare. For lengthy trips above the tree line, where even foodstuffs must succumb to the precept of ruggedness, I trashed the crackers in favor of traditional pilot biscuits. If you're not familiar with these once-popular shipboard staples, suffice it to say that, contrary to popular belief, they can indeed be broken. All you need is a full-sized ax and a good head of steam!

Despite years of dependence on this nutritious fare, I now gag at the thought of ever consuming it again. Indeed, I have asked Manitou to strike me dead if another pilot biscuit or squish of tube cheese ever again creases my lips.

Figure 16-1 Add a dash of water to the hot skillet part way through cooking. The "steam" will cook your food to moist perfection.

The noon repast should be politely civilized. The humble bagel provides the nucleus of the meal, at least for a day or three. Bagels lack preservatives, so they grow harder by the hour, ultimately sprouting a rich green growth of penicillium after a week out. Vacuum-sealing helps (inexpensive units are available), but not enough. Figure on a maximum shelf life of three days and you can't go wrong.

Pita (Mediterranean pocket) is avowedly my favorite lunch bread. The ones sold in Mediterranean food shops are by far the tastiest, but these usually lack preservatives and so keep only about as long as bagels. You'll find additive-packed pitas, which will last two weeks or more, on the refrigerator shelves of most large supermarkets. Again, vacuum-sealing markedly increases shelf life.

No need to rely on plastic-tasting synthetic cheeses. Good block cheddar, Colby, or Monterey Jack will keep at least two weeks in the heat of summer. Cheese should be vacuum-sealed or wax-coated to ensure freshness over the long haul. Simply trim surface mold when (if) the need arises.

I abandoned beef jerky long ago in favor of hard salami. There are other tasty meats that don't require refrigeration. Ask your grocer about them.

There's no substitute for good jam. I'll drive 50 miles to get the best Canadian preserves. What's good at home is great afield.

To the above items add a stash of chunky peanut butter and a favorite granola, salted nut roll, or fruit bar. (Have you tried Cotlets, Aplets, and Grapelets?) A splash of mustard will turn your meal into an adventurous picnic.

On into Supper

Scenario: For three days you've been pinned in a quiet cove by an icy, 30-mile-an-hour wind. It's only the first week out and you've already exhausted the two-day supply of extra rations you brought along for just this purpose. Should you put your crew on half rations? Not if you can creatively conserve food without cutting down. The following Dumpling Soup recipe provides an alternative.

Ingredients: Instant soup, any flavor; Minute Rice; Bisquick; cheese; dehydrated hamburger or canned chunk chicken, if you have it.

Preparation: Add 20 percent more water than called for in the soup directions. Fail to do this and you'll have glue, not stew! Bring the soup mix and water to a boil, add 1 cup Minute Rice for every four servings, then drop marble-sized Bisquick dumplings into the stew. Add dehydrated hamburger and meats at the start of cooking. Simmer five minutes or until dumplings are done. Add up to ¼ pound cut-up cheese during the last minute of cooking. Mmm good!

Note: You can beef up food value and "environmental effect" by adding noodles, spaghetti, or elbow macaroni. Potato buds can be used as a stock thickener or to make tasty dumplings. Pancake batter and fish breading can also be pressed into service for this purpose. Try diced, fried summer sausage (lunch leftovers) in your dumpling stew.

Note: Dehydrated hamburger provides the basis for dozens of trail meals—spaghetti, chili, stroganoff, or tacos, to name a few. A simple, low-cost dehydrator is all you need. Brown and drain the hamburger, then pour boiling water over the meat (optional) to remove as much grease as possible (the water will strip some nutrients). Place ground beef on a dehydrator tray lined with several thicknesses of paper toweling. Dry at 140 degrees for twelve hours or until hard. Most folks can't tell dehydrated hamburger from fresh when it is used in stew and sauces.

Tip: To make dumplings without soiling your hands, pour batter and water into a Ziploc bag. Seal the bag and knead the contents until they are mixed. Cut a slit in the bag bottom and squeeze the mix—use the bag like a cake decorator—into the soup. Afterward, burn the bag.

Hors d'Oeuvres

Pita Melt

Cut pita bread in half and fill the pockets with grated cheese. Heavily sprinkle garlic powder and oregano (optional) over the cheese. Fry the pita halves in a well-oiled (I prefer olive oil), covered skillet for about twenty seconds. Then flip the pitas and quickly add a dash of cold water to "steam-melt" the cheese.

Cook for an additional 20 seconds and serve immediately. So good, it could be a main meal!

You can substitute tortillas for pitas, if you prefer. The result is a lighter, crispier snack. Pack all the ingredients into the rolled tortilla, then fry and steam it as suggested above. What a great way to start a meal!

Baked Fish Fillets

This mouthwatering entree is the invention of Bill Marcouiller, a wilderness canoeist from Battle Lake, Minnesota. Serve as an hors d'oeuvre or full meal.

Ingredients: Split fillets of your favorite fish; margarine; salt and pepper; ½ teaspoon dehydrated parsley flakes; 2 tablespoons diced, fresh onion; 2 ounces or more of your favorite cheese; 1 teaspoon bacon bits.

Preparation: You'll need to rig an oven of some sort. Set the fillets on a thin layer of margarine, then smother them with more margarine, salt, pepper, parsley flakes, and onion. Cover the oven and bake ten minutes or until done. When the fillets are nearly cooked, spread cheese over them and add bacon bits on top. A dash of garlic flakes livens flavor. Bake until the cheese is melted. You won't believe how good this is.

Popcorn

Adjust your stove to medium-high heat and barely cover the bottom of your largest cooking pot with vegetable oil. Add a half-dozen kernels of the best (I use Orville's) popping corn to the uncovered pot. Don't add salt to the popper, as this encourages sticking and burning. When all the "maidens" have popped, the oil is at the right temperature. Add enough corn to cover the pot bottom, no more. You'll have tough popcorn if you don't allow steam to escape during the popping process, so find some way to vent the pot cover. Continuously shake the pot with a twisting motion until the cover is forced away from the pot, then immediately pour out the popped corn into a large paper grocery sack. Season with margarine and fine-grade popcorn salt. Shake the paper bag to mix.

You'll find other neat recipes and cooking tricks in the newly revised edition of my book *Basic Essentials:*

Gourmet treats on the Arctic tundra, Northwest Territories, Canada.

Cooking in the Outdoors (Globe Pequot Press, 1999).

Meal Management

Remove all excess packaging (like cardboard boxes) on foodstuffs and repack each meal separately in a large Ziploc bag. If you place plastic bags in color-coded nylon stuff sacks (I use green for breakfasts, yellow for lunches, red for suppers), you'll avoid much pack groping at mealtime.

Each packaged meal should be a complete unit. It should not be necessary to search for sugar, instant milk, or cocoa. All items should be premeasured in the correct amount necessary to serve the group.

The best way to pack breakables and crushables like crackers, candy bars, and cheese is to place them inside rigid cardboard containers (milk cartons are ideal). Place onions, green peppers, and other vegetables in a paper or cotton sack and carry them inside your coffeepot.

Cooking Gear

For a party of four, you'll need three nested pots with covers, a teakettle and a Teflon-lined skillet. Most skillets sold in camping shops are awful. Get a standard 12-inch Mirro with Silverstone finish and make a removable handle for it. My books *Basic Essentials: Cooking in the Outdoors* and *Camping's Top Secrets* (Globe Pequot Press, 1998) show you how. Chosen Valley Canoe Accessories* makes a commer-

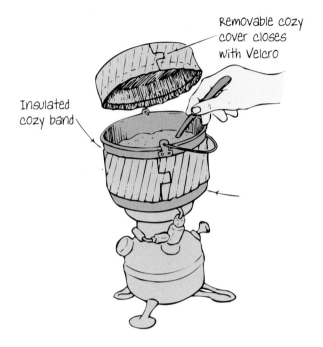

Insulated cozy band

Removable cozy cover closes with Velcro

Figure 16-2. "Cozy cooking."

cial kit based on a design I adapted from the once-popular Bendonn Dutch oven, which is no longer manufactured.

Each person should have an insulated cup, plastic bowl, and spoon. A stainless-steel Sierra cup makes a great ladle.

You'll also want insulated cozies for all your pots. These retain heat and save stove fuel during cooking, and they keep food hot long after the stove has been shut down. I make my pot cozies from quilted cotton material or insulated ironing board fabric. But any thick, reasonably flameproof material will work.

A two-piece cozy—top hat and belly band—is better than a one-piece model, because the wide band insulates the pot sides when you remove the cover to stir. The skirted top hat can also be used (skirt-up) alone on top of a skillet when frying.

Here's how to use your cozy:

1. Velcro the band tightly around the pot before you

begin cooking. Position the bottom of the band above the bottom of the pot so the band won't scorch when the stove runs full blast.

2. Measure water for the meal into the pot. Then cover the pot and put on the cozy. If you're making a freeze-dried or dehydrated entree, add meat, spices, and vegetables to the water. *Don't* add sauce mix, rice, cereal, or pasta yet.

3. Turn the stove to high and do other chores. The cozy will reduce the boiling time and save stove fuel.

4. When the water boils, turn the heat down to a simmer and add the cereal, rice, pasta, or sauce mix. Stir vigorously till the fixin's are blended and the water is boiling again. Then turn off the stove and set the pot on a square of closed-cell foam. Put on the cover and top hat, and work the belly band down till it covers all the bare metal of the pot. Your food will slow-cook in twenty minutes and stay hot for an hour.

This setup is lighter, more compact, and more efficient than mechanical heat-saving devices like the popular MSR Heat Exchanger, which only works with MSR pots. CLG Enterprises* in Minneapolis now produces a commercial version of my cozy design. I've

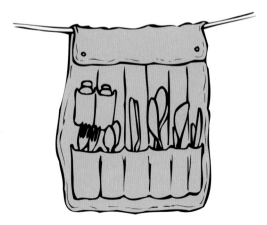

Figure 16-3 When rains come, hang your fabric utensil roll from a tight line strung beneath your cooking fly. Now everything you need to prepare meals will be clean, dry, and instantly at hand.

seen the prototype, which is made of pure wool. Very nice and reasonably priced. I receive no gratuities from CLG for use of my design.

Kitchen Accessories

A graduated plastic pitcher tied to a canoe thwart doubles as a canoe bailer and a mixing container for instant drinks and soup. Silverware and spices are best kept in a fabric utensil roll that can be snapped or tied to an overhead line (figure 16-3). Duluth Pack* makes a nice canvas model.

When rains come, run a tight line just beneath your cooking fly and hang your utensil organizer from it. Now everything you need to prepare meals will be clean and at hand. Package a few sheets of paper toweling with breakfast and supper meals. The towels are handy for drying cookware and cleaning the stove.

Ovens

In the days of large campfires, I used a folding reflector or Dutch oven for all my baking. Now, however, I cook almost exclusively on a stove, so my baking methods reflect this bias. An oven constructed of a large ring aluminum gelatin mold (figure 16-4) provides excellent results. To use the gelatin mold for baking on your stove:

1. Grease the mold and pour your bake stuff into the outside ring. Decrease the suggested amount of water by up to one-quarter for faster baking.

2. Bring the stove to normal operating temperature, then reduce the heat to the lowest possible setting. Center the mold over the burner head, top it with a high cover, and relax. Cooking times are about the same as those suggested in the baking directions.

3. Cool the mold by setting it in a shallow pan of water for a few minutes.

The Triple-Pan Method

The triple-pan method of baking works well on a stove or fire. You'll need two nesting skillets, a high cover, and a half-dozen small nails or stones:

1. Evenly scatter the nails or stones onto the surface of the large (bottom) frying pan.

Figure 16-4 **The gelatin mold oven: It works on any trail stove.**

2. Place your bake stuff into the small frying pan and set it on top of the nails (the two pans must be separated by nails or stones to prevent burning).

3. Cover the unit and place it on your stove. Use the lowest possible blue-flame setting. *Warning:* Don't use this method with a thin aluminum skillet on the bottom; you'll burn a hole right through it!

Sanitation

For short trips where there are few portages, all garbage should be bagged in plastic and packed out of the wilderness. When this is impractical, as on lengthy outings, the best method of disposal is to burn it in a good, hot fire. Please pick aluminum foil out of the flames before it melts all over everything!

In populated areas fish entrails should be buried well away from the campsite and at least 100 feet from water. In remote areas they may be left for seagulls on a large boulder, *well away from human habitation.* The exception to these rules is when you're camping in remote country where grizzly bears are about. The slightest odor may bring these big bears to you! The best plan here is to throw entrails well out into the river or lake.

Human waste should also be buried, preferably under a 4-inch cover of soil to maximize decomposition. Burn toilet paper and sanitary napkins and carry a water bottle to be sure flames are dead out!

And please, don't throw food—or anything else—into forest service box latrines or chemical toilets. Bears commonly upset latrines to get at the food they want.

Dishes should be washed on land, well away from the water's edge. Greasy dishwater is best poured into a small hole in the ground and covered with soil.

Water Purification

Most authorities recommend that you boil, filter, or chemically treat all water taken from a questionable source. That's sound advice, providing you have the necessary chemicals and/or equipment plus the self-discipline to use them. Although I occasionally boil (160 degrees will kill almost everything) my drinking water on backcountry trips, I confess to laziness in this respect. As often as not, I drink untreated water, but I am very careful where I get it. Here are the guidelines I religiously follow:

- Go well away from shore to get your drinking water. If you are camping at a spot that is frequented by humans or animals, go upstream of the source to get your water. On lakes a minimum of 150 feet from shore is recommended.

- Decay organisms (bacteria and protozoans) generally prefer the shallows, so the deeper your water source, the better. On large lakes I often weight a cooking pot with a rock and let it down 30 feet or more by rope. Avoid any water that has a green or greenish brown color. Water with a green tinge contains algae and is usually loaded with microorganisms.

- Don't take water from backwaters and stagnant areas. These are breeding places for microbes.

- Don't take water near beaver dams or lodges. Beavers are the favored host of *Giardia lamblia*—a small protozoan that will make you plenty sick!

A Final Thought

As you paddle the rivers of North America, you will surely come upon thoughtless people and their refuse. Tin cans, bottles, mattress springs, car bodies, and worn-out appliances are but a sampling of the debris I've observed in my travels. Once, in the Boundary Waters of Minnesota, I was awakened at midnight by an enterprising trumpeter. On another occasion a teen group sang ribald songs the whole night through. Many times I've put out other people's abandoned campfires and cleaned their trashed fireplaces and campsites. But my efforts are not unique: Everyone who cares about the future of our wild places follows suit throughout each and every camping trip. Doing battle with environmental idiots is a never-ending, non-rewarding process.

Nearly everyone who paddles America's rivers ultimately develops a profound respect for them and an abiding disdain for those who abuse them. Nonetheless, it's important to realize that those who violate the backcountry usually do so out of ignorance, not willful disrespect. To this end, I offer the suggested Backcountry Ethics Quiz in appendix 3. Use it as you wish. Reproduce it in any number you like, and share it with as many people as you can. Education may not be the total answer to eliminating environmental abuses, but it is a start.

CHAPTER 17

Weathering the Storm

I pitched the old Eureka Timberline tent on a gentle knoll amid a clump of birch trees. There was a much better spot about 20 feet away—a well-worn site where hundreds of tents had stood before. But the barren place was in a slight depression that was devoid of ground cover—a good rain could mean a flooded tent. Besides, a long-dead spruce tree, its limbs poised menacingly overhead, stood nearby waiting patiently for the first big wind to send it crashing down.

At about 7 P.M. it began. Slowly at first, with a gentle rain that lasted an hour. Then the storm intensified; soon rain fell in thick sheets, driven by gale-force winds of 60 miles an hour!

For a while I just stood complacently in the prestorm drizzle and watched the chilling blackness expand across the sky. Then, methodically, I began to make necessary adjustments.

First I pulled a coil of parachute cord from my pack and strung two taut guylines from each tent peak to trees nearby (the Eureka Timberline is self-supporting and theoretically does not need to be guyed). Then I weighted each stake with heavy rocks that I dragged from the streambed below.

Within minutes it struck. The big Eureka shook and groaned as the initial swish of the wind tore at her. But she stood fast.

The heaviest part of the storm passed quickly, but a steady 40- to 50-mile-per-hour wind continued relentlessly throughout the night.

We awoke the next morning to the scene of disaster. Trees were down everywhere. The dead spruce lay about where I predicted. And every depression was overflowing with water. Smugly, my wife and I exchanged glances. We'd weathered the storm!

Admittedly, stormproofing a camp requires luck as well as skill. Really, what would I have done if that clump of birch hadn't been there? Or if rocks or brush prohibited placing the tent on high ground?

It's unrealistic to expect any woodland tent to withstand sustained winds of over 40 miles per hour, regardless of how you pitch it. But rain is another matter. A sophisticated expedition tent that's pitched badly or set in the wrong spot is sure to admit water, while a simple forest tent that's rigged correctly won't. In the end your skills at coping with the weather are much more important than your gear.

Know the Shortcomings of Your Tent and Correct Them

Blowing Rain and Flowing Groundwater

Blowing rain or flowing groundwater is most likely to enter a tent through ground-level or exposed perimeter seams. Naturally, all tent seams should be waterproofed, with either a special seal glue or a liquid compound. I prefer Thompson's Water Seal, a brush-on chemical formulated for waterproofing concrete floors. TWS is flexible and stable in all temperatures and it's available at most hardware stores. The product is also useful for waterproofing maps and clothing. One application with a foam varnish brush does the trick.

Note: Some new tents come with factory-sealed (taped) seams—a good idea. Still, production realities often make it impossible to seal all seams. That's why a bottle of seam sealant (glue) comes with every tent. The bottom line is that seam-sealing compounds and machine-applied tape won't substitute for a weatherproof design—that is, a tent whose seams and zippers are covered by waterproof fabric. Remember this when a salesperson argues that sealing the exposed seams of an inferior tent will keep out rain!

Waterproof coatings eventually peel and seam glues give way—in time, *all* tent floors leak. The solution is to *always* use a plastic groundsheet *inside* your tent. Water that gets through a leaking floor will be trapped beneath the ground cloth and you'll sleep dry.

Some "experts" suggest that you place the ground cloth under the floor to save the floor material from abrasion and puncture. Don't do it! Groundwater will become trapped between the plastic sheet and floor and be pumped (the weight of your body creates a pressure differential) into the tent. You'll really have a sponge party if this happens!

An interior ground cloth will also nearly eliminate holes and abrasions in your tent floor. If you don't believe it, begin a trip with a new plastic groundsheet in your tent. At the end of your trip, count the number of holes in it—holes that would otherwise be in your tent floor! Old ideas die hard.

Wind

The best way to improve the wind stability of a tent is to run extra storm lines from the poles and fly. How and where you apply these lines depends on the design of your tent:

- *For tents that have traditional I-poles:* Run twin guy-lines from each peak, as illustrated in figure 17-1a. Extend the lines outward at 45-degree angles to the poles. Don't mess with the original tent guy. You want *three* lines emanating from each end of the tent.

- *For self-supporting A-frame tents like the Eureka Timberline and its derivatives:* Attach twin lines directly to the poles and crossbars, as shown in figure 17-1b. Stake the two lines about a foot apart if the tent is facing into a headwind. If a quartering wind develops, center one guyline and stake the other into the wind. Eureka Timberline and similarly styled tents will manage quite a blow if storm lines are applied in this fashion.

- *For self-supporting dome tents:* Sew nylon storm loops on the face of the fly, in line with the tent poles (figure 17-1c). Back what you sew with heavy material. Sew a Velcro tab to the inside of the fly,

opposite each storm loop. Seal all seams with Thompson's Water Seal.

When a wind blows up, Velcro the loops to the poles and run a guyline from the loop to the ground. This will transfer wind stress from the nylon fly directly to the poles.

If possible, attach all guy and stake lines to a tree or boulder. Or weight the stakes with rocks or logs so they won't pull out when the ground softens from rain. Two stakes per loop—each through a separate hole and at a different angle—doubles the surface area and holding power in soft ground. *Tip:* Tie 3-foot lengths of parachute cord to each stake loop before your trip and you won't have to mess with cutting and tying these anchor lines in a rainstorm!

- *Optional:* Attach loops of shock cord to stake and pole loops (the extra guys are added only during a storm, but the shock-cord loops should be a permanent part of your tent's anatomy). The elastic loops will take the wind stress normally reserved for the tent's fabric and stitching.

At home take a hard look at your tent's design. Pitch it tightly on level ground and check out the lay of the fabric. If you have an inexpensive tent, there'll probably be some sag along the roof line. You can string out the ridge so it doesn't luff, but only at the expense of the base. If the fly sags along its border (looks as if it needs more stake loops to support it), it probably does. Get out your sewing machine and add them—as many as necessary to make the fabric drum-tight and wrinkle-free. Use the storm loops like you'd use reef lines on a sailboat—only in rough-weather emergencies.

While you're handy with the needle and thread, reinforce questionable stitching, especially at the corners and peak of the tent. Afterward, carefully waterproof all the seams you've sewn!

The Rainfly

Waterproofing and windproofing your tent is only half the solution to weathering a storm. The other part is providing a dry place to cook and relax. Customize your nylon rain tarp as illustrated in figure 17-2. Perimeter loops should be spaced no more than 18 inches apart. Add extra loops if you need them.

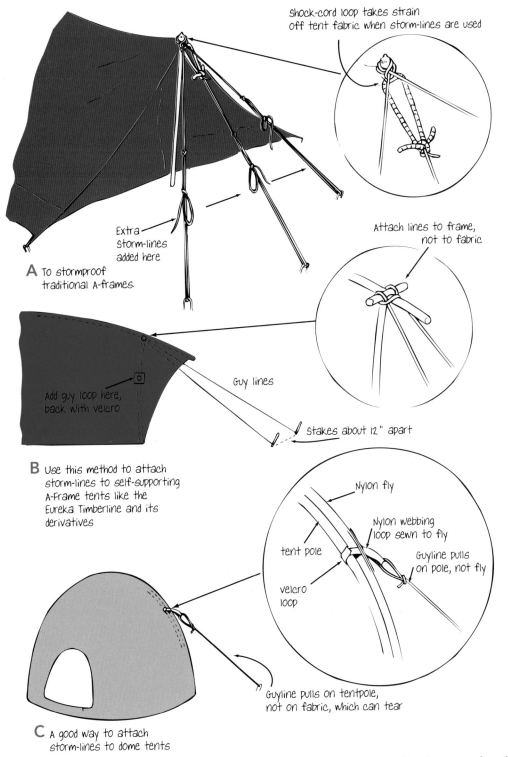

Shock-cord loop takes strain off tent fabric when storm-lines are used

A To stormproof traditional A-frames.

Extra storm-lines added here

Attach lines to frame, not to fabric

Add guy loop here, back with velcro

Guy lines

Stakes about 12" apart

B Use this method to attach storm-lines to self-supporting A-Frame tents like the Eureka Timberline and its derivatives

Nylon fly

Nylon webbing loop sewn to fly

tent pole

Guyline pulls on pole, not fly

velcro loop

Guyline pulls on tentpole, not on fabric, which can tear

C A good way to attach storm-lines to dome tents

Figure 17-1 Stormproofing the tent.

Only the center guy-and-pole loop is essential; the other four face loops allow you to pitch the tarp in a variety of geometric configurations. Back loops with heavy material so they won't rip out in wind. Be sure to seal all the seams you sew.

Thread 2 feet of parachute cord through each loop and knot the cord near the loop. The long tails of these cords can be tied directly to an overhead line or daisy-chained to a long guyline, as conditions demand.

If you plan to use a center pole, sew two opposing butterfly loops to the inside center (pole) patch. To use the butterfly pole loops, center the pole in the socket and tighten the cord lock. Now your pole will remain firmly anchored in high winds.

You can buy a customized tarp, like the one suggested here, from Cooke Custom Sewing* in forest green or high-visibility multicolor checkerboard.

Rigging procedure. The majority of campers are pretty haphazard about fly pitching, and, as a result, the first good wind that comes along rips the corner grommets right out of the fly. Consequently, some canoeists believe that tarps should never be set up in a wind-driven rain. Unfortunately, that is when you need their protection most.

After years of experimenting I've come to prefer this simple, strong, and efficient method of rigging (figure 17-4).

Materials. A fly customized like the one shown in figure 17-2; 50 feet of nylon rope; six lightweight aluminum tent stakes; two trees, not over 30 feet apart.

1. Locate two trees about 15 to 20 feet apart. String a drum-tight line between the trees about 5 feet off the ground. Use two half hitches at one end of the rope and a power cinch with a quick-release knot at the other end (see chapter 10 for a review of knots).

2. Take the pair of ties at one corner of your fly and wind one tie of the set around the rope in a clockwise direction and the other tie in a counter clockwise direction. Take at least four turns around the rope. Secure the ties with a simple overhand bow.

3. Pull the other corner of the open end fly tight along the rope and secure it with the ties, as in step 2. The wrappings will provide sufficient tension when the fly is buffeted by the wind.

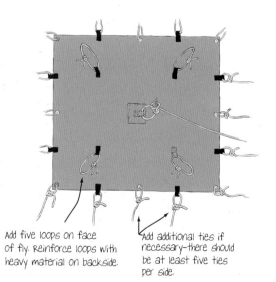

Add five loops on face of fly. Reinforce loops with heavy material on backside.

Add additional ties if necessary—there should be at least five ties per side.

Figure 17-2 Customizing the rain tarp: Add ties to all the grommets and sew five equally spaced loops to the face. This will allow you to pitch the tarp in a variety of geometric configurations.

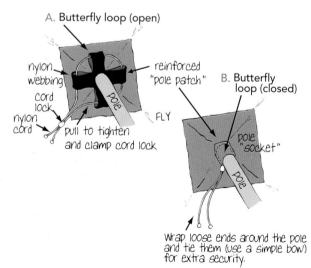

A. Butterfly loop (open)

nylon webbing
cord lock
nylon cord
pull to tighten and clamp cord lock

reinforced "pole patch"

B. Butterfly loop (closed)

FLY

pole "socket"

Wrap loose ends around the pole and tie them (use a simple bow) for extra security.

Figure 17-3 Inside view of tarp center.

Tie edge of fly to a tight line with a simple bow knot.

Quick-release knots.

Figure 17-4 A customized rain tarp can be rigged in less than three minutes and will withstand 30-mile-per-hour winds.

4. Secure all remaining ties to the rope with a simple overhand bow. (By securing the fly at several points along the length of its open end rather than just at the corners, as is commonly done, you distribute the strain across a wide area, thus increasing the strength of the fly.)

5. Go to the back of the fly, pull it out tight, and stake it.

6. Run the center cord over a tree limb or a rope strung just above and behind the fly. Snug up the center cord (use a power cinch with a quick-release knot) to pull the center of the fly out. Or use the pole and butterfly arrangement (figure 17-3).

7. Secure the sides of the fly with extra cord. Complete all knots with a quick-release loop. You now have a sturdy, rain-free shelter that won't flap in the wind. Total rigging time? Under three minutes!

You'll find more fly-rigging tricks in my book *Camping's Top Secrets* (Globe Pequot Press, 1998).

Twin flies make a cozy camp, Fond du Lac River, Saskatchewan.

CHAPTER 18

Bugs, Bears, and Bothersome Beasts

Bugs

Repellents

The most effective bug repellents contain deet—a chemical that contains N,N-diethyl-m-toluamide. Generally, the more deet a repellent has, the better it works. However, too much deet can burn sensitive skin and dissolve plastics. Children should use a mild citronella-based repellent or one that is about 20 percent deet and 80 percent soothing skin lotion.

My experience in the Canadian bush suggests that 25 to 30 percent deet, in a mixture with other ingredients, will keep away most insects. Pure deet is essential only if you're tripping in the barren lands where billions of black flies cloud the sky.

Tips for Applying Repellents

1. Bugs will avoid your face if you saturate your bandanna with repellent and tie it loosely around your neck. Spray the underside of your hat brim, too!

2. Try this if you have sensitive skin and are canoeing in blackfly country, where high-deet repellents are essential: First, rub sunblock deep into your skin; wait ten minutes; then apply the powerful repellent. The sunblock keeps your body from absorbing too much of the chemical. If possible, choose one of the new bonding based sunblocks, which penetrate deeper than common film based kinds.

3. Liquid or cream repellents are much more potent (a better buy) than sprays.

4. After a bite, Benadryl is the best nonprescription medication you can buy for allergic reactions.

Head and Body Nets

A small head net is a must in buggy country. Bulky, military styles with draw-cord hems that button down to breast pockets are a nuisance in canoes, where head nets are put on over life jackets. A simple rectangular net that can quickly be wadded to fist size and stuffed into a hat crown or shirt pocket is best.

It's difficult to see through light-colored bug netting. If you can't find a dark-colored head net, buy a light-colored one and darken the eye panel with black Magic Marker or dye.

Protecting your torso is another concern. A layer of lightweight long underwear, worn tight against the skin, discourages most bites, except on exposed ankles and wrists, which are easily protected by repellent. Your armor is complete when you've tucked your pants into high-top boots and sealed shirt-cuff openings with mating strips of Velcro.

Color counts, too. Dark shades tend to attract; light colors have no effect. Navy blue is by far the worst color you can wear in the woods!

Bug Jackets

Bug jackets made from tightly woven cotton or no-see-um netting work fine on cool days, but are sweaty when it's hot. A porous nylon wind shell works as well. Canadian paddlers mourn the passing of the wonderful Shoe-Bug jacket, which was soaked with pure deet (and allowed to dry). Some fishing stores still have these jackets in stock. Please let me know if you find a source—I'll send a check immediately!

Bug Tents

A small military surplus bug tent encourages sanity when lounging in buggy country. Campmor* carries a number of different models that are easy to rig. Or try the two-person Susie Bug Net, designed by my wife, Sue Harings. It's available from Cooke Custom Sewing.*

How to Bearproof Your Camp

Ask any newcomer to the Boundary Waters Canoe Area what he or she fears most about camping out, and you'll hear, "Bears!" Some folks are afraid they'll be eaten alive; others are worried that a bear will get their food. And backcountry managers offer small consolation, for their advice is often predicated on outdated conditions.

For example, here are some suggestions from U.S. Forest Service publications that are distributed to canoeists who enter the BWCA. All except one will get you into trouble. Can you tell which one?

1. Hang your food pack from a tree limb that is at least 10 feet off the ground or suspend it from a horizontal pole set between two trees. Some campsites have a "bear pole" that everyone uses. Please leave the pole as you found it as a courtesy to the next person who occupies your site.

2. Don't leave food in your tent!

3. Leave tent flaps open so that a bear can walk in and check the place without resorting to brute force.

4. This recommendation comes from the canoeing literature: Place food under an overturned canoe. Pile some pots on top to function as a night alarm system.

If you said number 2, you are correct. All the rest are wrong—dead wrong! Here's why: consider number 1: Bears are creatures of habit whose behavior is programmed by past experience. They quickly learn where and in what campers put food.

For example, I once saw a black bear tear apart a pack that was filled with sleeping bags and tents. This pack had never been used for food, so there was no odor. Past experience robbing other camps had taught this bear that food comes in packs and packlike objects. It was the *shape* of the container that attracted the bear, not the smell! Same with tin cans, which bears learn about at the local dump. How else can you explain why they will bite through sealed tin cans that have no food smell on them?

Bears also learn that food packs grow on trees—*certain trees*. At popular campsites there is usually only one tree with limbs that are high enough to discourage a determined bear, and invariably every camper suspends his or her food pack from this tree. "Soon as it gets dark, I'll climb up there and get it," thinks the bear. Consider this scene—which I witnessed some years ago:

A big sow bear and two youngsters waddle into camp and make a beeline for the "bear tree." The food pack is hanging from a limb, maybe 12 feet up and 3 feet out. Mama sidles up to the tree trunk, stretches out, and begins to climb. She goes up a few feet, then slides down. She's ticked. Real ticked! So she woofs and snaps as she circles the tree, her eyes fixed on the dangling morsel.

Meantime, one of the cubs gets wind of the food and starts to climb. Six feet up, it stops and begins to bawl. Seconds later, Mama shimmies to the rescue and nudges junior's behind. The kid scoots the remaining distance, stretches out on the limb, and hooks a pack strap. Seconds later, the cub and pack fall to the ground and everyone enjoys a tasty meal, courtesy of some camper who "followed the rules."

Moral? Tree your food if you like, just don't use the same tree as everyone else!

Next, let's check out number 3, "leave your tent flaps open so a bear can walk in." This one dates back to the 1950s when campers cooked fresh foods on open fires within yards of their canvas tents. Cotton holds odors tenaciously, and a curious bear might just check them out. So it probably was wise to leave the door flaps open so a bear could look around without tearing the place apart.

But nylon tents and fire don't mix, so now we pitch our shelters—and do all our cooking—out of range of windblown sparks (and food odor). Modern campers know better than to cook or eat around their tents, and bears know better than to waste their time looking for food in places that have not been productive in the past.

Closed tent flaps *will not* discourage a black bear, but

they will keep out insects, snakes, and the weather. The feds should've trashed this idea long ago!

Now, let's address number 4, "Place food packs under an overturned canoe and set pots on top as a night alarm system." This idea dates back to the days when campsites were not so heavily used and before camp bears became conditioned to the ways of humans. Today's camp bears are well educated. They're not afraid of man, woman, or clanging pots. A man told me a big black bear once tried to get at some food stored under his aluminum canoe. When the bruin couldn't connect, it began to jump on the craft. Damage included a broken seat and several pulled rivets. Just think what the bear could have done to a Kevlar canoe!

Now that I've shown you that traditional rules can't work, here is a nontraditional one that does: *Break the classical conditioning habit: Don't put your food in the same place as everyone else!*

What I do with my food depends on where I'm camped. If I'm deep in the Canadian bush where bears are heavily hunted—and generally afraid of humans—I just stash my food under a nearby tree or under my rain tarp. I've never had a problem.

Canoeing in populated areas like Minnesota's Boundary Waters and the Quetico of Canada requires foxier measures. Here I simply take food packs out of the immediate camp area and set them in the deep woods or along the shoreline, taking care to keep them out of sight and away from game trails. I usually separate packs by several yards for additional security. Bears don't see very well, especially at night, so as long as they can't smell food or see a container that they think might contain food, they'll leave things alone.

All of which brings me to the matter of a clean camp. Leftovers should be burned or buried well away from camp and water. Every spaghetti noodle and grain of popcorn must be gathered and disposed of. The feds are right about number 2: Bears will tear down your tent to get at food!

Let's review the real rules for bearproofing your camp:

1. Seal all foodstuffs in plastic so there is no odor.

2. Break the classical conditioning habit by putting your food where others don't.

3. Don't keep food in your tent. In grizzly country the cooking area should be at least 100 yards from where you sleep!

4. Keep a scrupulously clean camp and you'll find that what works for bears also works for ground squirrels, mice, and birds.

I've made more than a hundred canoe trips in bear-inhabited country. Trips have ranged from three days to thirty-one. No bear has ever gotten my food. Or clawed a pack. Or damaged a canoe. I've never had a problem. Not one!

What to Do if a Bear Comes into Camp

Stay calm. It's your food the bear wants, not you. Over the years I've confronted a number of black bears, and my nonchalant procedure goes something like this: First I yell or blow a whistle. A wild bear will hightail it at the sound, but an experienced camp bear won't even look up. Secure in the knowledge that my food has no odor and is out of sight beyond the camp boundary, I maintain a safe distance and watch the show. After the bear checks all the usual places and finds nothing, it will move on in search of more productive fare.

Again, let me emphasize that you *will not* scare off a determined camp bear with screams, whistles, or cherry bombs. It will leave only when it's sure there is no food around!

On the other hand, don't be too laid back. There are crazy bears like there are crazy people. You could run into one with an injury or with a nasty disposition. Unprovoked bear attacks are rare, but they do happen. So stay cool, keep your distance, and identify a getaway route in the unlikely event that things get out of hand.

During the summer of 1987, a man was mauled by a small female black bear in the Boundary Waters Canoe Area of Minnesota. The attack was unusual because the man and his son watched the bear peer at them from the edge of the forest for several minutes before she attacked. Convinced that the bear was just curious, the man sent his son to gather firewood. As soon as the boy was out of sight, the bear attacked. She followed the father into the lake and kept chomping away. Fortunately, he survived the mauling. When forest service personnel later killed the bear, they discovered she was starving!

If you are confronted by a black bear, stretch out your arms (so you'll appear bigger than you are) and yell, "*Whoa bear, stop monster,*" or something that suggests you're in command. *Do not* look the bear in the eyes. And *do not* run. Bears are mostly bluff—a "charging" bruin will almost always stop short of you, then turn tail and run.

The danger signs are woofing and clacking. If you hear loud hiccuping sounds with the clacking of teeth, the situation is deteriorating. The bear's mad and unpredictable. If there's a tree handy, climb it now. If the bear follows, break off a limb and poke it in the nose and eyes (really). If you are attacked, fight back! Grab a sheath knife, an ax, or a sharp stick. Do not play dead with a black bear. If the bear gets you on the ground, roll facedown, hands clasped behind your neck, legs spread-eagled. Don't let the bear roll you belly-up!

A very small number of bears are out to get you. Most attack during daylight, so keep moving if you see a bear that won't go away. Bears are very smart (much smarter than dogs), so they weigh their odds for success before they strike. Note that in the 1987 Boundary Waters mauling, the black bear bounded in from the bush only *after* the man's son left his side. This calculated observation, and hundreds of other incidents like it, suggest that solitary travelers and small children are most likely to be targeted by predacious bears. There is safety in numbers.

Space precludes an in-depth treatment of bears. You'll find more information in my book *Camping's Top Secrets*. For the whole story, read these books: *Bear Attacks, Their Causes and Avoidance*, by Stephen Herrero (Lyons and Burford, 1985); *Bear Encounter Survival Guide*, by James Gary Shelton, (self-published, 1994); and *Bear Attacks, The Deadly Truth*, by James Gary Shelton (self-published, 1998).

Pepper Spray

Pepper spray (sometimes called "bear Mace") con-tains 10 percent capsaicin—the flaming ingredient in red pepper. If properly used, it will stop bears about 75 percent of the time. Most upscale sporting goods stores have it.

Use pepper spray only on aggressive bears. *Do not* spray your canoe or camp to keep bears away! Recent studies suggest that while bears don't like to be sprayed with pepper, they do like the taste of it. Evidently, bears like spicy food, too.

There are a number of formulations of bear Mace. I rely on Counter Assault, which you can order from Bushwacker Backpack and Supply Company.* Get the 1-pound can, which costs about forty dollars. A quick-draw holster is a must!

Grizzly Encounters

In 1984 I was charged by three grizzlies on the Arctic tundra. As they galloped toward me, I dropped to the ground and played dead, certain that the ploy would soon become fact. The bears came within two canoe lengths then wheeled off into the highlands. I later learned from a wildlife biologist that my behavior was textbook perfect.

For years I thought that the old advice "play dead if attacked by a grizzly, fight back if you're mauled by a black bear" was the right thing to do. After all, I had played dead with three grizzlies and survived their charge. Then I read Herrero's and Shelton's books and learned that "bearhavior" is not simple science. The fact was, I was hidden among thick willows and my odor was masked by that of thousands of caribou grazing nearby. The bears just lost their target.

In summary, you'll avoid most bear problems if you simply keep a clean camp, don't store food in your tent, and store odor-free food packs where other people don't. If you tree your packs, don't use the same tree as everyone else. If you're camping in a popular park, such as Yellowstone, where bears have learned to break into cars (they are especially expert at invading Hondas and Toyotas), *don't* keep food in your car. Indeed, you may be wise to avoid the parking lot even if you *don't* have food in your car! Remember, bears are creatures of habit; they enjoy being entertained—and breaking into cars (even those that don't have food) is probably fun. As I mentioned, I never hang my packs in bear country. But I keep a scrupulously clean camp, and at night I put my food in an out-of-the-way place. I've lived by these simple rules for forty years, and in that time neither I nor anyone in my charge has ever lost food or equipment to any animal. And that, friends, is the "bear" truth!

CHAPTER 19

Planning a Canoe Expedition

In his wonderful book *Survival of the Bark Canoe* (Farrar, Straus & Giroux, 1975), John McPhee pokes fun at master canoe builder Henri Vallaincourt. McPhee describes Vallaincourt as a talented man who is so consumed with his canoes that he is unable to focus on the mundane chores of preparing for a canoe trip.

Minutes before the event, Henri allegedly dashes about and stuffs his pack with whatever he can find. No margarine? Jam will do. Out of cooking oil? We'll bake instead of fry.

An attitude like this can get you in big trouble on a remote river. You absolutely cannot afford to forget a thing when help is an airplane ride away!

You'll need some time to round up what you need for a lengthy expedition, but the chore will make you smile. Indeed, experienced paddlers often begin to assemble their outfit weeks or months before the grand experience—not because they must, but because it's so much fun. Naturally, they use a check-list like the one in this book. Be aware that it's not complete—you need to brainstorm with experienced friends to cover all bases.

Choose Gear You Can Fix with Simple Tools

You're ahead if your equipment can be fixed with simple tools. A lot of new gear can't. The throwaway syndrome began with shoes and now runs rampant across equipment land. Still, natural materials like leather, wood, canvas, and brass remain popular because they are so easy to repair. The trick is to know when to go high-tech and when to follow tradition. Experienced trippers usually have a mix of old and new. For example, on dicey days I wear a wool shirt and pants plus wool or Thermax long under-wear. I switch to fast-drying nylon river pants and a polyester T-shirt when the weather warms. I bring four hats—a wide-brimmed Tilley for sun, a nylon sou'wester for rain, a wool stocking cap, and a fleece-lined Gore-Tex cap. You can never have too many hats on a canoe trip!

Before a group trip everyone gets a detailed equipment list that they must follow to the letter. For example, a poncho or fishing shirt won't substitute for a rugged rain suit. Long wool or polyester underwear, wool shirts and pants, and warm stocking caps and gloves are essential items. I encourage everyone to bring three sets of footwear—knee-high rubber boots, neoprene or canvas wading shoes, and comfortable camp shoes.

I use a mix of canvas Duluth packs and nylon portage packs plus a variety of pack baskets, plastic wanigans, and dry boxes. I prefer upright baskets for fragile items like eggs and optics, and wanigans (dry boxes) for hard gear like stoves and cookware. Why? Things slide around when wanigans are tipped up to portage. Baskets aren't tipped.

I value products that provide an escape route when things go wrong. For example, my parkas have storm flaps *and* zippers, tents have twin entries, and cooking tarps have more attachment points for storm lines than I'll ever need.

Ounce Foolish

Some paddlers go to extreme lengths to save weight, which may be a bad idea. For example, if you have to whittle dry kindling from the heart of a wet log to start a campfire on a rainy day, you'll wish you'd brought a 1-pound ax. Constant wear means frequent holes, as you'll soon discover if you wear your Gore-Tex parka for both wind and rain. You can patch the holes, of course, but not until the storm is over and you've recovered from hypothermia. Better to bring a light, porous garment for wind and a fully waterproof one for rain.

Here's what can happen when you go to the nth degree: I used to cut off and discard portions of my maps that did not include my route. This saved considerable weight and bulk. But I stopped this practice three years ago when I bought a GPS and discovered that the coordinate values I had removed were needed for positioning! Now I'll have to buy new maps if I take old trips again.

Prepare for Worst-Case Scenarios

These include days of cold, persistent rain; a capsize; sweepers (downed trees in the channel); high, fast water; low, impassable water; hordes of insects; fearsome portages; and a medical emergency. Develop a battle plan for each.

You'll Discourage Danger if Your Eggs Are All in Order

The canoeing literature is rich with advice on how to avoid dangers. To wit: Don't paddle when the wind is up; stay close to shore on big lakes; line or portage dangerous rapids; et cetera. You'll rightly find this stock advice in all canoeing texts, including mine. Still, experienced paddlers would be lying if they said they always do the prudent thing.

Case in point: In 1998 I led a Science Museum of Minnesota–sponsored canoe trip down the Tha-anne River in Canada's Northwest Territories. Now Hudson Bay rivers are known for their nasty, unpredictable weather; if there's an axiom for them, it's that the wind always blows upstream—and it's usually accompanied by rain. As expected, headwinds wreaked havoc with our schedule all the way.

The lower Tha-anne is a mess of huge (Class III to VI) rapids and falls that begin just beyond Hyde Lake, which must be crossed. Hyde Lake is shallow and has few islands to break the wind. A small breeze produces big waves. It's nearly 7 miles to the far shore; if the weather is calm, you can easily canoe that distance in two hours. But it's much safer to paddle 25 miles around the north end of the lake and hug the shore all

the way. Once you leave Hyde Lake, it's a rigorous two days to Hudson Bay.

The wind was blowing bloody murder when we arrived at the headwaters of Hyde Lake, so we camped and hoped for a clear sky in the morning. Two days remained to make the bay where we had arranged for charter boats to pick us up. The wind continued to blow all that night and the next day. When it finally quit at 3 A.M. on our last day, we found ourselves in a serious predicament. Hyde Lake, plus 22 miles of rapids and falls, lay between us and Hudson Bay. Could we do it all in one long day? It seemed impossible.

We studied the map. Prudence suggested that we paddle around the lake, which would take six hours and foil our plans to make the bay on time. A thin fog and barely perceptible tail breeze suggested that if we made a beeline across the lake right now, we'd be out of harm's way by sunrise. What to do?

A vote was taken and we agreed to power straight across the open water. I programmed the outlet of the lake into my GPS and determinedly paddled into the mist. An hour later we had completed 5 miles and the shoreline loomed ahead. Suddenly, a squall came up and we steered into the teeth of it, grateful for our full splash covers. Seconds later, the squall passed and the sun came out. Hyde resumed her composure and allowed us to proceed without incident. We continued downriver and arrived at Hudson Bay at 10:40 P.M., minutes before the sun went down. We had been in the saddle for 19 hours, longer than any of us had ever paddled.

The point is that there are serious pressures associated with "being where you have to be when you have to be." Had we taken the longer, safer route around the lake, we would not have made the bay on time, and our chartered powerboats would have returned to the Inuit hamlet of Arviat, 50 miles away, without us. Yes, they would come back another day (but who knows when?) and rightly double our $1,000 charter fee. We would miss our flight to Churchill and the train that runs to Thompson every other day. Some people would have to reschedule their commercial flights home, and everyone would miss some work. It would be a mess.

Here's why we thought the beeline plan was best:

1. The sky was clear and the weather looked stable.

2. We were experienced paddlers and had full splash covers on our big Royalex tripping canoes.

3. It was too far and too foggy to see the outlet of the lake, but we knew exactly where to go. GPS doesn't lie! We could run a straight, unerring course all the way.

4. The slight tail breeze would speed our progress. We figured we could make the run in around 90 minutes. We loaded our canoes slightly stern-heavy to ensure control if the wind picked up.

The moral is that *you will discourage danger if you have all your eggs in order*. We had apparently stable weather, an experienced crew, splash-covered canoes, an unerring route, and two hours till sunup. Still, we took a chance, and we should be thrashed for doing so.

Here are some other things you'll want to consider when you outfit for an expedition:

Is your canoe properly rigged for dangerous water? Are bow and stern lines coiled and secured under loops of shock cord on the decks, as suggested in chapter 2? Is your spray cover snapped down all around? Can you reach your sponge and bailer? Is rain gear easily accessible, or will you have to grope for it? Have you secured your plastic pack liners so they won't leak in rain or a capsize? Can you quickly get to your change of clothes and fire-making materials if hypothermia rears its ugly head? Are map and compass and GPS where you can see them clearly?

Small things count, too: Do you have a security strap for your eyeglasses and a small chamois or cotton handkerchief to clean and dry them? Paddle rapids in a misty rain and you'll see why these are so important.

Versatility Matters

I once rented Royalex canoes from a Canadian outfitter for a trip in the Northwest Territories. The canoes had one-piece splash covers that fastened with laces that had to be painstakingly threaded through small loops. Tall packs had to be set flat on the floor of the canoe, because the covers did not expand. There was no access to gear when the covers were laced down.

Our covers were durable and reliable, but we grew to hate them because they were so much trouble. One crew refused to use them at all, even when life-threatening situations loomed ahead. We all yearned for the easy accessibility of the three-piece expandable covers I designed. Too bad we couldn't make them fit our canoes.

Color Counts

You're well into a portage and lose the trail, so you set your green canoe into the green bushes and go exploring. Minutes later you find the way and return for your canoe, which is nowhere to be found. Ultimately, the whole crew joins in the search. Two hours later you find the craft, right where you left it.

Or maybe your floatplane pilot has agreed to pick you up at a certain place. Will he see you from the air? Probably not if all your stuff is olive-drab or forest green.

Bright colors count if you're going in harm's way. Believe it!

What's Best?

I'm often asked which pack, paddle, raincoat, canoe shoe, and so on, is best. Fact is, you can get by elegantly on an expedition with discount-store gear if you have good judgment, a flexible schedule (you're in no hurry to get somewhere), and outstanding paddling and camping skills. Quality gear won't substitute for knowledge—though it will smooth the way, and good stuff is always a pleasure to use. There are regional preferences, however, and everyone has good ideas. For example, it's Duluth packs in Minnesota and dry bags in Colorado. New Englanders want wicker baskets and Canadians prefer pickle barrels. Choose what pleases you and develop a foolproof system that won't fail when things go bad. When I discover a reliable product or procedure, I stick with it until hell freezes over or something better comes along. Some people say that's being opinionated. I call it wisdom!

There's Merit in Uniformity

If you have two identical stoves, you can scavenge parts and get one running if both go down. One spare pole is enough for all your tents if they are alike. My five Royalex tripping canoes have matching portage pads that attach to the yoke with aluminum bars and wing nuts. It takes just a minute to replace a broken pad with a good one. The Fastex buckles on my dry boxes and wanigans are interchangeable, as are the AA batteries in my flashlight, headlamp, GPS, VHF radio, and waterproof camera.

Don't Put All Your Peanuts in One Bag

Boundary Waters paddlers often put their food in a single pack, which they dutifully hoist into a tree each night—supposedly to discourage bears. (If you read the last chapter, you know there are better ways!) And what if a bear gets your only food pack? Or you capsize and lose the unit that contains your tents or cooking gear? Doesn't it make sense to spread good things around?

I don't understand why some paddlers prefer to put all their food in a single pack that, for an extended trip, can weigh 100 pounds. Who would want to carry such a load? Besides, dissatisfaction often rears up when a few people routinely carry more than others.

If you want to know what works and what doesn't, seek the advice of those who regularly canoe wild rivers. It takes some time and experience to sort things out. What works for years hangs around.

My dad was a quality control engineer. In his office hung a large sign that read: ACCIDENTS DON'T JUST HAPPEN; THEY ARE CAUSED! Ditto a successful canoe expedition.

APPENDIX 1
Canoe Terminology

Aft: Toward the stern (back) end of the canoe.

Amidships: The center or middle of the canoe.

Bailer: A scoop (usually made from an empty bleach jug by cutting off the bottom) for dipping accumulated water from the bottom of the canoe.

Bang plate: On aluminum canoes, a curved metal plate running from deck to keel; it holds the metal skin together and takes the bangs. The bang plate is called the stem band on canoes of wood-canvas construction.

Beam: The widest part of the canoe. It generally occurs at or slightly aft of the waist (middle) and just below the gunwales.

Bilge: The point of greatest curvature between the bottom and side of a canoe.

Blade: The part of the canoe paddle that is placed in the water.

Bow: The forward (front) end of the canoe.

Bowperson: The forward or bow paddler.

Broadside: A canoe that is perpendicular to the current of a river, thus exposing its broad side to obstacles in the water.

Broach: To turn suddenly into the wind.

Carry: To carry a canoe and gear overland, either to a distant watershed or to safer water. *Carry* is synonymous with *portage*.

Deck: Panels at the bow and stern that attach to the gunwales.

Depth: The distance from the top of the gunwales to the bottom of the canoe when measured at the beam (sometimes called *center* depth, as opposed to the depth at the extreme ends of the canoe).

Draft: The amount of water a canoe draws.

Flatwater: Water without rapids, such as a lake or slow-moving river.

Flotation: Styrofoam or other buoyant material set into the ends, along the inside bilges, or beneath the decks and gunwales of aluminum and fiberglass canoes to make them float if upset. Can also mean any buoyant material, such as life jackets, beach balls, and inner tubes.

Foot brace: A wood or metal bar against which a paddler braces his or her feet. Foot braces help secure the paddler in the canoe and so add to the efficiency of strokes.

Fore (forward): Toward the front end (bow) of the canoe.

Freeboard: The distance from the waterline to the top of the gunwales at their lowest point. The greater the freeboard, the greater the ability of the canoe to handle rough water, assuming the canoe is well designed.

Grab loop: A loop of rope that passes through the hole or painter ring at each end of the canoe. It gives you something to "grab" when you capsize.

Grip: The top end of the shaft of a canoe paddle, where you grip it.

Gunwales (pronounced "gunnels"): The upper rails of the canoe.

Hogged: A canoe with a bent-in keel.

Inwale: That part of the gunwale that protrudes into the inside of the canoe.

Keel: A strip of wood or aluminum that runs along the center of the canoe. Keels prevent lateral slippage in winds and protect the bottoms of canoes from damage in rocky areas. However, their main purpose is to stiffen the bottom of a canoe. There are two types of keels in common use: *Standard, fin, or T-keel*—a deep keel that extends an inch or more into the water. It is an ideal choice where travel will be limited to large, windy lakes. *Shoe (whitewater) keel*—a rounded or flat strip of metal or wood designed to protect the bottom of a canoe from damage. The smooth contours of shoe keels allow water to flow over them with little resistance. Thus they permit quick turns in rapids.

Leeward: A sheltered or protected place out of the wind. In nautical terms, *leeward* is the direction toward which the wind is blowing.

Line: Rope used to tie up a canoe or pull it around obstacles in the water. Also refers to working a canoe downstream around obstacles in the water with the aid of ropes (lines) attached to the bow and stern.

Outwale: The part of the gunwale that protrudes over the outside of the canoe hull. Outwales are desirable for canoes that will be used in whitewater, as they help deflect spray when the bow of the canoe plunges in rapids.

Painters: Lines attached to the bow and stern of a canoe.

Planking: Lightweight boards nailed to the ribs on wood-canvas canoes. Planking runs perpendicular to

the ribs of a canoe. Its main purpose is to support the canvas.

Portage: See *Carry.*

Ribs: The lateral supports that run at right angles to the keel on the inside of a canoe. Ribs provide hull rigidity and structural strength and are necessary on aluminum and wood-canvas canoes. The trend is away from ribs in canoes of modern construction, as the new synthetics are very strong and do not require crossbracing for support.

Rocker: An upward curve of the keel line of a canoe. When placed on a level surface, a canoe with rocker will, like a rocking chair, rock up and down (fore and

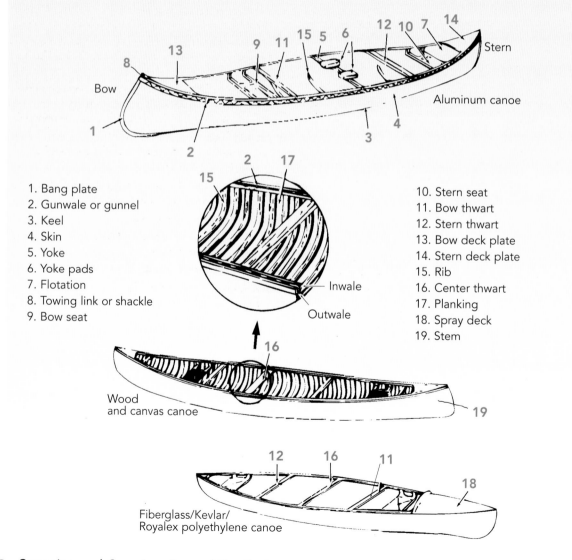

1. Bang plate
2. Gunwale or gunnel
3. Keel
4. Skin
5. Yoke
6. Yoke pads
7. Flotation
8. Towing link or shackle
9. Bow seat

10. Stern seat
11. Bow thwart
12. Stern thwart
13. Bow deck plate
14. Stern deck plate
15. Rib
16. Center thwart
17. Planking
18. Spray deck
19. Stem

aft). Canoes with rocker turn more easily than those without rocker.

Rock garden: A shallow place in a river that has many scattered rocks.

Seats: Generally, there are two seats in a canoe. They may be made of wood, fiberglass, plastic, or aluminum. Wood-framed seats, which are strung with cane or nylon webbing, and tractor-type molded fiberglass seats are most comfortable. Aluminum seats are least comfortable and get cold in cool weather. For greatest warmth (and comfort), cover aluminum seats with waterproof foam and secure the foam to the seats with waterproof tape. You spend long hours sitting in a canoe; consequently, more than a passing consideration should be given to the seats.

Shouldered tumblehome: The canoe's sides are extended upward to a double-radiused shoulder, as illustrated in figure 1-3.

Sliding seat: A canoe seat that can be moved forward or aft to adjust trim. Most of the best canoes now feature sliding bow seats as a standard or optional accessory.

Skid plate: A piece of thick Kevlar that is glued to the bottom ends of Royalex canoes. It prevents abrasion of the vinyl skin of the canoe. Skid plates are a desirable addition to Royalex canoes that will be used in shallow, rocky rivers.

Skin: The outer covering of the canoe. It may be wood, canvas, aluminum, or other material.

Splash cover: A fitted cover designed to keep water out of a canoe. Splash covers are useful in rough rapids and big waves. Even small, sporty canoes are suitable for wilderness use if they are covered.

Spray deck: An extra-long deck equipped with a cowling to deflect water that comes over the ends of a canoe.

Spray skirt: A waterproof fabric sleeve that is attached to the splash cover at one end and is secured around a paddler's waist by means of elastic shock cord at the other end.

Thwart: A crossbrace that runs from gunwale to gunwale. Thwarts give strength and rigidity to the hull.

Toe blocks: A feature of whitewater canoes. Wood or foam blocks glued to the canoe's bottom support the paddler's feet and keep him or her from sliding around in the boat while maneuvering.

Thigh straps: A feature of whitewater canoes—a webbing harness that runs from the gunwale or seat frame through a ring on the canoe's bottom. The paddler pushes his or her knees tight against the straps to lock them in place—a very secure arrangement, especially when combined with toe blocks.

Tracking: Working a canoe upstream, against the current, with the aid of ropes (lines) attached to the bow and stern.

Trim: The difference in the draft at the bow from that at the stern of a canoe. A properly trimmed canoe will sit dead level in the water. Trim can be adjusted by weighting the bow or the stern.

Tumblehome: The inward curve of the sides of a canoe above the waterline.

Tumpline: A strap that is secured just above a person's forehead to help support a pack or canoe.

Waist: The middle of the canoe.

Waterline: The place to which the water comes on the hull of the canoe when it is set in the water.

Whitewater: Foamy (air-filled), turbulent water.

Yoke: A special crossbar equipped with shoulder pads for portaging the canoe.

APPENDIX 2

Equipment List for Two People for a Trip of One Week or More

Group Equipment

- tent (preferably with double entries (two doors))
- plastic ground cloth for use *inside* tent
- coated nylon cooking fly, 10 feet by 10 feet or larger, and telescoping poles
- three Duluth-style packs (number 3), or two Duluth packs and a pack basket or wanigan
- at least 100 feet of nylon parachute cord
- waterproof liners for packs
- 100 feet of ⅜-inch nylon rope
- hand ax or small "forest" ax in sturdy sheath
- one compact folding saw
- repair and miscellaneous kit: pliers with wire cutter, fine copper wire, silver duct tape, needles, thread, instant epoxy, 12-inch square of fiberglass cloth for canoe or paddle patching, six hammer-driven rivets, two aluminum carabiners, one nylon pulley, small file for sharpening the ax, whetstone and honing oil, 3-inch square of scrap canvas for repair, small piece of leather for repair, sharp sewing awl, safety pins, sandpaper, Leatherman or similar multitool
- six heavy-duty rubber ropes with steel S-hooks attached
- large sponge for bailing
- cook kit and oven
- graduated 2-quart plastic shaker
- biodegradable soap and abrasive pad for dishwashing
- stove and gasoline
- matches in waterproof container; cigarette lighter
- several candles
- first-aid kit (See *Wilderness Medicine* by Dr. Bill Forgey [Globe Pequot Press, 2000] for a complete list of first-aid items and their use)
- GPS (optional)

Individual Equipment

- life jacket
- two paddles, one straight, one bent
- sleeping bag and foam pad
- two pairs of military field pants (choose wool pants in spring and fall)
- two long-sleeved shirts, one wool, one nylon
- one medium-weight wool or fleece jac-shirt or three sweaters
- one polyester or cotton T-shirt
- one pair of long johns (spring and fall trips)
- four pairs of wool socks
- one light nylon wind parka (not waterproof)
- one waterproof two-piece rain suit
- one brimmed hat for sun; wool stocking cap for chilly days; sou'wester hat for rain
- extra glasses (if you wear them) with security strap
- three changes of underwear
- one small towel
- two cotton bandannas
- one pair rubber-bottomed boots
- one pair of canvas sneakers or other soft footwear for camp use
- one pair of lightweight leather or polyester gloves (for arctic trips use leather-faced wool, Gore-Tex, or neoprene gloves)
- one flashlight, extra bulb, and batteries
- sheath knife or heavy-duty pocketknife
- toiletries (include hand lotion for chapped hands)
- orienteering compass
- map set in waterproof case
- insect repellent
- insect head net (essential for trips into northern Canada, otherwise unnecessary)
- binoculars/camera (optional)
- butane lighter or matches in waterproof case

A P P E N D I X 3

Backcountry Ethics

Here's a not-so-simple quiz that will test your understanding of backcountry ethics. Answers and rationale follow. *Hint:* Some questions have more than one right answer, and some answers are open to interpretation.

I hope you'll duplicate this quiz (permission is granted by the publisher) and share it with friends, with church and Scout groups, with anglers, hunters, birders, hikers, canoeists, and with everyone who cares deeply about the future of our wild places.

Neglect and the Proper Way

Questions

1. The best way to dispose of fish entrails is:
___ (a) Throw them into the river or lake.
___ (b) Bury them at least 100 feet from water.
___ (c) Leave them on a prominent rock (well away from camp area) for seagulls.
___ (d) They are biodegradable so it makes no difference how you dispose of them.

2. To properly dispose of human waste:
___ (a) Bury it at least 12 inches deep, 100 feet from water.
___ (b) Human waste degrades quickly; it should not be buried!
___ (c) Bury it 4 to 12 inches deep, at least 100 feet from water.

3. It's okay to dispose of biodegradable wastes (food scraps and such) in forest service outhouses, box latrines, and chemical toilets.
___ (a) True.
___ (b) False.
___ (c) Open to interpretation.

4. What's the correct way to dispose of steel and aluminum cans?
___ (a) Burn out the cans, pound them flat with the back of an ax or rock, and pack them out in a strong plastic bag.
___ (b) Burn out the cans, then bury them!
___ (c) Bury them at least 100 feet from water.
___ (d) All of the above methods are acceptable.

5. How should you dispose of glass bottles in the backcountry?
___ (a) Break them into fine pieces and bury them.
___ (b) Pulverize them to a powder and bury them at least 100 feet from water.
___ (c) Burn them out in a hot fire then bury them.
___ (d) If you bring bottles into the backcountry, pack them out!

6. To keep water from entering your tent in a heavy rain, dig a shallow trench around it so the runoff will drain harmlessly away.
___ (a) True.
___ (b) False.
___ (c) Open to interpretation.

7. If you have a small amount of uneaten food, toss it into the bushes. Animals will dispose of the food quickly and completely.
___ (a) True.
___ (b) False.
___ (c) Open to interpretation.

8. It's okay to construct log benches and tables at your campsite as long as you use cord, not nails.
___ (a) True.
___ (b) False.
___ (c) Open to interpretation.

9. The best way to dispose of aluminum foil is:
___ (a) Bury it.
___ (b) Burn it.
___ (c) Pack it out.
___ (d) Any of these methods is satisfactory.

10. It's okay to play loud radios during daylight hours.
___ (a) True.
___ (b) False.
___ (c) Open to interpretation.

11. Pounding nails into trees so you'll have places to hang things improves the campsite for the next party.
___ (a) True.
___ (b) False.
___ (c) Open to interpretation.

12. Leave your ax or hatchet at home: It is not essential to your comfort or survival.
___ (a) True.
___ (b) False.
___ (c) Open to interpretation.

13. Bright-colored equipment—canoes, tents, packs, and clothing—detracts from the wilderness experience. Choose earth tones instead.
___ (a) True.
___ (b) False.
___ (c) Open to interpretation.

14. You may bathe and wash clothes and dishes in a waterway as long as you use biodegradable soap.
___ (a) True.
___ (b) False.
___ (c) Open to interpretation.

15. Always bring a strong plastic bag for garbage . . . and pack out the contents!
___ (a) True.
___ (b) False.
___ (c) Open to interpretation.

16. Use a camp stove for all your cooking. It is unethical to build fires in wilderness areas.
___ (a) True.
___ (b) False.
___ (c) Open to interpretation.

17. You are responsible:
___ (a) To check the remains of your fire by hand before you leave the area; if ashes are hot enough to burn your hand, they're hot enough to burn a forest.
___ (b) To bring the right gear and clothing for the worst conditions you may encounter.
___ (c) To help others who are in trouble.
___ (d) To educate others in the proper way to treat wilderness areas.
___ (e) All of the above.

18. Ecology-minded outdoorspeople will row or paddle rather than use motors. The noise of motors frightens wildlife and the oil/gasoline scum and carbon monoxide exhaust is harmful to fish and aquatic organisms.
___ (a) True.
___ (b) False.
___ (c) Open to interpretation.

19. To ensure a restful sleep, the wise camper will always place evergreen boughs or a bed of green leaves beneath his or her sleeping bag.
___ (a) True.
___ (b) False.
___ (c) Open to interpretation.

20. You are responsible to call unsafe and illegal practices that you observe to the attention of the person(s) involved, and to report violations of land- and water-use regulations to the appropriate authorities (if practical).
___ (a) True.
___ (b) False.
___ (c) Open to interpretation.

Answers

1. B is correct, though c is acceptable if you are in an area where seagulls are common, and the water way *is not* heavily fished. A would be correct in grizzly country.

2. C. The top foot of soil contains the greatest number of decay organisms (bacteria and fungi), so breakdown will occur most rapidly in this area. The idea is to bury wastes deep enough so animals won't dig them up, yet shallow enough so they'll decompose quickly.

3. Absolutely false! Garbage should be buried or packed out, never thrown in latrines. Bears commonly upset latrines to get at food buried among the human waste. The mess that results is indescribable!

4. A is correct. Steel cans degrade in around seventy-five years. Aluminum cans require hundreds of years! Cans should *always* be packed out.

5. D is correct. It may require one million years for a glass bottle to "return to nature." For this reason bottles should always be packed out! Better yet, they should *never* be brought into the backcountry.

6. False! Trenching creates soil erosion. It is unethical and, in most places, illegal to ditch tents. Use a plastic ground cloth inside your tent and you'll stay dry in the heaviest rains.

7. Absolutely false! This upsets the ecology of animals and causes them to become dependent on humans. Chipmunks, squirrels, and raccoons get used to being fed and will chew through packs and boxes to get at food. And bears will become bold and downright dangerous!

8. False. Many people take to the backcountry to get away from the trappings of civilization. Your "improvements" may be interpreted by them as full-scale "development"!

9. C. It requires a very hot fire to burn aluminum foil completely. Partially oxidized foil is the scourge of the backcountry. Bottles and cans have been outlawed in many federal wilderness areas because people won't pack them out. Aluminum foil may be next!

10. No way! It's never all right to inflict your noise on others.

11. False. It's unethical, illegal, and it hurts the trees!

12. This is debatable. Purists would say "true," but I disagree. When the woods are drenched from a weeklong rain, you need a small ax, saw, and a knife to make fire. First, saw off a 12-inch length of dead log and split it with the ax to get at the dry wood inside. Then slice fine shavings (tinder) from the heartwood and you'll have a roaring fire in no time.

Axes don't damage forests; irresponsible people do! Score your answer correct if you are in philosophical agreement with either viewpoint.

13. C (purists would disagree). Bright-colored equipment is essential to the safety of an expedition in remote country. If you float local streams and never make remote trips—and are bothered by bright colors—you may wisely choose earth tones. Otherwise, vivid hues simply make good sense. I don't mind seeing an orange tent or a red canoe. But I do mind litter, noise, and graffiti!

Score your answer correct if you agree philosophically with these viewpoints.

14. No way! When bacteria attack biodegradable products, they reproduce and use up oxygen, which harms fish and aquatic organisms. Just because a product is biodegradable doesn't mean it is good for the environment.

15. True! A responsible outdoorsperson *always* packs out his or her trash.

16. C. Many outdoorspeople (myself included) prefer to do all their cooking on a stove. However, it is ethical and legal to build fires in most publicly owned wilderness areas, and that includes sand- and gravel bars in navigable rivers. Nonetheless, you are strongly encouraged to use a stove instead of a fire whenever possible, especially in well-traveled and ecologically sensitive areas. No conscientious outdoorsperson would think of making a campfire on delicate vegetation.

Score your answer correct if your heart was in the right place.

17. E. Don't take these responsibilities lightly. You are responsible for any forest fire you cause, and penalties are severe. So make sure your flames are dead out! If you don't know what to bring on a canoe trip, read a book about it before you go. And do help others in trouble and educate everyone you meet about "neglect and the proper way."

18. False. The sound and smell of motors is certainly offensive to many people—the reason they are banned from some lakes. However, motors do little, if any, damage to lake and river ecosystems.

19. Absolutely false! It is illegal and unethical to cut green trees. Use an air mattress or foam pad; it's more comfortable.

20. True. Whenever possible, use the "honey rather than guns" approach. Most damage to ecosystems is the result of ignorance, not wanton vandalism. People will usually do the right thing once they've been properly and patiently educated. Be a spokesperson for the environment. And practice what you teach!

Scoring the Test

Each question is worth one point. A score of 20 is possible.

19–20	Environmental expert!
17–18	First-class scout.
15–16	Knowledgeable tenderfoot.
13–14	Fun-loving loafer: Sorry, your good times are being had at the expense of the environment!
12 or less	Backcountry bumpkin! You need help. Take someone along who earned a higher score.

A P P E N D I X 4

Sources of Products Mentioned in This Book

Bell Canoe Works

25355 Highway 169
Zimmerman, MN 55398
Factory: (612) 856–2231

Superb tandem and solo canoes, canoe yokes, and the excellent Bell/Grey Owl straight canoe paddle.

Bourquin Boats

Jeannie Bourquin
1568 McMahan Boulevard
Ely, MN 55731
(218) 365–5499
www.wcha.org/builders/bourquin

Jeannie Bourquin was a member of the first all-women's team to canoe the South Nahanni River. Her story is in my book *Canoeing Wild Rivers*. Jeannie builds exquisite wood-canvas canoes (no solos). Her portage yoke pads are comfortable and breathtakingly beautiful. They work on any canoe.

Campmor

P.O. Box 700P
Saddle River, NJ 07458-0700
(800) CAMP–MOR

Hundreds of camping items, plus personal-sized bug nets.

Camp Trails Division

Johnson Camping, Inc.
625 Conklin Road
Binghamton, NY 13902
(800) 847–1460

Portage packs and camping gear.

Cascade Designs, Inc.

4000 First Avenue South
Seattle, WA 98134
(206) 583–0583

Fax (206) 467–9421
Waterproof bags and packs. Makers of the Therm-a-Rest sleeping pad.

Chosen Valley Canoe Accessories

P.O. Box 474
Chatfield, MN 55923
(507) 867–3961
>k2carr@aol.com

Source of the slick removable pot handles I inspired, as well as a high-tech yoke that works well on light-weight canoes.

CLG Enterprises/Superior Packs

3838 Dight Avenue South
Minneapolis, MN 55406
(800) 328–5215

Superior tripping packs and rodeo accessories. Also manufactures a tough dry box (the Hard Pack) and the insulated pot cozies I designed.

Cooke Custom Sewing

7290 Stagecoach Trail
Lino Lakes, MN 55014-1988
(651) 784–8777
cookecustomsewing.com

Cooke manufactures some of the best packs, tarps, canoe covers, and paddling accessories around. I'm proud to say I've had a hand in some of the designs. Cooke gear emphasizes practicality, utility, and killer strength for the long haul. Good stuff!

Counter Assault

120 Industry Court
Kalispell, MT 59901
(800) 695–3394
www.counter@counterassault.com

Source of Counter Assault bear repellent (pepper spray).

Duluth Pack

365 Canal Park Drive
Duluth, MN 55802
(800) 777–4439

I love this wonderful old company that, until recently, was officially known as Duluth Tent & Awning Company. Duluth Pack has so many wonderful things, you'll just have to get a catalog.

Empire Canvas Works

P.O. Box 17
Solon Springs, WI 54873
(715) 378–4216

Serious gear for serious outdoorspeople—modern canvas summer and winter tents, mushing clothes, warm wool long johns, and the best universal-fit hardworking portage pads around. The super-size pads I inspired are wonderful.

Fast Bucksaw, Inc.

Paul Swanstrom
110 East Fifth Street
Hastings, MN 55033
(651) 437–2566

Best (and by far the most beautiful) folding camp saw I've found.

Forestry Suppliers, Inc.

205 West Rankin Street
Jackson, MS 39204

All sorts of tools and navigational aids for the professional forester.

Fox 40 International Inc.

Worldwide Head Office
20 Warrington Street
Hamilton, Ontario
Canada, L8E 3V1
(800) 66–FOX40
www.fox40whistle.com

The world's loudest, most reliable, and most popu-laar river whistle.

Fox 40 U.S.A. Inc.

4600 Witmer Industrial Estate
Niagara Falls, NY 14305
(888) 66–FOX40

Gougeon Brothers, Inc.

P.O. Box 908
Bay City, MI 48707
(517) 684–1374

West System epoxy, fiberglass, and other boat repair materials. Ask for their *Building, Restoration & Repair* manual.

Grade VI

P.O. Box 8
Urbana, Il 61803
(217) 328–6666

CEO Charlie Wilson is part engineer, part philosopher, and one of the best freestyle canoeists in North America. His Grade VI paddling luggage deserves a hard look if you want great stuff that lasts almost forever.

Gransfors Bruks, Inc.

P.O. Box 818
Summerville, SC 29483
(800) 433–2863
Fax (803) 821–2285

Absolutely the best axes on the planet. Hand-forged, superbly balanced, and razor sharp.

Granite Gear

P.O. Box 278
Two Harbors, MN 55616

Impeccable packs and paddling accessories that will stand up to the hardest use. Proven in Minnesota's BWCA and well beyond.

Grohmann Knives

P.O. Box 40
Pictou, Nova Scotia
Canada BOK 1HO
(902) 485–4224
Fax (902) 485–5872

Source of the wonderful Russell/Grohmann knives, which have won numerous international awards. Note: Carbon steel versions are available only from Duluth Pack.

Idaho Knife Works

Mike Mann
P.O. Box 144
Spirit Lake, ID 83869
(509) 994–9394
Cell (509) 994–1633
Source of the carbon steel Cliff Knife that I designed. Makes some great fillet knives, too!

L. L. Bean, Inc.

Freeport, ME 04033
(800) 221–4221
Is there anyone who hasn't heard of L. L. Bean?

Mad River Canoe Company

P.O. Box 610
Mad River Green
Waitsfield, VT 05673
(802) 496–3127
State-of-the-art canoes and accessories.

Marathon Canoes

P.O. Box 549
Marathon NY 13803
(607) 849–3211
Grumman canoes are back in business under a new name! Marathon canoes are identical to those your granddad paddled. What fits a Marathon canoe will fit your aging Grumman.

Northwest Canoe Company

308 Prince Street
Street Paul, MN 55101
(651) 229–0192
www.visi.com/~nwcanoe
Here's where to go if you want to build your own fiberglass-covered wood-strip canoe. Building plans, precut wood strips and trim, Ad-Tech epoxy resin and accessories—shipped to your door. The company will repair any nonaluminum canoe or kayak.

Old Town Canoe Company

58 Middle Street
Old Town, Maine 04468
(207) 827–5513
Modern fiberglass/Kevlar, Royalex, and polyethylene canoes and canoe accessories.

Orion Safety Products

28 Sloan Street
Roswell, GA 30075
(770) 650–8991
Colored smoke, flares, whistles, and other signaling gear.

Ostrom Outdoors

RR #1
Nolalu, Ontario
Canada POT 2KO
(807) 473–4499
Superbly designed high-tech packs and paddling accessories for those who demand the best. Bill Ostrom makes good stuff.

Pakboats/ScanSport, Inc.

P.O. Box 700
Enfield, NH 03748
(603) 632–9500
www.pakboats.com
America's source of expedition-ready folding open canoes.

Pelican Products

23215 Early Avenue
Torrance, CA 90505
(800) 473–5422
Pelican waterproof boxes are extremely reliable.

Solo Playboating by Kent Ford

Performance Video & Instruction
550 Riverbend
Durango, CO 81301
A superb instructional video for those who are serious about canoeing whitewater. Kent Ford is the former director of instruction of the Nantahala Outdoor Center. He's an ACA (American Canoe Association) instructor-trainer and a member of the World Champion C-1 team, 1983, 1985, 1992, 1996.

Steger Mukluks

125 North Central
Ely, MN 55731
(800) MUK–LUKS
Wonderfully warm and comfortable winter and summer mukluks, made in traditional Native American styles. Great for canoeing in winter!

Stormy Bay

P.O. Box 345
Grand Rapids, MN 55744
(218) 326–5104
Manufactures the excellent Stormy Bay Wanigan—
formerly E. M. Wanigan

System Three Resins, Inc.

P.O. Box 70436
Seattle, WA 98107
(206) 782–7976
A very popular epoxy resin for laminating wood and
fiberglass.

Thrifty Outfitters

c/o Midwest Mountaineering
309 Cedar Avenue South
Minneapolis, MN 55454
(612) 339–6290
Everything you need to build a canoe splash cover,
make a tent, or repair your stove or Gore-Tex rain
gear. If Thrifty doesn't have it—or can't fix it—you'd
best forget it.

TrailBlazer Outdoor Quality Products

2736 Robie Street
Halifax, Nova Scotia
Canada B3K 4P2
(800) 565–6564
trail@istar.ca
One of the best folding saws around. It's big enough
to cut thick logs.

UDAP Industries, Inc.

13160 Yonder Road
Bozeman, MT 59718
(800) 232–7941
www.udap.com
Source of Pepper Power—a highly effective pepper
spray for use on aggressive bears.

We-no-nah Canoe Company

P.O. Box 247
Winona, MN 55987
(507) 454–5430
www.wenonah.com orvfg
wenonah@luminet.net
Racy We-no-nah canoes and canoe accessories.

Zaveral Racing Equipment, Inc.

242 Lockwood Hill Road
Mount Upton, NY 13809
(607) 563–2487
www.zre.com
zaveralb@zre.com
In my opinion, the best graphite canoe paddles on
the planet. Zaveral paddles are also available from
We-no-nah Canoe.

Canoeing Associations

American Canoe Association

7432 Alban Station Boulevaard, Suite B-226
Springfield, VA 22150
(703) 451–0141
The ACA has been around since 1880. Emphasis is
largely on training, racing, freestyle, and poling, but
there's stuff for everyone.

Canadian Recreational Canoeing Association

P.O. Box 398, 446 Main Street West
Merrickville, Ontario
Canada K0G 1N0
(613) 269–2910
http://www.crca.ca/
staff@crca.ca
CRCA offers trips and canoeing instruction and has
a huge inventory of canoeing books and trip guides.
Canadian and American members receive the
bimonthly magazine *Kanawa*, which alone is worth
the price of membership. The CRCA paddling center in Merrickville, Ontario is a knockout. If you
love wilderness canoeing, you'll love the CRCA.

Minnesota Canoe Association

P.O. Box 13567, Dinkytown Station
Minneapolis, MN 55414
The MCA is the largest canoe club in America.
Emphasis is on building your own strip canoe. MCA
has great canoe building plans (solo and tandem) and
the best canoe building book around. *HUT!* magazine—loaded with tips and trips—comes to members
each month. Members in fifty states and Canada.

INDEX

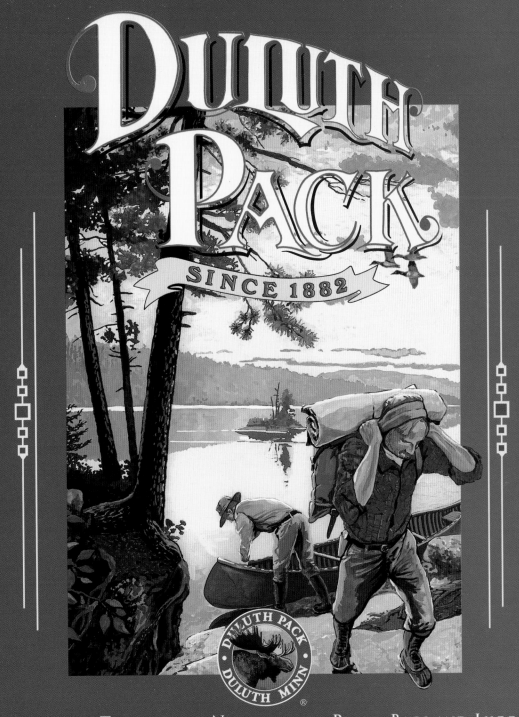

**PURVEYORS OF TRADITIONAL NORTHWOODS PACKS, BAGS AND LUGGAGE.
ORIGINAL MANUFACTURER OF THE FAMOUS DULUTH PACK SINCE 1911.**

CALL FOR OUR **FREE CATALOG** OF NORTHWOODS GEAR

1-800-777-4439
www.duluthpack.com